Is Love Worth the Wait?

BY DAVID E. CLEMONS

The contents of this work, including, but not limited to, the accuracy of events, people, and places depicted; opinions expressed; permission to use previously published materials included; and any advice given or actions advocated are solely the responsibility of the author, who assumes all liability for said work and indemnifies the publisher against any claims stemming from publication of the work.

All rights reserved
Copyright © 2023 by David E. Clemons

No part of this book may be reproduced or transmitted, downloaded, distributed, reverse engineered, or stored in or introduced into any information storage and retrieval system, in any form or by any means, including photocopying and recording, whether electronic or mechanical, now known or hereinafter invented without permission in writing from the publisher.

Dorrance Publishing Co.
585 Alpha Drive
Pittsburgh, PA 15238
Visit our website at *www.dorrancebookstore.com*

ISBN: 979-8-8902-7076-4
eISBN: 979-8-8902-7574-5

Is Love Worth the Wait?

A Bit of Information About Why This was Written:

Is Love Worth the Wait? was inspired for me to write about it and speak about love, as many who will take the time to read it to see what it is all about will see. One night as I was in a long deep sleep, I had a dream as if I was in the midst of this whole triangle, looking in the face of two young individuals who were different races, but for some reason, they didn't see it that way as they were young and played together as a sister and two brothers, one brother was the sister's brother and the other was a neighbor who lived across the road from each other not having a clue about what is and what is not because that was the way society had structured itself. As I continued to dream, the whole fantasy became true in a life in the deep south to show anyone who looks in a different way that life can be beautiful as for this young white guy and the young black girl he admired so much he wanted to marry her.

A bit of information about the person who sat down to write this book. First, I am an educator, who holds an LLB law degree as well as a master's degree from the University of Chicago, Illinois and an online doctorate degree in psychology.

I served a stint in the military in Germany for four years before returning back stateside to teach a few years in school and later moving on over to becoming a federal government official, holding the position as a comptroller with the Department of Defense. After I completed my years there, I spent a few years giving back to students to help them to fulfill their time learning all they possibly could in order to become successful in life. After all that I have done with my life, I reside here in Virginia where I spend my time writing and supporting my church affairs.

Foreword

Having a wandering mind as I do, I came up with the idea of reflecting back into the early part of my life when I first came to know and to understand about how things back in the fifties and the sixties were being implemented, as far as the race of people of various colors were concerned. As I grew up and became more understanding of the situations being carried out in all southern states in the south, I thought to then create in my mind why were those things happening especially when little white boys and little black boys played all day in and around their neighborhoods not feeling a care in the world as well as little white girls and little black girls played with dolls not being mindful of who they were only to know that they were friends and children. The only part to their situation was they could not have dinner together because they were not allowed to because that was not a part of the white society. As years flew by and as all things were beginning to take shape, there was love on the rise and it didn't matter if that person was a white boy looking into the eyes of a beautiful little black girl to see a different world, one to whom he knew he would be happy living in and it didn't matter what society of the white man said. With so many ups and downs all through the years, something happened when a white family moved close to a black family and they became friends as their children connected as they played that started the whole thing that lasted until it was time for a young white boy to reveal to his parents that he had fallen madly in love with the black girl he grew up with and he wanted her to become his wife. This white boy, as he is mentioned in this book, and the black girl to whom he was in love with are the sole script of this book.

Acknowledgements

Is Love Worth the Wait? is an inspiring, made up story from the viewpoint of my mind as it is a fictional story, but it could have been a non-fiction story back in those days, but no one dared to write about it, afraid that it would get into the wrong hands and thus cause a lot of trouble since it all started and took place in the southern state of ole Mississippi, as we all know what type of harsh and bitter things that really took place back there in those days. If all who read this book and come to the understanding of what it was like back in those days will have an open mind to understand that those days should have never been dark days but instead light days for all races of people. To whom this white boy is or was in those days with his determination, I hold high esteem too, because it was he that possibly changed the way things were being carried out there in that racially divided southern state of dear old Mississippi, who vowed never to be brought down, but it shows that nothing remains the same as people with great integrity will make sure that changes will happen for the good of all people.

Introduction

This fictional novel was not easy to start off writing about something that you know you had ideas about nor that you had no idea that any of this ever existed, but back in the deep part of my membranes, I just kept getting these ideas in my mind as I slept that these ideas that kept coming into my subconscious thoughts should be better served if I had the courage and time to write about something that just might took place back there in those days undercover that no one knew about. All I do know is this: something did take place because as I look around not only into the race of other people but I took a deep look into my own family history to find out that I came from a family of mixed up races to include French, Indian, Jamaican, white, and you name it as I called my family a melting pot of colors.

 I can truly say this much, how much I can appreciate all of this because regardless of how the white race might feel about other races of people, they are a part of it all because they are the ones who got this all started and since this did happen in years gone by, they should be happy to know that we are all connected in some form or fashion and there is nothing anyone can do about it. I know that one day and it will soon happen that there will be no separation in people because we will be the same. I dedicate this book to all opened minded individuals who have learned to accept things as they are and to move forward in ensuring that all lives will be as the creation intended.

Episode One

THIS DOCUMENTATION IS WRITTEN AS A PLAY OF WHAT SHOULD have taken place early on if the main character had known all about the intent of the other character and if all the facts were presented to her by the one main person who had an infatuation of pure love for her.

The main characters who carry this play and all episodes will be centered around are as follows:

Wayne Hunt - a white boy who grew up as a neighbor living close to the girl that had always inspired him to want to become a part of life even though there would be a lot of rejections he just might face.

Sandra Logan – a beautiful young black girl who was his neighbor, who had no desire to become involved with a white guy, nor did she think of Wayne as anything else but just neighbors as they rode the same school bus and were in the same classroom as small children.

Wayne's parents were Samuel and Florence Hunt, who didn't give a thought about any love affair between their son and their neighbor; Elijah and Catherine Logan's daughter, Sandra because they viewed themselves as good neighbors sharing things together with one another and both mothers would get together as other good neighbors would do to show the world that people of different colors could be as one. The two parents never thought anything that just might one day lead to a possibility this play start out in Melbrook, Mississippi, a little old southern town with a small population that evened out equally with blacks and white, thus making it a rather closeknit little community surrounding where everyone knew and worked together without any mention of what was taking place in the other parts of the world. The government there made it possible for everyone to be together because of their religious faith as they followed what had been written in the bible that everyone should be treated by the laws that were laid out.

Since all children grew up and played together as well as attended the same school to get a good education taught by both white and black teachers, it made it much easy for all students to be only aware of what they needed to learn and become good and outstanding citizens. In this whole setting there were two families who lived about three blocks from one another and had a close tie as families, not colors. The Hunt family only consisted of father, mother, and son, therefore allowing him to become closeknit with their black neighbor Logan, whose father and mother were fortunate to have two wonderful and loving children, a daughter Sandra who was a beautiful brown complexioned girl with long wavy black flowing hair as if she was made up of many races, and their handsome young baby son who name was Greg also would one day break the hearts of many women because of his looks. I guess you can say they got their looks from both parents because somewhere down the line, their fore parents were of a mixed color and so those genes just flowed downward.

As time passed on and the children of both the Hunts, the white family, and the children of the black family, the Logans, grew and spent many weekends playing together within their surroundings while their parents entertained each other whether sitting out on the front porch of their homes watching over them as their children ran all around the front yard playing hide and go seek. Nothing ever came up to say maybe one day a change in the children would change to come together to be as one where families just might be as one. While the children played, the parents talked about work and how their planted produce would turn out because since they were so closeknit, each of the parents owned a small plot of land next to one another therefore allowing them to work together in making sure they keep the stores supplied with their harvest of vegetable sand fruits as raised on their land.

Since the children spent time entertaining one another, sometimes after school, they would join in to help out when needed to help do something with the vegetable and fruit crops. It seemed as if time was moving fast as the children were going up to soon become young adults where Sandra, being the oldest of the Logan family, and Wayne, the only child in the Hunt family, were headed toward completing school and it was sure they would be headed off to separate locations to attend college. By this time, Wayne had already developed some feelings for Sandra as he watched her every mood and remained close to Greg and her, not letting his feelings step out of line as it would probably mess their family relationship up so he had made up in his mind to just maintain himself until the time would come and he had no doubt that the right time would come. Greg, Sandra's brother was fourteen and she was seventeen and ready to graduate from high school as was Wayne.

Before graduation time, she and Wayne would spend time together sitting out on her parent's front porch talking about their plans and what college each would attend. As the two of them swinged laughing and talking, Greg would come out and sit with them to introduce his silly talk. Wayne's parents never had to worry about him because they knew where he was at all time, down the street at the Logan's home enjoying himself with their children until it was time for him to come home. The whole time while being in the company of Sandra, Wayne's feelings for her were making him to want to tell her, but he dare not to at least not yet because the timing was not right.

Episode Two

AFTER GRADUATION, THE TWO OF THEM SPENT THEIR LAST SUMMER together before it would be fall time and the two of them would depart and enter the college of their choice, Wayne being accepted to attend the University of Mississippi to study agriculture so one day he just might be able to guide farmers on what steps to take in planting their crops. Sandra had decided to enroll into the University of Arkansas to study English with a minor in pre-law. Sandra decided upon this field to be able to obtain a job in another field if she did not get a job teaching English in a high school there in her hometown.

After the two of them had talked it all over with as far as their intent, Wayne had to say goodnight to Sandra because if he did not and remained there sitting and talking with her, he just might slip and let her about why he hung around her and her brother Greg so much, not because of good friendship as though the three of them were sister and brothers, but because of his fond feelings for her. Wayne decided that he would just act normal around the two of them because he knew Greg had a very skilled mind and if he acted as if he had feelings for his sister, Greg would possibly let the cat out off the bag. "Well guys," Wayne said, "it is getting late and I have to get going or else my mother will be calling over here to your mother to tell me to come on home so I am going to say to the two of you goodnight."

After Wayne had left, Greg said to his sister Sandra, "Sometimes Wayne acts very strange when he is around you more so than when he is around me. I wonder what that is all about?" he said.

Sandra said to Greg, "I guess it is because he will not be around to be close by you as well as me because I too will be going away so all the good times we three have had as we grew up will not be that way any longer. My little brother, you will be here all alone once Wayne and I are gone away for four years."

Greg said to her, "Don't you worry your pretty little head off because we will always be together whether here or away. It is not that you or Wayne will not return because once you two finish with your college education, I am sure you will get a job in this area teaching school as you have always wanted to do and our adopted brother Wayne will be here involved with teaching all these farmers on raising their crops."

"Greg what about you?" Sandra asked.

"By the time you two finish with your college education I will be graduating from high school to be ready to start out on my future. Who knows Sandra I might even get married and raise a family," he said smiling.

"Do you expect me to believe that about you getting marry and raising a family? Now you know Mother and Daddy will not go along with that because just as I am about to do, you too will enroll into college because the two of them will not take no for an answer."

"My dear sister Sandra what will I do once you and Wayne leave? I will be here all alone."

"Believe me Greg you will be just fine, besides you do have some friends that live close by where you can visit and have good times with don't you?"

"Yes I do, but it will be nothing like having you and Wayne around."

"Greg the reason you are feeling this way because the three of us grew up together and we were always around each other."

"You tell me Sandra how do you feel about it?" asked Greg.

"Well, I will at first miss having Wayne around all the time but I will definitely miss being around you because you are my brother. Wayne is just a good friendly neighbor who happen to be blessed to know good people as we are. That is how I see him and nothing more you know." You know Greg once I graduate from college, it is a possibility that I just might want to move on maybe to New York to obtain a job there since I will have a minor degree in pre-law. Who knows, working for a law firm just might be a good idea there, I could really grow to become someone and meet interesting professional people. You know little brother that I will always come home especially on holidays to spend time with my family. Tell me about what you desire out of life other than remaining here in this little homeland?"

"Sandra my dear sister, as time passes and I reach the age of making up my mind as to what my intentions will be, I want make a fast dash from at least spending some time with our parents so they will not be so lonely since you will be far away as it is a possibility and then I will decide about my life once I too have completed college to be ready to face my future."

"Greg do you think you will ever get married and maybe have children to make Mother and Daddy happy with grandchildren?"

"I suppose if the right girl comes into my life. Enough about me, tell me all what you are thinking and if you will marry."

"Like all young girls brother, I think if I meet and fall in love with the right guy then it is a possibility I too will become a mother to have several children to make our parents happy grandparents. Right now, I have to direct my mind strictly on my education and you know just about another month, off to college I go and you will be left here to carry on to keep our parents joyful and laughing."

As Sandra and Greg sat talking, up walked Wayne as he said to them, "What were you two talking about before I walked up?"

"Wayne we were talking about our lives and our future," Sandra answered. "By the way now that you are here being nosy, tell us what are you planning on doing once you finish college in the field you chose to go into?"

By that time before Wayne answered, Sandra and Greg's mother opened the front door to say to Wayne, "Good morning my second son, how are you doing this morning?"

"Mrs. Logan, I am fine."

"Have you had anything to eat yet because if not you know you are welcome to come on in and place your feet under my table as you always do," she said smiling.

"What on your parents' agenda for today Wayne?" she asked.

"I think they are planning on going into town to take care of some business."

As Sandra and Greg sat still swinging, Wayne jumped up on the porch and pushed his little adopted brother Greg aside and joined them. "Wait a minute there Wayne now! I know you think you belong to our parents at times, but you just cannot take over the swing our father hung for my sister and me."

"Greg stop and don't go there because you yourself come over to my home and act just like my parents are yours as well so you see, you and I are the same.

All I am trying to let you see is how overprotective I am of Sandra, our sister," Wayne responded.

As Mrs. Logan stood listening to Wayne and Greg go after it with one another, she finally said to the two guys, "No fighting now because you are allowing the food I prepared to eat get cold so come on in."

Wayne said to Greg smiling, "You see, I won."

As the three of them made their way into the house Wayne held the door open for Sandra to walk in and said to Greg laughing, "Brother where are your manners? Don't you know that females are always first? It is a thing you call respect."

As they all sat down to have a delicious good breakfast, Mrs. Logan asked Wayne about whether or not he was really to go off to college this fall. "Yes, I think I am but I will be a little sad because I will be leaving Mother and Daddy behind."

Greg said to him, "Listen my brother, stop saying that because they want you to go if they did not, would they be making all of those preparations for you? Don't be silly Wayne you have finished high school and now they want you to move forward."

Greg's father Mr. Logan, said to him, "Son don't be so hard on Wayne because you are forgetting one thing, he is an only child and I can relate to what he is going through because if you have not forgotten, I too was an only child and my parents were very lonely once I left home." As everyone talked, Sandra remained calm because she did not want to get into a fighting contest with her brother and Wayne so she decided to remain silent.

It was not that Wayne would be missing his parents so much as he would be missing the dream of his life Sandra which had not come into play as of yet because he wanted to be sure of himself that when and if the time came forth, he would not be let down by hurt so he had to play his cards right. As they continue to eat, his little mouth adopted brother Wayne said to him laughing,

"Think about it brother man, on campus you will have your pick of girls to date as I heard being in college, there are a lot of girls from everywhere to choose from. I have to tell you my little adopted brother Greg when I go away to college I don't think I will be there just to get involved with girls but rather to get a good education in the field of agriculture to be able one day to assist many farmers on how to grow their crops better to produce more without using a lot of chemical pesticides that harm the human race."

Greg father said to him, "Son, is that the only thing you have to share with us over this nice meal your mother made?"

"No Daddy, I would like to ask my big sister what she will do after graduation from college?"

Sandra spoke up to say to her brother, "Why I don't see where that is any of your business, first my little caring one, you have to complete your high school before you can even think about venturing of into something you know nothing about. If you have not thought about it just yet, when I am in my last year in college, you will be in your last year of high school so you see, Mother and Daddy will have to attend two graduations."

As they continued to talk, Wayne just took everything in because he himself knew he would be in the same position as Sandra, his hidden love. He keep saying over and over in his mind that he knows once Sandra graduates and is not lucky enough to obtain a job in the school system here as she so much wants to then without even thinking on it she will move away maybe to a big city where the employment is greater for her as she would not be looked upon by her color, but merely by her smarts. "As for myself and how I wish this was not the case but I think it will be easier for me to get a job in town with the State Agricultural Department because of the field I chose to go into. I know in my hear that Sandra will make a great English teacher and I know she can open up a whole new avenue for everyone, but that is water under the bridge that will pull her away from me and just might not allow her to return back here in this nice little southern atmosphere where we all grew to love one another because of who we are. Just looking over at her while I eat, I can see how much I want to tell her as well as my parents as well as hers, how much I have fallen in love with her as it started out while we were young and grew up together. I don't think I will ever date any other girl whether white or black because my heart belongs to Sandra. I loved her from the first day we met in school as youngsters. Each night as I lay in bed, I just cannot seem to fall asleep without thinking about her and how wonderful our lives would be, but this is just not the right time to get off into that just yet. I know there will be many twists and turn that she and I must go through in life to be worked out. I can understand others will soon be asking me about why I have not started dating yet. I keep asking myself what would I tell them or if I let them know that I am in love with Sandra how would they handle it knowing both families are so close to each other? I am quite sure I will find some way to tell them that I will soon."

"Mrs. Logan, I really appreciate this good breakfast and I thank you so much for having me to eat with all of you."

Greg said to Wayne, "Man you know you don't have to let my mother know how much you appreciate her breakfast because you eat here all the time as I find my feet under your parents table as well."

"We are a big family my brother, although you are a white boy but who cares? You are still my brother and that is all that matters."

"Why thank you back my little black half-brother because it indeed is a pleasure to have a sister and brother," he said. laughing.

Mr. Logan said to the two of them, "I wonder what you two guys are going to do once you have settled in your own lives"?

Wayne said to him, "I think you won't ever get rid of me because I think I will always be around looking over my sister Sandra here. I don't know about Greg because he probably will be a wild guy running all around looking for something."

"Wrong my brother Wayne, I will be running around checking on what you are doing," he said as the two of them laughed.

"I think I better walk back to the house as my parents will soon be coming back. I have to do a few things around the house that Mother wanted me to take care of before she returns".

Once Wayne had departed as Sandra and Greg said their goodbyes once he stepped off the porch to head home, Greg said to his sister, "Now there goes a good friend to you and me. Sandra do you ever think about how blessed the two of us are by having someone like Wayne's parents being white to walk into our lives to act as if they were a part of our family?"

"Of course I do Greg, but what is the point? To me he is just an ordinary white boy who just so happened to be raised up in the midst of a black family, I don't see anything other than that, unless you have something better to say about it."

"No sister, I do not because I feel the same as you besides, I know he is feeling a little scared as I can sense it because just over another month, he will not be here around to spend time with us because he will be away in college. Not only him but you as well and we won't come together until holidays or school breaks." Soon Wayne had gotten out of sight and home and Sandra and Greg walked back inside to be with their parents to continue a family conversation.

As the two of them sat down to finish up their breakfast, their father Mr. Logan decided to ask them why it took so long for them to return.

"Well Daddy, I can tell you this, your little son here always have a lot to say whenever Wayne is around always trying to get into his business as if he can sort out whatever is going through his mind."

"Daddy, all I said to Wayne was he will be happy to be entering college where he could meet a lot of girls to maybe find a girlfriend."

"Greg," his mother said to him, "I don't think you should be trying to encouraging him about that especially when he has not gone yet. First of all my dear little son, you need to concentrate on your schooling because you know when school opens, you will become a freshman you know and your father and I expect the best out of you just as your sister has shown."

Greg sai, "Mother, I got this and don't you and Daddy worry yourselves because just like Sandra, I too will graduate with a good grade average so I will be accepted to the college of my choice."

"Mother," Sandra said. "That is exactly what I keep on telling him and stop trying to make Wayne think that he is some sort of king fish, as he is not. I understand how he might be feeling now having to leave home to leave his parents behind for four years with no other sibling to fill in for him while he is away. Besides being in college studying hard to pass exams, his mind would be focused as well on them. This I don't think Greg has a clue about."

"Son," his father said to him. "Listen to what your sister was saying because everything made sense. You see, for your mother and me, it will not be as hard as for us as it will be for Wayne's parents because we still have you for the next four years until you graduate and off to college you will go. Now, try to be a good son and a good adopted brother to Wayne as the two of you call yourselves to build up his spirits and to let him know that although he will be away but he should not worry too much because you as his little brother just as you are to Sandra will be there for his parents."

"Daddy, Mother, I have listened to all what you guys have said and I promise you that I will take all of it into consideration to assure Wayne that I will be available to assist his parents while he is away. Besides that is exactly what brothers are for isn't it?"

"I don't believe it," Sandra responded. "Greg has finally seen the light so I am going to see how far this is going when Wayne is around," she said smiling.

"Big sister, you will see as I will not beat up on Wayne to make him feel down."

"Well, I think this family has really shown love toward Wayne as well as his parents," Mr. Logan said. While the Logans were all having a joyful time, Wayne had other thoughts running deep in his mind not knowing just yet how to deal with them because it was too early and not the right time to let go and tell his parents. The only one thing he knew he had to do at this particular time is just continue to act around Sandra as he always has not letting on to her about how he felt about her to keep her thinking that she was his little sister and Greg was his little brother. Wayne realized soon there will be a lot of questions to be asked of him by his own parents and even Greg about why he does not have a girlfriend or why he does not date. Wayne already knew he would have to handle it in a diplomatic way to throw everyone off.

Of course this would be the hardest thing he would probably have to face in his life, but he knows that time is on his side and he is determined to hold out until the end before he would bring it all out and when he does, he is hoping the best for him and he will come out on top. Wayne had made up in his mind when he walked over to the Logan's home tomorrow at some point and had time to sit down and have a brother bonding time with Sandra and Greg, he will act as he has always acted to not let anything slip out of place for them to detect. "In order to beat these feelings I have now I will just have to suppress them even when I am away in college to know what I am there to obtain and then after my four years are over with I can regain those hidden feelings. At that time, I will be much stronger and motivated to succeed my mission. By then Sandra just might move away to gain employment someplace else thus making it even harder for me to convince her how I feel about her. I guess right now I should not be thinking too far in advance because anything is possible. I have heard that things like this did happen in the past when two people were just friends and later on became loving couples. I think it can happen to Sandra and me, regardless if this world is so upside down about the color of a person's complexion. If you put a lot of thinking into it, does it really matter? Love is love and I think if the world could see how love is meant to be shared then what does it matter? I realize there will be many twists and turns in her life and mine but if this is meant to be then it will happen. Sandra is a pretty girl and she has so much going for her not only her looks, but her smarts as well that way I am overjoyed. I don't know how she will take all of this once she know that I have been in love with her since day one and I don't know how her parents as well as my parents will feel about it especially all these years we all have been just like one big family. I do hope and pray that all of them will look at the whole situation as something positive that just might had meant to be. Sandra is the main one that I will be concerned about because I am sure all of this will surely catch her by surprise and throw her for a loop."

As time moved quickly on, the summer was closely coming to an end and the two families of the children often got together to talk about the future of their children sitting out on the front porch of the Logans. Wayne's mother would often bring up the idea of how she and her husband Samuel would like to see their son Wayne start off his career once he has finished college. Sandra's mother Catherine asked her exactly how would she like for Wayne to begin his career.

"Well, since he is our only child, I would like or should I say, would hope that he finds a nice young educated girl to fall in love with and maybe get married and give us some grandchildren before his daddy and I pass on." As they talked, Wayne Sandra and Greg just sat still in the midst of one another on the other end of the porch listening to everything they were saying.

With all the conversation being said, neither Sandra nor did Greg gave it a moment of thought because to them at this time it did not apply to them. On the other hand it did apply to Wayne because after all was said and done, it was all geared around him. Wayne would find himself looking directly in Sandra's eyes as she would ask him if there was something wrong from his stare. To cover himself, he would say to her that he was just thinking all about how things were going to change once they go off to college, not being able to spend time together as they all are now.

Sandra said to him, "I know and I too have been thinking a lot about it too as the three of us will not be sitting out here laughing and talking about things we have done as we grew up." That was the way Sandra viewed it but Wayne it was different because sooner or later all of his feelings for Sandra would surface and both families would surely be shocked not ever thinking something like this would happen.

In Wayne's mind, he kept asking himself how his parents would take it knowing all these years they were all good friends and never for one moment thought their only son would be in love with their best friends' daughter.

Not only thinking of himself, but he too was thinking about how would Sandra's parents and little brother Greg feel about him being in love with their daughter and sister after all these years they all were seen as brothers and sister. "I am quite sure it would be a shock to them, but as I have been told and from what I learned from my reading, you cannot change the feelings of a person for another doesn't matter who they are or from where they came from. Love is love as I see it so I know in their time, they would come to accept it as I hope once Sandra becomes confronted with it, she too will accept and welcome it. For now, I think I better remind myself not to let her see me staring into her eyes not to give myself away too quickly."

"Finally, my father asked Mr. Logan about what he thought about mixed marriage; why he asked that, I don't know. Maybe he just wanted to get his take on it."

Mr. Logan returned an answer to say, "Samuel, if two people are madly in love with one another, I don't see why society will put so much dislike on it. If it be God's will then it will be. Samuel, why did you bring that up to me after all the times we have been in each other's company?"

"Elijah, I can't tell you why all I know that the thought just came up in my mind." Of course in Wayne's mind his father was not wrong, and maybe his father has sensed something through the way he has been acting around him.

"My father knows that I think the world of Sandra as well as Greg and I am sure the Logans feel the same way too, but a relationship with their daughter, I don't think they even given it any thought about I was or could ever be in love with their daughter. The truth of the whole matter is, I am and there is nothing I or anyone else can do about it. What will be will be because that is a part of life and if your life has been mapped out for you to go down that road then you will and you won't look back. The night was getting on and we all had to face another day and after my parents and I decided to greet the Logans good night to return to our home, my feelings for Sandra will still remain."

As Wayne tossed and turned all night struggling with the feelings he had for Sandra it was soon daylight and he realized he had not at all slept any through the night because he was so much in love with his little adopted brother's sister as the three of them grew up together as a family. Before his mother knocked on his bedroom door to let him know that breakfast was ready and he should come to join them, Wayne had to make himself look as if he had a good night sleep so they would not see anything that was different about him once he sat down at the table to start breakfast. Wayne knew how much his mother observed everything about him so he had to try to hide anything from her. When he finally joined his father and mother for breakfast as they would always wait until he sat down before they started to eat, his mother asked him how did he sleep. "Mother, I think I had a rather good night."

"Son," his father said, "you look a little tired and worried, is there anything wrong or going on with you that your mother and I should be concerned with?"

Wayne knew if he told them the whole truth, they would just might fall out of their chairs so he lied and said, "I guess the nightmare I sometime have that makes me look so tired."

"Honey," his mother asked, "what type of nightmare?"

"I really cannot say Mother at this time because everything with those nightmares seems so far away and I just cannot bring them into play but I can handle them as they really come only few and far in between." He knew he was lying out of his teeth, but he had to because this was not the time to let the cat out of the bag to destroy everyone's life and especially Sandra's. As the three of them ate breakfast, Wayne said to his mother how wonderful everything tasted and he really liked the apple preserves.

"Well son, it came from Catherine, if you remember when she and I were busy in her kitchen making peach and apple preserves about three months ago while you, Sandra, and Greg sat out on their front porch laughing and talking all about school."

:Oh yes, I do remember now. You three kids were laughing so hard until Catherine and I were wondering what was going on."

"Wayne, I would like very much if you can help me this morning with something," his father said to him. "And after you have finished you can join your two best friends for the day as I know that is where you want to be that is if your mother doesn't have anything for you to do to help her out."

"No Samuel, I don't have anything for Wayne to help me with so he can spend his remaining time with Sandra and Greg at least we know where he is."

Those words were exactly what Wayne wanted to hear as he agreed to help his daddy out for a while. This way, he knew he would be near to Sandra as he wanted to and to use Greg as a cover up. Wayne knew how fast time was moving so soon he would be away in college as Sandra will as well so all the available time he could get to spend with her he felt would make things even better for him once the time came to expose it all to everyone.

Wayne at nights would sit in his room and ponder whether he was doing the right thing by keeping all of his feelings stored up inside of him instead of telling Sandra but he was so afraid of the rejection he just might receive from her as he knew she only viewed him as a dear close friend over the years and maybe there could be nothing any more than that on her part. There was one thing for sure Wayne knew, once he was away in college, he could prepare himself to better handle the situation because he would not be around her as she will not be around him and then it would be a real possibility that she will think so much about him and develop some feelings. Of course this was a wishful thought on Wayne's part. Whatever happened through the years and time they would not be in each other's circle, he would have to prepare himself for the outcome whether good or bad as he will always hope for the good.

After breakfast and Wayne had finished with helping his father, he said to him, "Daddy, I think I will walk over to see the Logans."

"Do you mean son, you will go over to spend time with Sandra and Greg?"

"If you put it that way Daddy, not Mr. and Mrs. Logan, but Sandra and Greg," he said laughing.

"Have a nice time then" his father responded.

After that moment, off walked Wayne out of his home driveway onto the street to head toward the Logan's home because there he would be happy because there he would be happy. Sometimes Wayne wished that he too had a sister to sit and talk things over with as he could not do with his parents. Being in the company of the girl he had always been in love with, it was easier for him to say certain things that Sandra never paid any attention to because she saw it as Wayne being like a second brother who was just making comments. Once Wayne had gotten to the Logan's home, he walked up on the front porch and sat in their swing as always because he knew out of the house Greg would come out to say, "Hey man, you are here early today, what's up?"

"Oh well, I thought since I had finished helping my daddy with his work, I decided to come over to spend time with my second family."

"Wayne," Greg said to him. "I think if your parents would let you, you would move in with us wouldn't you?" By that time Sandra walked out because she had finished helping her mother in the kitchen with the breakfast dishes.

"Hello Wayne," she said to him. "How are things going with you today?"

Looking directly at her not to give himself away, he said to her, "I guess I am fine, now I know I am because I am here with my sister and brother so lets you and I talk about college, you know we have about three more weeks as you and I will be leaving right in the last week before classes start to get settled in."

"I know and I am so looking forward to it."

"Hey, wait just one minute," Greg said to the two of them. "What is going to happen to me because once you two guys leave, I won't have anyone to spend time with."

Sandra and Wayne said to him, "Brother you will be entering school as a freshman and you will meet lots of new faces where you will bond with to make a lot of friends."

"I think being absent from you my little brother will be a good thing for me," Sandra said to him. "That way, you will be able to become more dependent on yourself and less on me."

"That is so right little brother because I too will not be around so that will make our bond even greater," Wayne said to him laughing.

Sandra continued the conversation by saying to both Wayne as well as her little brother Greg, "You know guys I too will be moving into my dorm room at the same time you will Wayne so you see, Greg will not only miss from having me around him, but he will miss having you around as his big brother as well Wayne." To Wayne all of what Sandra had said sound good and to her it meant a lot, but to be honest Wayne was not at all concerned whether or not he would be missed only as a dear friend, he wanted to be missed as Sandra's possible future husband to make her happy in every way he could, knowing the backlash he and she would receive from the public there in Mississippi, because it still had a very long ways to go before all of the back ideas would be washed away because of things to come that will make changes in the way people come to learn and accept people for who they are.

Wayne often would say to himself that he was so glad to have been raised by parents who did not completely see things as other people did just because who people was. "I think by my upbringing has made me to see things as they should be seen. Here we are two races of people just loving one another and sharing all that we have to support one another. Now, I think I was meant to fall in love with Sandra from the first time I laid eyes on her as we made our way through school and now, we are about to go off into our separate ways striving to make a better tomorrow for everyone. Oh god, how I hope and pray that one day we will be together but until then, it is education that now stands in front of us that will delay me from coming out to tell her exactly how I feel and why I want to marry her. If I am going to take on this role as being a husband to live according to my beliefs, I will have to be prepared because I know Sandra will take on her life seriously to help make this world a better place. I have already braced myself that in the next week when she and I roll up out of this place and head off to the chosen college of our choice, it will be a while before we set eyes on each other again except for holidays and college breaks."

"I know in my heart it will be tough but I have to continue maintaining my strength to not give myself away until it is time to open up this heavy can of worms. It is a scare for me that the can of worms may never be opened because I suppose it will all lie in the hands of Sandra if she will be willing to accept me as a husband since all these years we have seen each other as family. I just keep asking myself, will she accept me for who I am or will she not accept me other than what she has always viewed me as? Although I will be struggling with my studies but somewhere between learning all I can about agriculture, there will be Sandra in between."

"I know in my heart that Sandra has no need to concentrate on me because as it stands now she is just a good friend and sees me as another brother to go along with her now little brother who I have become very fond of. As much as Sandra and I have talked about college, I know she will be there for one thing and one thing only that is to get a good education to be able to help mold other children. She had always talked about becoming an English teacher to help students within the area to learn things in a more suitable atmosphere that will broaden their horizons. Not only did she talk about being an English teacher, but she had also always wanted to concentrate on the legal field and if she could not obtain success in one opportunity maybe she would in another so with a double major she would be sure to make it."

The three of them spent their almost last good times together because come Monday, they would be leaving early in the morning being driven by their parents to their home away from home for the next four years. Sandra and Greg both asked Wayne if he had everything he needed to take with him all packed. He answered by saying, "I suppose so and all that I leave and need I guess I could have Mother and Daddy bring it to me one weekend or I probably could wait until I come home on break."

Wayne asked Sandra if she had all of her things packed. She said smiling, "Yes I do and I am looking forward so much to a long vacation from my little brother Greg."

As Wayne was about to leave to go home after spending his long time friendship with Sandra and her brother Greg he almost let it slip out of his mouth to Sandra as she walked him out of the house for the last time to say good bye to tell her how he really felt about her and how he had always loved her from the time they were growing up and played together. He wanted to tell her so much how she was the only girl for him and it did not matter if she was black or not because love has no color, but to be on the safe side for a while, he pulled himself back into reality to not make it known just yet because he knew there would be many hurdles to jump over before it would come to be presented not only to Sandra, but to his own parents as well as her parents and her brother Greg.

"Well Sandra," Wayne said to her. "I guess this is the time where you and I say good bye and good luck with our college studies to wish each other the best," Wayne said to Sandra as he placed his arms around her as a brother would do as she would see it that way to give her that last everlasting reminder that she has always been his sister as she would see it, but on another side of it, Wayne would take it as something different.

"Wayne," Sandra said to him as he started walking toward his home. "I wish you the best and I want you to know that I will miss you, but come college breaks we all will see each other to share our excitements at college."

"Okay Sandra, I will be looking forward in sharing my time with you as well as your brother." Wayne looked around to ask her what time will her parents be leaving tomorrow morning to take her off to college.

"We will be leaving really early to beat the traffic you know. What about you and your parents Wayne?"

"We also will be doing the same thing, leaving early to beat the traffic. Be sure to let Mr. Logan know that I will miss him as he will miss me as well," Wayne said to her as he walked out of sight and Sandra returned back inside to relay to Mr. Logan Wayne's message. To Wayne, departing from each other was a bittersweet as it was also for Sandra as he was her big brother she had known and been with for many years.

Sandra said to her brother Greg, "You know little brother, the three of us have been through a lot as a family because it has not matter whether Wayne was a white boy or not because you and I never for one moment thought about that."

"Big sister, it is all about the way our parents as well as Wayne parents taught us that God almighty had created a rainbow color and it was up to each individual to look into that rainbow to understand it. I think you, Wayne and I have learned in order to live together as one, we must abide by that rainbow."

"You are so right Greg but now you as well as I will miss Wayne because through all of our growing up years the three of us were real sister and brothers." As they were talking their parents walked into the room to ask the two of them what were they talking about.

"Well Mother and Daddy, it is like this, Sandra and I were saying how much we were going to miss Wayne from being here and how much I too will miss my sister because tomorrow she will be gone off to college. Mother and Daddy, what am I going to do? I will be all alone with no one to share my thoughts with?"

"You will have other friends at school to build a relationship with."

"I know that, but it will not be as if I am with Sandra and Wayne." Greg's father said to him about how life works and if not Sandra as well as Wayne then it would be something else. "Think about it my son, after your sister and Wayne finish college the two of them will not be here as before to sit out on the porch swinging and just talking because they will have a career to attend to."

"Greg," his mother said to him. "Look at yourself, in another year you will be just like Wayne and your sister, off to some college as they are. Greg your father and I, as well as Wayne's parents should be asking ourselves, what are we going to do? If you have not given it a thought by now, soon both parents will be back just like it when we first started out, just ourselves."

"I know mother, but you and Daddy will be able to handle it because just think, if Sandra goes off after college to get married after she lands a good job somewhere then you two will hope for some grandchildren to spoil. I am sure Wayne's parents are thinking on the same line."

"I think that's enough of that talk for now." So Sandra's father asked if she had packed all the things she think she will need for college for leaving.

"Yes Daddy, I can think of nothing else."

"Okay Greg why don't you take Sandra's baggage out to the car and place it in so we won't have to do it come tomorrow morning? The four of us can sit down to our last good breakfast together before leaving."

"Daddy, maybe I should run over to Wayne's home to see if he need some help packing," Greg said.

"No I don't think that's a good idea because he needs to be alone to accept being in your absence come tomorrow morning. Besides, the three of you have said all goodbyes. There will be holidays where you guys will unite for old time's sake."

"Sandra I am really going to miss from having you around here to greet me when I get home from school."

"Greg you can call me or even write if you think you need some of my advice pertaining to those hot girls there at school," she said laughing.

"I guess you have a point there and I am sure that will happen to Wayne as well with all those lovely girls there on campus. Wayne just might forget all about you and me once he become involved with one of those white chicks there on campus," he said to Sandra.

"Little brother that has crossed my mind but then it will be a good thing." Little did Sandra know that it would not happen that way because Wayne has always been in love with her and he will not take a chance of losing that because she is what he wants. Well, as the Logans were preparing to call it a night to get a good night sleep for an eventful upcoming day, the Hunt family was busy sitting around spending their last night together as a family because their son Wayne will be an empty space in their home come tomorrow night once they drop him off to college and return.

Episode Three

After a long night of tossing and turning by Wayne fighting his emotions over the one girl he loves but dared not to let on to his parents afraid of what they just might say about the whole thing about this type of behavior should not be with him, Wayne realized in the south and in this time, things of this sort just did not happen because the south whites would not tolerate a white boy falling in love with a black girl. This could never be because this is not the way southern whites were brought up from longstanding ways. As Wayne laid sleepless all through the night trying to put his emotions in order, he kept thinking about how he allowed himself to come to this point in his life to fall in love with a beautiful black girl when he could be entertaining some white girl as society says it's the right thing to do for all purposes.

After thinking hard on this line for a while Wayne fell off to sleep with a complete solid mind knowing his decision was based purely on pure love from the first time he met Sandra as when they were small children. His puppy love for her as children grew as the years passed which blossomed into something more concrete. One would say, how could a white boy keep such a thing hidden without giving himself away? Wayne fought many battles when he was in the midst of Sandra and her brother Greg pretending just to be close friends as they were, but all the time Sandra never picked up on any indication about the way Wayne felt toward her, only as a sister to him and a big brother to her and her brother Greg. Even both parents never thought of anything but good old neighbors where many meals on both sides were shared.

Wayne said to himself if he had opened up and alerted Sandra's family about his feelings for their daughter, would they allow him to come over to spend time with them? Or if he revealed it to his parents, how would their relationship with the Logan family be? He knew there were a lot of factors at state her and they only way to not change the course of things between the two families would be to let things ride as they are now, at least until a few years had gone by maybe once he and Sandra had completed their college studies. On Wayne's part, this would be a waiting game as it will not be for Sandra because she had no knowledge of what was going on in his mind concerning her.

Soon morning was in sight and it was time for both households to get up to enjoy a good last breakfast together before both cars would roll out onto the streets to head into their separate ways to introduce two bright students to the college way of life for the next four years. As Wayne and his parents had finished with breakfast, it was time for them to get started as they loaded up into their car and slowly backed out of the driveway to slowly pass by the Logan's home as they too were loading up to take Sandra to college. As they drove up Wayne's mother and father said to the Logans laughing, "Well here we go to dump of our kids."

Wayne yelled out the window to Sandra to wish her the best as Greg yelled back to him to say, "So now you and my sister are leaving me to be here all alone."

Wayne replied back to say to Greg," I will be home come the first holiday to find out what you have been doing."

As they were pulling off, Sandra yelled out the window to Wayne to say to him, "I do expect you to do well as I know you will"

The two cars separated themselves in different directions on the way to the university where Wayne will be attending, sadness was over his face as his mother asked him as she looked back at him to say, "What is wrong son?"

"Oh its nothing mother except I am feeling a little homesick already because I will not be there for you and Daddy." The reason he said that to his mother because he did not want to let on to her that the reason why his sadness was upon him was that he would be missing Sandra. In his mind he was saying, "My dear Sandra has left me but I know in my heart that one day she and I will be together but first I have to work out all things that just might stand in our way. There's a lot of understanding that has to be done with both parents in order to make this relationship work." Once when Sandra and I are finally together as one, we will need their support so this will be a long lasting relationship." Wayne's father looked back through his rearview mirror to notice that something did not seem right with his son, because going off to college should be a happy time because this will be the turning point in his life, but his father noticed something different.

"Son, is there something you need to discuss with me?" he asked.

"No Daddy, I don't think so."

"The reason why I asked because you don't seem to be happy about entering in college."

"Oh no daddy, I am happy I just have a lot on my mind to think about."

Wayne was surely not thinking about college because he knew he would do well once he got himself all settled in, the love of his life was entering college in a total place far away from him and the only time he will see her would be when the two of them are home for the holidays and breaks. Going off to college could not have been any better for Sandra because a love affair was not the thing on her mind as she only wanted to concentrate on becoming a good student in her classroom work to become a good English teacher as she wanted so desperately to teach in the schools there to get school students to understand English grammar. Once Wayne's father drove up onto the grounds of the university where he would be attending, they got out of the car and reached the site where he would be staying to make their way inside the building to get him registered in before moving on to the dorm where he would be sharing a room with another person. After everything was taken care of and Wayne was given his key to his dorm room, they headed out to meet the dorm attendant who was the manager and overseer over all rooms there in the dorm building. After meet and greet then Wayne started to go down to the car with his daddy to retrieve his things as his mother remained inside the room talking with his roommate. "I think you two guys will be happy here at this college," his mother was speaking to his roommate. "I know you two will support one another in your studies and watch out for one another. My son Wayne is a very quiet person and he is a dedicated young man so if there is any problem you might have, you can always count on my son to help you out. By the way, I never asked you your name young man."

"My name is Danny." By then Wayne and his daddy walked in with all of his luggage and other things to get settled down before his parents had to get back on the road to return home before dark.

"Wayne my darling son, do you have everything you will need here?"

"Yes mother and if I need anything else I will call you to either bring it or just mail it." After spending quality time there with their son, it was about time for the two of them to leave for home because the longer they remained there the more sad his mother would get knowing her only child has left her.

Wayne's parents decided it was about time to say their goodbyes to get back on the road for a long journey home before nightfall. As Wayne walked his parents to their car and hugged and kissed and thank them, he made it a point to let them know that there should be nothing for them to worry about because he would be just fine while studying at the University of Mississippi. The only regret he had being there was the absence of Sandra attending too. In those days school had not fully accepted integration so therefore, Sandra had to enroll at a predominantly an all-black university in Louisiana, which was a well thought about educational school.

Once Wayne's parents pulled off from away from the university, he turned to walk back inside the dorm to get really acquainted with his roommate. After a night of being away from home and a place where he could just breathe and think about his beloved Sandra, things were getting to feel much better with him knowing he could prepare to complete his assignments and make preparations once he graduated to make it known to everyone that he had a surprise to tell everyone. All though he had made up in his mind what he plans to say and do, this was still four years away and he had to be very careful how he would tell it. He thought for a moment if he should get very close with his roommate to tell him what he was about to do with his life or not since he didn't know exactly how his roommate felt about interracial marriage. As Wayne did some heart searching, he thought this was not the time so he would not open up about it to anyone not just yet because if he did, this probably would cause him to be dismissed from the university because of it so a shut mouth would be his best weapon.

In the meantime, Sandra, her brother Greg, and their parents had gotten to the university of her chosen place in Louisiana to get started with her future. Sandra already had her room and she knew who would be her roommate because the two had been connecting before now so this would be easy for her once she had checked in and given her key to her dorm room where her roommate Mary was already inside to welcome her. As Sandra and her mother made their way to her room, her daddy and brother were busy getting all of her luggage and other items from the car to take inside. As Sandra and mother walked inside, Mary welcomed her with open arms to say, "Girl I am glad we are finally meeting and I know we will be good together as you and I have decided to study the same field."

Sandra introduced her mother to Mary then went on to say, "This is my father and little brother Greg," as the two of them were walking in loaded with her things.

Mary said hello to the two of them as Greg responded to say, "Mary, make sure my sister will be doing the right things while she is here."

"Mary, please don't listen to my brother because he feels a little out of it because he has to return home without me."

"Don't worry Greg, Sandra and I will just be fine besides, we won't have too much free time because when you decide to go into the English field, there is quite a bit of work to do and learn."

"I am sure of that," Greg said. "But I am speaking about these guys on this campus and believe you me, I just laid my eyes on a lot of them."

"Greg this is a coed college," Mary responded. "But I don't think Sandra or I will have any problems."

"If you two do just call on me," Greg said laughing. Sandra's mother Catherine asked Mary about her mother because she would love to meet her.

"I am so very sorry but my parents brought me here early this morning and they had to hurry back home to be with my two small sisters. I am sure you will meet her in time."

"Sandra," her mother asked. "Do you have everything you think you will need?"

"Mother, I am good and all I ask of you and daddy while I am away is to make sure Greg get his homework completed because you know how he is at times."

"That is easy for you to say because now I don't have anyone I can run to for help since you and Wayne have left."

"Who is this Wayne?" Mary asked.

"He is our big white brother that has been in our family since day one so we are really just like real families where we depend on one another," Greg responded.

"So where is this Wayne brother of yours?"

"He enrolled today as we speak at the University of Ole Mississippi."

"It sounds as if your two families are one in the spirit," Mary replied.

"Mary, I introduced my mother and brother's names but not my daddy. His name is Elijah, a really sweet Daddy too."

"Hold on there my sister, don't get carried away because now since you won't be around I believe Elijah and Catherine Logan will be all mine," Greg said laughing.

"Well be that as it may but for now, I am here surrounded by many people. Just don't you bring home any of these guys to say they are boyfriends now big sister," Greg warned her.

As Sandra hugged and kissed her mother and walked over to do the same with her father she whispered in his ear to say, "Daddy, get him out of here before he makse me cry as it is hard enough to see you guys leave me here."

"Okay guys, I think we have been here long enough and I feel good and at ease because I know my baby girl will be alright because she has a good roommate."

"Mr. and Mrs. Logan, Greg too, please try not to worry about Sandra too much because she will be just fine because she and I will have each other's back. We will be fine."

"Now you said that, I feel much better so come on guys, let's get going because we have a distance to travel you know."

As the three of them walked out of the room as Sandra followed, Greg said to her laughing, "I mean what I said about these guys because I don't think Mother and Daddy are ready to entertain your boyfriends yet."

"Greg will you please cut it out because that is not what I came here for."

Once to the car, the four hugged again and as they loaded up to pull away, Sandra stood by waving her goodbyes as Greg had his head out of the window yelling, "We will see you the first holiday sister." At that moment in Sandra's life, it hit her that now she was no longer home but now in a completely new surroundings. As she walked back inside to her room to be with her roommate, she kept telling herself that she would be just fine and she hoped Wayne would be also although nothing of how he felt toward her was even in her mind.

As the Logans drove home, Greg was very quiet as his mother asked him what was his problem. Greg stuck his head between his mother and father to ask them this question. "When it is time for me to go off to college, what will you and Daddy do in my absence?"

"Well son," his father replied. "I think your mother and I will be just fine knowing that we did what parents need to do to give their children a start in life. We will want the best for you just as we do with your sister. She did everything she had to do in order to make it to college and you must follow in her footsteps."

"I am feeling really sad now because nor Sandra or Wayne are around making it feel as if I am at a lost."

Greg's mother spoke up to say, "You are not alone nor are you at a loss because now we three have to make sure Wayne's parents are jolly enough so they will not worry too much about him not being there. I don't know about Sandra's intentions but I do know that Wayne will return back home to this location once he graduates to work in the agricultural department to teach farmers how to grow their crops. Now, once your sister finishes, she hopes that she will be able to teach English at one of these schools, but you know how things are now about blacks teaching white students. I hope by then things would have changed and she will not have any problems."

"You know son, you will also be in college into your third year once Sandra graduates," his father said.

"That is right daddy."

"Have you given it a thought as to what you plan to major in?"

"No I have not just yet Daddy because I think I still have time to think about it since this is my last year of high school."

"Don't wait too long," his mother said.

"Our first night at home without Sandra," Greg said. "The house will be empty."

"No it will not son, and I don't want you to keep talking that way. We will have a lot to do and prepare for and besides you won't have to fight over who will have the last cheese biscuit."

"You are so right about that because I will have my choice," Greg said laughing.

"Greg," his father said to him. "When we get home I want you to go over to Wayne's parents and see how they are handling having Wayne away. Sit down and spend some time with them to build up their spirits to let them know everything will be alright because we are in the same boat as they are."

"No problem daddy, I will; besides it will give me a chance to eat some of Mrs. Hunt's apple pie."

"Greg is that all you think about is eating?" his mother asked him.

After Wayne's parents had dropped him off at Old Mississippi University, they returned home a little sad because the only child they were able to have has now left home to enter college thus leaving them all alone to face each day together as if it would be like the time when the two of them became husband and wife. As they drove up to their home and as Florence, his mother, got out of the car and looked toward the Logan's home to see if they had made it back from dropping off their daughter Sandra so she could walk over to talk to ease her loneliness only to see they had not arrived. Standing beside the car looking in a distance, her husband Samuel looked toward her to ask, "Florence, why are you standing still as if you are in a daze?

"Samuel, I am just thinking how I already miss our son who has been our life from the time he was born and now he is all grown up and is making his own way in life."

"Well Florence," Samuel replied. "You should have known that one day it would all come down to this, besides we raised him the best you and I knew how to so let's hope the best for him and hope that in the coming years he will make sound judgements and find a nice girl to marry and give us some grandchildren. Don't you want that for him Florence"?

Florence turned toward Samuel to say, "Now won't that be great having some grandchildren around so you as well as I can just spoil them?"

"It won't happen Florence if we don't give him that chance and let him make his own decisions. Regardless of how you might see things now, but in a couple of years it will all change. Maybe while there on the college campus, he will find a nice girl to court and marry after he graduates."

"Now you hold on there Florence, let you and I remain out of his decision about what he should decide on because that will strictly be his choice."

"I know Samuel, but it would be a nice thing if we could introduce him to a nice young girl."

"All I can say about this whole thing Florence, I hope you won't be blindsided with who he marries and you will be able to accept it. Besides honey, we are only parents and we cannot make up our children's decisions. Enough said, come on let us go inside and wait until the Logans get back from dropping off their daughter Sandra so we will have a lot to talk about. You know Greg will be coming over here as often as he can to eat up your home cooked apple pies, taking Wayne's place. Think about it Florence, although Wayne is away, we still have Greg here with us for another year to fulfill our needs as well as his own mother's and father's."

"Greg is just like our son as well and Sandra our daughter too because we have treated them just like we did Wayne as our own. You know Samuel, I am so glad we have a loving relationship with them because all these years living close to each other has really opened our eyes to many things to life to show color does not matter when you are so connected and share the same values. If you have not given it a thought Florence, this young generation of kids are going to change the way society has built it and they intend to break all values and go after whomever they like so brace yourself because I feel a lot of changes are coming down the pipe. Think about it, come next year, Elijah, and Catherine will lose their baby boy Greg. He too will depart from their nest and go off on his own to the college of his choice to start mapping out his life so they two will be just as you and me as they started out. I think with all three children gone away, this will bring the four of us closer together to welcome our kids when they come home to visit whether married or just on vacation from their jobs once leaving from college."

"I am sure Samuel that is exactly what you and Elijah will talk about once you two get together in your spare time after work."

" So Florence, you act just like you and Catherine won't be doing the same thing," he said laughing. Just as Florence and Samuel were about to walk up the steps to enter their home, they heard the sounds of the Logan's car to turn to see they too were driving up. As they got out of the car, Florence yelled to them to tell them stand still because Samuel and she are coming over. When they got there, they all took a seat on the porch to just embrace and talk about how it will be around there since their kids are gone.

"Florence," asked Catherine. "How do you feel knowing that your only daughter is no longer here?"

"Well to tell you Florence, it is too early to feel her absence because I suppose still having our son Greg here will make it much easier for Elijah and me. We will miss her I think starting tomorrow morning when we all sit down to the breakfast table to have breakfast that's will I will know she is no longer here."

"I know it will not be the same with Samuel and I when we sit down to have breakfast because there will be an empty chair there."

Greg spoke up to say, "Don't remove that chair because I will eat here and then run over to your home to eat there too, so you and Mr. Samuel will think Wayne is still here."

"That is so nice of you Greg but if you ate that much then you will not be able to fit into your clothes and then your mother and I will have to go out to buy you new ones," Florence said laughing. Finally, Elijah and Samuel opened up to say that this is the time where these two families ave to stick close together because of their children and believe that things will be alright as they will see because both kids are away in college, but look what they will accomplish in the next four years.

Samuel said, "My son will come home with great ambitions in the agricultural field to involve himself in teaching farmers how they should plant and attend to their crops."

Elijah said, "My daughter Sandra will come out with her degree in English to teach kids how to use their grammar."

After their brief visit with the Logans, Samuel suggested to his wife Florence that it was time for the two of them to go home to try and have a goodnight without their son Wayne being there. "This is something Florence, you and I will just have to get used too for these next four years and after that we might just have to come to the realization that our son will not take up housing here with you and me ever again because if he is going to be working with the agricultural department, you know he will have to be close to his job in town."

"Samuel, I understand but I thought when the time comes, we would at least have him back with us for a short while until he gets things in prospective."

Catherine said to Florence, "Try not think ahead of yourself at this point because they just enrolled into college and this is all new. Besides, you and I have plenty of time to bake cookies to send to the two of them to share with their friends there. Try to go home and have a good night sleep without worrying so much about Wayne because he will be alright just as Sandra will."

"Alright Catherine," Florence replied,. "I will take your suggestion and if I wake up having a hard time sleeping, I will call you."

"Catherine, Samuel said. "Please don't worry about Florence calling you because I will hide the telephone from her," he said laughing as the two of them walked toward their house after saying goodnight. After that, the Logans decided to go inside and sit down to try to deal with their daughter and sister's absence. Once inside Greg asked his mother if he could have a piece of cake with a cold glass of milk.

"I suppose so and cut a slice for your father, so the two of you can enjoy a man talk. I think I will go into the bedroom to change out of this dress into something more relaxing before I join the two of you." When Catherine returned and sat down she said to Elija, and Greg how Wayne being away from home will cause Catherine to go into a deep depression if she doesn't get it together.

Elijah said to her, "This I think is where you come in to make sure that doesn't get to that point."

"That sounds all good, but tell me, what am I supposed to do to keep her from thinking about him so much Elijah?"

"Well honey, I am going to leave that up to you and our son Greg," he said laughing.

"I think while Samuel and I are out busy working and you and Florence are home and when Greg gets in from school, I am sure that you two will keep her involved with things to take her mind off him so much. Why Catherine, you and Greg are busy taking care of putting up vegetables for the winter time you mean Florence and I because Greg only hangs around to get what is left to eat, right son?"

"Well Mother, you know Daddy did say, let me help and that is my intention," he said laughing.

"I tell you what my darling wife, why not prepare dinner and have the two of them over tomorrow night, your delicious dinner will surely bring smiles on her face. You know how much she and Samuel like enjoying your food. That just might be the start of something that can help restrain her from going depressed."

"Okay Elijah, I am on board with that suggestion."

"So am I too Dad," Greg said.

"I can imagine if we didn't have Greg I just might feel the same as she does especially with only one child, but we were blessed to have this greedy son which I love dearly to help the two of us from feeling that way. Catherine, before Florence realizes it those four years will be over with before she can say what happened. The big bang that will really get her is when Greg graduates and takes control of his own life. With our only daughter, we will feel somewhat the same way because I am quite sure after Sandra graduates and apply for a teaching job here in this location and she is turned down, I don't expect her to hang around here without working for what she went to school for. Think about it, she has cousins in New York and other places where she could go to obtain work. Wayne, on the other hand, only has relatives in this state because they never moved away and then too, they are not really that close where he would feel comfortable living with them. When the time comes Elijah, we will deal with it."

"Catherine, I am quite sure whatever happens after the two of them graduate from college will be good because wherever they land the two of them will find success whether here or their new embarkment," Elijah assured his wife.

:As you know we are still in the early part of the sixties where so many new things have not yet been put into practice and I hope by the time our son makes his way into society, things will turn around where everyone will have his or her rights to decide on what they want to do," Catherine implied to her husband and son.

"That sound all good for now but Catherine, you know so many people will not be ready to turn around from the way they were brought up to make a complete change where everyone will be judged on their accomplishments not on their color," Elijah replied.

After listening to all the talks from both sides of his mother and father, Greg decided to chime in to say, "By the time I am about to complete my college career I hope things will be new and everyone will have an opportunity to mingle with whomever they wish to be involved with." While they were all talking about how changes will surely happen in a few years, they never even once gave it a second thought about whether their best friends' white son whom they had seen as a second son to them was in love with their daughter. If they knew, how would they act? Little did either parents know, very soon they would be shocked with the news and everything just might change between them if they did not remain positive with changes. For now, this is merely a wait and see cat game being laid on both sides by the one person who is the center of it all, as it is a secret for now until the time is right.

Is Love Worth the Wait?

In the meantime Wayne's parents Florence and Samuel had settled in to accept the absence of their only son as he engaged himself in studies at Ole Mississippi University, preparing to learn all there was to know about agriculture that would allow him to engage himself in the process of teaching farmers there in the county on how best to grow their crops. While Wayne was having such a hard time dealing with his emotions, Sandra, the one girl that he had loved from day one was busy at the University of Louisiana, studying to become a good English teacher with a minor concentration in legal affairs because she wanted to learn all about things in the legal field, but her main determination was to become a good English teacher to teach schoolchildren the right way to write and speak so they would be recognized that they were taught by a good, educated, black English teacher who held a lot of pride within herself to make sure all who she came in contact with would excel.

Sandra was so busy focusing on her education that she never once gave it a second thought about Wayne being in love with her, besides how could he because to her he was just her big brother as she, her brother Greg, and Wayne always hung out as family. Being at the university, Sandra never thought for one second that a boyfriend was an interest to her because she was only there for one thing and that was to get a good education to move forward. Besides, what would this do to her if she found out now since she was in the prime of her life? This is why Wayne was determined to keep everything a closed secret until the two of them finished up their education and just then maybe he would expose it to his parents as well as Sandra's parents. How so much he hoped they would be happy and understand that he cannot live in the past of the ways society has proposed for so many years.

Wayne had decided to break the frozen ice and let it melt to run down the hills once the cat was out of the bag. He have already embraced himself of all the possible repercussions that just might hit him, but if he was to better himself and let everyone know that to him, color did not matter then everyone who just might be against it would see it his way and come around to include his own parents as well as Sandra's parents to become one. Wayne, has dug back into his history books to find out for many generations passed, there has been a mixture of races because of all the various complexions around today. Once Wayne took a look into what had happened in those years past, he then realizes that if what happened in those years as things were kept as secrets why then those secrets cannot be broken and brought out because if many people have never realized it, mixed marriages were long established, but society did not make a big notice of it because of status.

Foe now Wayne will just have to place it on hold until the time and day is right to expose it all to his parents hoping they will take into consideration that this is what he wants and there is nothing they could do about it because he is his own man. On the other hand, knowing Sandra's parents and brother the way he does, he feels as if he will not have any problems because of their fondness for him through all the years they have known him. Surely Greg will not because he is next in line to marry whomever he desirse too. The only one that will need a lot of convincing will be Sandra because this whole thing is center around her and how she will accept it. Wayne is hoping and praying that she will honor his decision and accept all that he will have to offer to her so they will have a glorious life together to make both sets of parents happy to have some grandchildren to carry on both legacies. For now, Wayne understand that he has four years to make it all right and to wrestle with his feelings.

To put all of this thinking aside for a while, Wayne could hardly wait until the university had its first holiday break where he could rush home to be there to greet Sandra as she comse in so the two of them and Greg can just sit outside on their first porch and talk about how things are going in college for them. This too will be a highlight of some of his thoughts of her. At some point in time, Wayne will find a way to ease into their conversation to ask about whether or not she has met a college fellow on campus. The reason why he would ask that to see if it would be a possibility for him. Wayne just wanted to make sure of himself that one day he would get Sandra to love him and become his wife. While on their short vacation break, Wayne knew he had to make sure he did not expose himself too fast but, however, move very slowly in all what he says or does so Sandra would not notice anything out of the norm about him. This Wayne thought would be very hard for him to do as he knew he had no other choice but to play his cards right or else fail.

Their first college break would be Thanksgiving as they would be home for about a week before they would return back to resume their studies so there would be plenty of time to enjoy his own parents as well as spending time with Sandra's family as well. Wayne was hoping that maybe the two families could share the Thanksgiving dinner together because his mother as well as Sandra mother could cook up mean dishes of foods. This he thought would be the ideal thing to do so when the decision is made by him to open everyone's eyes, it would be much easier for all of them to accept, but first this will be a while down the road before anything would take place because Wayne does not know whether Sandra will remain here in this location or leave for New York City or some other place to seek good employment that will pull her away from him, thus forcing him to marry one of those white girls there as he would not be happy, but because of what society says must be. He is sure if that happens, the marriage would surely fail, because it would not be Sandra.

Wayne said to himself, "How can I ever be in love with one of these country white girls when all the time I have only known a beautiful black girl whom I fell in love with from the time we met and spent just about our whole lives together getting to know one another and to know what each other likes? Sandra and I have always made it a point to do our school work together and shared many thoughts and secrets to one another. She and I have built up something stronger than anything I could ever see in a white girl because I love the qualities of a smart, black, young girl. I won't care what society says that this is the way it supposed to be remaining true to your own race but I don't care what it says because I have my own mind and I am the one to regulate it for the way I want to live my life. I am hoping that one day Sandra will find those same thoughts in me as I have found in her. Being together on school breaks will help build our relationship stronger although Sandra will not see it the way that I do but I am going to keep hope alive because I know it will surely come one day."

For that reason Wayne knew the only thing now left for him to do is remain positive and make sure while he is engaged into his studies, he is to learn everything possible about the field he set out to study and do it well once this is all over with so he will put his plan into action. Sandra, on the other hand, once home on break will go about her business as usual treating Wayne as she has always treated him, seeing him as her big brother no matter how hard it was for him to accept. Other than friendship, there was nothing else on her part because she never did see anything else but just that. The two of them will sit out swinging a tandlking about their first year in college and what things they have learned being away from home for the first time in their lives. Sandra would explain to Wayne how so afraid she was the first day her parents and brother drove her to the university. In turn, Wayne, on the other hand, would open up to say to Sandra how so hurt he was the morning when their families stopped side by side to let the two of them say their goodbyes.

Since Wayne has been away at school away from the presence of Sandra he has managed to control his feelings for her by seeking heavily into his classroom work and assignments to prepare himself to be able to move on up to the next year of his studies because he realizes it will soon be just a short stay there at the university before he will leave and return back home to begin his life just as he was doing before he enter the university, the only difference this time would be that he has set his goals high and he would be solely responsible for his own surroundings not having his mother to guide and direct him. While thinking this way, he also was thinking about Sandra's life as well, but this time after she too has met her goal she would not return home to spend her days doing nothing that is, if she did not get an opportunity to be assigned to a school there. Sandra would have to move on to the next location in order to use her tools.

Wayne was thinking way ahead of himself as if he and Sandra were involved in a close relationship other than friends. Of course, it would be nice if she knew all about his intention for them, but how could she when nothing of this sort has ever confronted her to decide? If it has, then who would know if she would accept such a relationship with Wayne due to the fact they grew up together and deemed one another as sister and brother? This thoughts and ideas were only in the mind of Wayne, not in Sandra's mind, in about another month, the two of them will come together because they will be out on break for the Thanksgiving holidays which will last for about four days before returning back to continue their studies. In that period of time, Wayne will make sure he spends as much time with Sandra as he can to see and find out if she has missed him in the absence period of their time. He is so much hoping that she will tell him how much she missed being around him, so he will take it that she is showing some sort of feelings for him.

Of course back in his mind he know that will not be the case, but it doesn't hurt to hope that it would be that way. A few days has passed before it was about time for the two college students to come home for their Thanksgiving break as both parents would drive to pick them up because back in the sixties, students did not have their own car to have on campus unless it was the rich kids so parents had to drive to retrieve the ones who could not afford to have their own vehicles. Early one morning while the Logans had finished with their breakfast and Greg had left for school, Catherine and Elijah were sitting out on their front porch talking before he left for work on his land when Florence and Samuel walked over to spend some time with them before he too engaged in his work to ask if they were ready to go and get Sandra from college for the holidays.

Elijah responded by saying, "If I don't that son of mine Greg will never let us live it down because each day when he gets home from school all he talks about is when are we leaving to get his sister?"

Florence turned to Catherine to say, "You do know that Greg really misses her and I do myself because not having her here seeing that beautiful smile on her face has made a lot of difference around here."

"I have to agree with you Florence, because living in a house with just two men and you are the only female makes the difference around here when it comes to doing things, at least when Sandra was here I really did not have to worry so much about Greg because he always looked to her to help him out whether locating his clothes or other things he misplaced. The two of them shared a great bond toward each other and now that she is not here it has made it hard for him to accept until he comes to grip with her absence."

"So Catherine," Florence asked. "What about your family and my family having thanksgiving dinner together? We all can have it here or we can have it over to our house, it won't matter just as long as we all are together and I am quite sure Wayne, Greg, and Sandra would love that.

"You and I can decide what each one should prepare and whoever house we decides to serve dinner we can bring our dish of the prepared food. Florence, you and I can make that decision in a few days."

Elijah said to Samuel, "What was on his agenda for the day as I noticed you driving your tractor out to the front?"

"Well Elijah," Samuel said to him. "Do you know that patch of land close to the house where I never did anything with?"

"Yes, I think so Samuel. I think I will turn up that soil upside down and plant some winter corn in it, I was thinking about doing the same thing with that piece of land I have not that far from the house myself. I don't know as of yet what I want to plant in it but I will think about it by the time I finish tearing it up," he said as he laughed.

"You know next week Samuel, we will have to go pick up our kids from college to have them here with us for the holidays."

"I know Elijah, and I can hardly wait until our Wayne is home, because we have really missed him from being here especially at nights when the three of us are sitting at the dinner table enjoying some of Florence's good old cooking."

"I know the feeling because by not having Sandra sitting at the table, I can see a difference on Greg's face as he asks for a dish to be passed because he was so used to his sister asking him like she was his mother if he would like to have more of this or that," he said laughing.

"Isn't it funny Samuel to see you have kids here today and when you turn around, they are gone," asked Elijah.

"That is true but as I concentrate on it more each day, I come up with this answer. It is all part of growing up and I have already informed Florence about Wayne's decisions once he complete his education that there is a possibility that he will not be returning back home to live with us because he will be looking into a new level of life. Each morning Florence will walk into his room I guess she is hoping that he will be there only to learn he has left and is away at college studying to better himself for a new life which he has to carry on."

"You know Elijah, neither you nor I will know what the future holds for our kids, but we are hoping that the future will give them a sense of good understanding as to understand and work hard to try and make things better for everyone, not just one race of people, but for all of humanity. You and I cannot tell them who to fall in love with or who to marry because that is a choice they have to make and if they make a choice, we as parents are to remain true to their decisions and accept what they have chosen."

"Now Samuel, you could not have said it any better because Catherine and I have long decided that we would not try and stop Sandra from marrying who she thinks is right for her just as long as he makes her happy and that applies to our son Greg as well."

"Once when Wayne gets married just then maybe Florence will be happy and thrilled to hope that she will get a chance to enjoy and entertain some grandchildren to make her life complete."

" Samuel, Catherine as well as I feel the same and Greg hopes one day he will have nieces and nephews to call him Uncle Greg. Now that will be something since he has not even mentioned anything about if whether or not he will get married after he completes his college education."

Florence said to Catherine, "Greg just might wind up coming back home to live with you and Elijah, you know because some kids rather be home around their parents to protect them."

"I don't think so Florence," Catherine said. "Because Elijah and I want him to make a life for himself just as we did when we were first married. It was hard to leave home but then we realized, we are now husband and wife and we must fly away from our parents to develop our own nest, so we did and now look, we have two wonderful children whom we love dearly just as you and Samuel did with Wayne. It's a wonderful thing to see how well you have groomed and mold your children to grow up to be strong women and men to be able to face life on their own with great enthusiasm."

"Listen, here the four of us are sitting out here on the porch on this cool fall like morning talking all the things that has not been discussed before of how we want our children to be knowing right now, we only have just a little while longer to spend with them and then they will be gone on their marry ways," Florence said.

"Don't get me wrong because I think what we are talking about is good and you are so right Samuel, we should prepare ourselves for what is to come and I try each day to keep in mind what you tell me all the time about Wayne. Sooner or later I know I will have to turn him loose so he can find his own thin line in life for himself because he is a man and he is subject to meet his goals without his parents looking over his back to tell him no son, please don't do that because that is not the right way or do not marry her because she is not the right one for you. I think whomever he fall in love with I will be able to accept it."

Catherine responded to her by saying, "Are you so sure of that Florence?"

"I think so," Florence said.

"What if she is a Chinese or Spanish girl he had met at college and decided to marry one of them, how would you feel then?" Catherine asked.

"I don't know because I am not use to seeing them around so I really cannot say at this time. How would you feel Catherine, if Sandra met and married a young man of color other than her race to marry, how would you feel?"

"Well, being like you I first would have to look deep inside my heart not because who that person is but to ask myself will he be a good provider for her and would he love her regardless of what color he is and never see her as being different from him? I think Florence that would be my only concern."

Florence said, "Here you and I are talking about that, but we have not asked our husbands how they would feel."

Elijah as well as Samuel both said, "We just have to deal with it and hope the best because as we have talked about it, there is nothing we can do to decide for our children, they have their own minds to make their ways in life, whatever choices they make for themselves, they will just have to live with."

Just after the Logans and the Hunts had finished having their early morning conversation concerning Thanksgiving and about their children, it was now time for everyone to start off with their own agenda for the day. Elijah made it his point to get started on what he had decided to do to his land for the day as did Samuel, thus leaving Catherine and Florence to decide on what each one would be preparing for the big dinner come Thanksgiving where each family would be sharing together. Without any complaint if Wayne knew what was being put into place, he would just be thrilled over the top of his head because now this would definitely give him more definition on the way he feels about Sandra just knowing this togetherness would close the possible gap between the two families if his plan works in the upcoming few years after graduation for both he and Sandra.

Once the two men had left, Catherine and Florence sat down side by side together in the porch swing with a piece of paper and wrote down what each one would be preparing. This way, they would not have too much of the same menu. Catherine said to Florence while they talked, "You know next week we will be going to pick up our child from college and I don't know about you but I can hardly wait to have my daughter home for a week."

"Hey not so fast there Catherine," said Florence. "You know as well that I too can hardly wait to have my son home to spend the absence with his father and me."

"Okay Florence, this is what I will prepare and you can tell me later what will be on your list to do. I will do the greens, mac and cheese, stuffing, yams."

"Since you will do all of that then it will be my duty to bake the turkey as you know I can burn on that smiling. I will make potato salad, rolls, mashed potatoes, and gravy, along with your son's favorite, a banana pudding. Why not let Sandra make the lemon tea as everyone loves it? Sounds like a winner to me so I suppose we have everything set if you agree Florence," Catherine said.

"Now, the decision is to be made where will we all meet, here at my home or at your home?"

"Well, you know you have the biggest dining room Catherine, so I think we will all have our dinner right here in your home. By having it here, it will give the three kids time to enjoy one another and I know Wayne will be thrilled."

"Don't you know Florence," said Catherine. "Because sometimes I think he feels that he doesn't have to go home when he is over here with Sandra and Greg."

"You do know Catherine, he feels as if he is a part of your family and especially seeing Sandra and Greg as his sister and brother."

Catherine said to Florence, "You know, I am so glad we live close to each other because we have really bonded as a family because we have not looked at each other by color and you have taught your son not to judge."

"Hey Catherine, don't you feel left out because you too have done the same thing as me not to judge or look at a person by his or her color?"

"I suppose it was meant for the two families to be united together although here in this state, it still have a ways to go to make changes because look at where my daughter has to go to college which should not be because there is one right here in this county, but she is not allowed."

"Catherine," Florence responded. "Don't even think about it that way because you know Sandra will be getting a good education where she us because from what I heard about the University of Louisiana, it is one of the greatest college around in this state as it turns out many smarter graduates that the University of Ole Mississippi. To my belief, I think she is better off just where she is going. The reason why Wayne is attending Ole Mississippi University is because it does have an outstanding agricultural department and he believes he can learn a lot by attending there. I do know if things were better, I know he would have enrolled exactly where Sandra is attending. Little did they know, if he could have, he would have to keep an eye on his future wife as he hoped so desperately that it would come to be once he have completed his studies and be gainfully employed by the City Agricultural Department to work with farmers.

Lord, help Catherine and Florence, if they knew about all the intentions of Wayne wanting to marry Sandra. Would this put a damper between the two of them or would this cause the two families to grow apart because of their color? Right now, Wayne is in a vulnerable state of mind because although he is not too much worrying about how their parents will react as so much as he will be worrying about how Sandra would accept his decision once he comes forth to tell her. Wayne seems to think that Sandra's little brother Greg will be over thrilled and he will welcome it with open arms for he would have the two of them always around. Wayne is really dealing with whether or not Sandra will even want to marry him since they have been like sister and brother all these years and to now come forth to break a different kind of world to her just might send her over the cliff as he hopes it will not. Wayne knows that it will be a lot for Sandra to digest, but given time he thinks she will come around especially if she have gone through so many relationships if she leaves the area and heads off to the big city where she is sure to meet some fast talking, charming guys that just might break her heart thus causing her to return back home to gain her momentum, before any thoughts even enter her mind about dating guys.

It is nice for Wayne to think about all those things way ahead in the future that just might happen but there are still three whole more years of schooling to go through and for Sandra it is only education for her and surely she is not on campus to gain the eyes of the guys that are attending there as well. So Wayne for now does not have to worry about her on that issue because she is true only to her books. No sleepy time on her part, only on his where at many hours through the night he wakes up not being able to sleep thus allowing his roommate to ask him what is wrong or what is going on with him. Of course Wayne dares not mention anything to his roommate about a girl he is in love with and she is black because the time in this state is not appropriate to discuss so he would tell him, "I just have a lot on my mind."

Wayne know that he definitely would not say anything other than that to his radical roommate because he sure does not trust him and especially about this issue. After all the nights he laid awake, it did not affect his studies because when it came to his work in his classes, he excelled because he wanted to be a sure thing for Sandra if ever she did decide to say yes to him and marry him as he wanted her to know that he was well able to support her and family if it came down to that. In another week, he will be going home on a week school break for Thanksgiving and this will surely build his confidence to glow around her to see how she looks and how the two of them will share what they have learned since entering college. This particular week will be the highlight of his life just seeing her as she and Greg sit out on the front porch together with him as the two of them swing back and forth just talking and laughing. Enjoying themselves will not give Sandra one single clue as to why he is having so much fun laughing and just talking about the students there at Ole Mississippi University as she speaks about the students there at Louisiana State University where she attended.

Wayne would say to Sandra and Greg, "Nothing could be finer that what we three are doing right now and that is sharing moments of love," he said as he laughed. The love he was really speaking about the love he has for her. His love for Greg was brotherly love.

Greg responded to say, "Hey brother, I think this is the first time I ever heard you say that about how you love my sister and me."

Sandra would chime in to say, "I guess one can let one know exactly how he or she feels especially when you have been close together for so long just like family." All these thoughts were running through Wayne's head and he decided to turn over and force himself to sleep because if he did not then he just might miss his morning class.

"It is nice to dream and think of all the things you would like to happen before it gets started. Lord knows, I am praying that all the things I have worked out in my mind will come to a head and I will be one of the happiest man around here in this god forsaken state."

In Sandra's mind, nothing of this sort ever appeared because as it stands Wayne was not even on her mind to think of something like getting married and having a family with him. The only concerns that were floating around in her mind were to graduate and hopefully be accepted to teach at one of the schools there which was mixed with students but not teachers. Teaching English in one of the schools there was her only intention, not to be married to Wayne and to have a family with him. Sandra knew if she put all of her emphasis on her studies she would graduate with honors and just then maybe one of the school districts would give her a contract to teach, but there is still a lot of work to be done to get to that point and she was leaving that fight to the power to be in the civil rights field. Even before she will graduate, she had already made a decision not to remain in that location if she will not be offered a position in a school.

Sandra had already discussed this with her parents about a possibility of leaving to obtain a position in New York City where her chances are much greater than in Mississippi, besides there, she has relatives there where she can stay until she is able to find employment. Not only did Sandra decided to major in English which is far and near to her heart, but she also decided to have a minor in legal affairs that way if she could not obtain a position in her major, she would be able to work with a law firm to help make things right. There again, Sandra will not be looking for any romance there in the city. Before any of this can take place, Sandra wants to be well established within herself before she makes any attempt to involve herself in dating. Of course while she is home on break from school this is one thing she feel she doesn't need to let her brother or even Wayne know. This is something she will keep to herself and she dare not ask Wayne about his love life on campus. To her, this is and will not be an issue for her to talk about. If she brought up the subject, Greg would just take it and run with to ask Wayne about those girls there on campus.

Episode Four

SANDRA KNEW BEING IN THE COMPANY OF BOTH HER BROTHER Greg and their good friend who has been with them all of their practical lives would just escalate Greg to be asking Wayne a lot of questions concerning his campus life so he didn't think bringing up anything that would set him off would be the best solution for the three of them that way for the short stay home before it was time for the two of them to leave would definitely be a plus in Wayne's world, at least for the time being. Thinking within herself wondering what it would be like for some lucky girl to meet and marry Wayne how he just might forget about ever being the adopted brother for her and Greg. Would he stop disassociating himself with them or not? Oh well, if that's what it would take to make him happy and dear to his wife, he was for one all for it.

Of course, these were all the thoughts she as well as Wayne had running through their minds before any of this would ever take place besides there are three more years to come to that point and by then the two of them would have all grown up as well as Greg and ready to move on into different phases of life.

"As I think about Greg and myself, I too have to think about my little brother and how all of this will play into his life as well because just another year he too will be entering the college of his choice to map out his future thus leaving our parents all alone as well as Greg will with his parents. I think if the three of us try hard enough we just might make things easier for our parents and they will not have to worry about whether or not we are at a standstill in life. I think for right now all of these future ideas I have all stored up in my thinking capacity should be placed on hold until I reach that point so I am just going to concentrate on the wonderful Thanksgiving time we all will have together."

"Come tomorrow, my parents and little brother will be driving up on campus to get me so I will be with them for Thanksgiving. All of the students here are so looking forward in going home to eat some real food because the food being served in the cafeteria here you can say is not the best and to get some good eating will be the best thing that has enter our mouths since leaving home. My roommate is all packed and ready to go as her parents will pick her up around nine o'clock tomorrow morning. Just like her, I will be sitting outside waiting for my parents and brother as well because all dorms doors will be locked and the housekeepers will be busy taking care of things so when we all return, the rooms will be operational. Will I be glad to see Wayne since it has been a few months, I suppose I will because I am sure he can hardly wait to see me to be asking me a lot of questions as to how I like the university and what about my classes."

As Sandra is thinking about everything he will be asking her, Wayne will be mostly studying her actions since they have been apart to try and see if there was anything he would pick up from her whether or not she had gotten involved with one of those campus young guys that would put a damper on his feelings. Little did he know, there would not be any indications whether Sandra has found and fell head over heels in love with one of the fellows there on campus. If he even brings up this to her, she will just tell him that the only reason she is enrolled at the university is to get a good education and to be able to use it in the right way to help a lot of students. She will also tell Wayne that at this point in her life, she is really not looking for any relationship because there are a lot of things she wants to pursue before even thinking about meeting and falling in love with someone. Wayne also will be told by Sandra that when the time come, and he knows it will someday, the guy has to be someone who she had come to know and has prepared himself for a good future if the two of them decide to get married and have children. This would be exactly what Wayne has always wanted to hear her say because now he knows it would be him.

If Sandra knew in her mind what she had just laid out would be how Wayne viewed it for his satisfaction, she probably would have put it into a different context. With this he now know that given time, he will win her over and she will become his wife as he had always dreamed it to be. Back in Wayne's dorm room, he and his roommate were speaking about what they plan to do on their Thanksgiving break home as his roommate said to him, "Wayne, I plan to spend most of my spare time with my girlfriend as I know she has been missing me since I left. Wayne what do you plan to do while you are home?" he asked.

"Well to tell you this much, I plan to eat a lot of my mother's and my neighbor's good old cooking and spend time with my little brother and big sister there because I have really missed them." One thing Wayne was sure not to let on that the sister and brother were black because he knew this would cause a problem with him and his roommate because he was pro white all the way.

Wayne's roommate said, "It looks as if your Thanksgiving time will be taken up by your family. What about a girlfriend there?" he asked.

"What about it?" Wayne asked him. "I don't see why I have to overlook my family just to spend time with a girlfriend." Wayne was not interested the least in what he was speaking about and wished him well in all the time he and his girlfriend would spend together. "I know one thing," Wayne said to him. "I can hardly wait to get out of here because these months being away from home seem like a lifetime and I can hardly wait to see it. Have you been some place and you missed your home so much that you thought you were losing your mind?" he asked his roommate.

"No my friend, I cannot say I did because to be honest with you, this is my first time being away from home and to tell you the truth, I sort of like it. At least I can take responsibility on my own without my parents telling me to do this and not to do that. Finally, I feel like I am my own man. I guess I should feel the same way as you because when I was home, my parents were the same as you, but for good reasons to make sure I did the right things."

"Now that I am home preparing to enjoy my Thanksgiving with my parents and hopefully with Sandra the girl I love along with her parents, I hope this big dinner will turn out to be the best thing that ever happened to me."

As Wayne and his parents drove by the Logan home, he said to his parents, "Do you think that Sandra has arrived home from school yet?"

His mother said to him, "Son, if she has it will only be a matter of time before her brother Greg will come knocking at our door to greet you and to say that his big sister has arrived. I can just see the three of you hanging out on the porch making up for lost time being away from one another."

"That will be the best part of it all my dear mother, when the three of us can once again reunite to talk about our days so far at college and Greg letting us know how his last year in high school is going." Wayne's mother did not mention it to him that the two families were planning on having Thanksgiving together over at Sandra's folks home. Of course Wayne will be very delighted to hear about that because this would give him lots of time to spend not only with Greg, but with the girl of his dreams before it would be time for the two of them to return to college to continue their education in separate locations.

It had been no longer than thirty minutes before there was surely a knock at the kitchen door as it was Greg standing there saying to Wayne, "Brother are you going to let me in or are you going to just stand there?"

Once Wayne opened the screen door, Greg embraced him with a big hug to say, "Man am I glad to see you because since you have been gone, my world seemed so far away." Greg standing there greeted Mr. and Mrs. Hunt by saying, "I did not mean to overlook you two but I just had to grab my brother to give him a big hug. As you already know since Wayne and Sandra both have been away things for me has not been the same no matter how much of your banana pudding you served me Mrs. Hunt," he said laughing. Wayne immediately asked Greg if Sandra has gotten home yet.

"Yes she is and she is now sitting in the living room telling mother and daddy all about her time in college. Greg did she say, she enjoys being there?" Wayne asked.

"Well, all I could hear her say is this: mother, I am so glad I made the right decision to enroll there to further my education. Wayne there was one thing she did say to them was, how much she admired all of her professors and her classes because she knew she would learn all that is to be learned to carry out her intended career. Enough about my sister Wayne, what about you and your classes? Are you happy being there at that Ole Mississippi University?"

"Little brother, it has all to offer what I plan to do there, but if I had a choice to be there at the University of Louisiana, believe me, I would be there, but since these southern states have yet to forget how things has been established here, I will study hard there to get out and hope to help change things so the next generation as yours will have the opportunity to enroll in any university of their choosing.

Wayne's father, Samuel joined in to the conversation to say, "I really hope it will be very soon because I am so proud of the two of you bonding together as one and calling each other brother. You know that's what life is all about and how it was intended to be so don't you two guys every forget that and never give up short changing yourselves because you are not the same tone of complexion."

"Greg I don't know if your mother has mentioned this to you or Sandra yet, but we all are going to have our Thanksgiving dinner together over at your home. Now won't that be grand?" she asked him.

"Oh boy," Greg responded. "And I know your banana pudding will be on the menu right?"

"Don't worry my dear little son, because you and Wayne will have your time to fight over who will finish off the last of the pudding," she said laughing.

Wayne said to his mother, "You are serious and not kidding are you?"

"Why would I tell you a thing like this if I was kidding son?" This was right down Wayne's alley because he would rather be in the presence of Sandra than being home with just his mother and father eating alone just the three of them. This way all seven of them would be sharing the dinner table together with all the trimmings that will fill their hearts. Wayne knew in his mind, once he would return back to college, his mind would be at ease not only because he spent time with his family, but his time spent with Sandra would make it alright with him as he gets up each morning to head for his classes knowing that Sandra too was doing the same thing that one day the two of them would be together with a lot to offer society that would definitely change things.

"Greg," Wayne said to him. "Why not let us go over to your house to see Sandra so she can tell me all about her classes as I will tell her about mine?" Little did Greg did not know that was not at all Wayne's intention. He wanted to be near to her because he had missed it.

"Okay you two guys," Wayne's mother said to them. "Don't tire out the Logans asking a lot of questions and please be back home in a timely manner, Wayne, for dinner because tonight I am going to prepare a favorite welcome home meal for you so the three of us can catch up on what you have been learning since being in college to let your father and I know that we are not wasting our hard earned money," she said smiling.

"Mrs. Hunt, I can promised you that I will make sure Wayne s back home for his special dinner even if Sandra and 1 have to join him in this meal," Greg said laughing.

"You know Greg you and Sandra always have a seat at our table too," Mr. Hunt said to him.

"Okay guys, now get out of my kitchen and go your way." Once Wayne and Greg walked out of the house you would have thought the two of them were back in grade school because as they walked toward Greg's home to two of them just pushed and ran around each other as though they were on the school grounds playing a game so glad to be back in the presence of each other. Once reaching Greg's home and walking up on the front porch, who met them at the front door was none other than Sandra opening the door to welcome Wayne in as she gave him a big hug and a kiss on his cheek. That threw him for a wild loop because a kiss on his cheek was nothing he ever expected. A hand shake was all he expected to receive from her.

"Wayne," she said to him as he walked inside the kitchen to take a seat. "Please tell me all about how you fared being away from home for the very first time."

"Wait a minute my sister, let Mother and Daddy be the first to ask him questions and then you can ask all the questions you want to," he said laughing.

Sandra responded back to her little brother to say, "As if you have not already asked him a million of your silly questions."

"Now wait a minute you two guys," said their father. "Let us show Wayne how grateful we are to have him back home for Thanksgiving to be enjoyed by everyone."

"Mr. And Mrs. Logan, I am so glad to be back home and the best part of it all is just being able to spend these off from school days with the two families I love so dearly."

"Why that is nice of you to say," Mrs. Logan, responded to Wayne's nice comment. "Now Wayne that you are on this side of the street, did your mother let you know that we all will be having Thanksgiving dinner here at our home together?"

"Yes she did just before Greg and left to come over and I said to her, I think that will be one of the best Thanksgiving I will ever have just being in the company of so much love."

Sandra said to Wayne, "Why don't you, Greg and I find ourselves out on the front porch so we can exchange our class excitements."

"Okay you guys," Mr. and Mrs. Logan said to them. "But please take it easy Greg on the two of these college students," they said now smiling. After that the three of them walked out to the front porch as Sandra and Wayne took their seat together side by side in the swing as Wayne decided to take another seat near them. This was exciting for Wayne because this is exactly what he wanted to be near and dear to the future wife he has envision one day to be.

Sandra said to Wayne, "Should I start telling you how much I have missed these moments just the three of us sitting out here talking and laughing?"

"I have to agree with you," Wayne opened up to say, "because being away at college has given me a lot of time to do a lot of thinking."

"What things to think about Wayne?" she asked.

"Well, not now because I don't think I have figured all the aspects of my life out yet." He almost slipped and said our lives, but he caught on to what he was saying. He did open up to ask Sandra after she graduates from college what are her plans if she will not be able to get a teaching job here in this state because how things are especially when it comes to a black teacher teaching white students.

"Wayne, I hope by the time you and I both graduate from college, things will have changed a lot but if I cannot be fully employed here as a teacher, I guess I will travel to New York to live with my cousins there to obtain a job there in the legal field as it will be my secondary major."

"Sandra when I graduate, I will do everything that in my power to see that you get what you want out of life because you deserve the best of everything if that means teaching all students."

"Wayne you will not have that problem because of who you are which is through no fault of yours, it is just the way things are right now. Heaven knows I rather remain right here to teach English because there are so many students in school today using the wrong grammar so if they have someone to teach them the correct way to speak then I do believe they will make better people."

"I agree wholeheartedly with you Sandra," Wayne said. "I would like to say something to you and I hope you will not take it the wrong way. I wish you will not have to leave from here in order to obtain a job in a big city being around a lot of strange people whom you don't know. I rather you be here, but it is not my decision only yours. Whatever decision you make will have my support."

"Why thank you Wayne for being so sweet and understanding." Those words were all what he wanted to hear because now he has reassured himself that one day he is sure to have a future with the girl he has always been in love with. What better way to have a coming home welcome that being in the company of a wonderful girl and a wonderful soon to be in the future brother in law?

"Tell me a little about your classes you are taking Sandra."

"Well, at first I was a little afraid to face my professors because I did not know how they would be in all of my classes whether they would be rough and less caring but to tell you the truth, they are so very helpful because they teach with a desire to ensure that all their students leave the university filled up with the knowledge taught to them. So far, I have made wonderful grades, all A's if you want to know," she said smiling.

"I knew you would excel in all of your classes because from the time I have known you, you have always been smart."

Greg said to him, "What about me my brother? I thought you said I too was a smart guy as well."

"You are Greg, and I know that but this is something different, college material I am speaking to Sandra about. Since you want to know about my sister's classes and her grades, what about you in your classes, my brother?" he asked.

"Greg," Sandra shimmed in to him to say. "I thought that was my job to ask Wayne not you."

"Big sister you were to slow to ask so I decided to do it for you," he said laughing.

"Neither of you worry yourselves about my classes and grades because like Sandra I too received all A's as I must make good grades to be able to know all that is to know about agriculture when I am out there educating farmers on the right fertilizers or dusting to use for their crops to be successful in their growth. You know Wayne before you and I both know it, we will have graduated and out there facing the world on our own. Please don't stop to tie up your shoe laces because I will be right behind you as you alluded."

"Little brother, I know this is your last year of high school, but have you given it a thought as to what field you are planning to enter or what college you are looking to attend?" Sandra asked him.

"I have thought about many colleges, but won't it be something of a surprise if I enrolled into the Ole Mississippi University? Now that would give everyone the scare and put this state on the map for sure."

"That would be nice if that happens," Wayne said to him. "But you must know what difficulties you would have being on campus with the way these evil people are. You will have to have security around you day in and day out. Now my brother that would be something else to see you there walking into those classes surrounded by security. It is nice to think that way and hope that someday someone will invade that ole campus," Wayne said. "The only reason I am there is because of the program. Greg my man, I want you to know that choosing to attend ole Mississippi university was indeed not my choice, but my parents because they thought that would be the best college to attend to get all the learning I needed if I was to make a good agriculture agent to help all these farmers in and around this county. You know I just could not disappoint them because to me, it would not have been the right thing to do since they worked so hard to save money in order for me to attend."

"You don't have to tell me all that Wayne," Greg said. "Because it was the same thing with my parents making sure Sandra would get the best education she possibly could at an outstanding university, and that is why she decided on attending the University of Louisiana. Wayne I think the two of you made wise decisions and when the two of you graduate you will realizes it was the right thing to do because you two would have gained all that you seek..

After a very long gathering just the three of them, Wayne decided that it was about time for him to return home because as he and Greg were told that his mother was preparing a welcome home meal for him to enjoy. "Guys, you two know if you like to you are most welcome to come on over to help me eat up whatever mother has prepared and you know you can plant your feet under our table at any old time."

Sandra said to him, "Wayne this is your night and I know how much your parents want you to enjoy the well cooked meal just the three of you. Besides as you know, we all will be eating together on Thanksgiving and then we three can see if you can eat the most. Now you run along on home to be with your parents. Greg and I are going to fight over our dinner tonight as the four of us will just sit back and fill our stomachs." As Wayne stood up to leave, Sandra like any good sister stood beside him to place her arms around him to let him know that she was glad he was home just as she was to be on school break, at least to be in the company of each other again. Placing her arms around him and giving him a kiss on his cheek was exactly what Wayne needed because now since this was his second kiss from the girl he had always loved, it reassured him that having her soon as his future wife is paying off. This was his thinking because Sandra didn't have a clue that her kisses were leading up to how he had decided that his life would be with her.

Was Wayne fair in keeping Sandra in the dark not letting her know exactly how he felt about her? The question would weigh heavy on his mind whether he was being fair to this whole love thing or would it bring trouble between the two of them, regardless if so much love was shown between the two families? Wayne knew in the next few years while he would be away at college, decisions would have to be solved and by solving them, this is where he would definitely have to bring his parents into the core of it all. For now, it has to remain a complete secret only allowing no one to know, not even Greg, Sandra's brother who he viewed as his little brother because of the long years they maintained friendship together as one. He already knew when the cloud burst, the rain will surely fall and what particular way the rain will flood, he is not sure but when it does happen, he has to be ready for the price he just might have to pay. The only thing that Wayne is concerned about will be will this destroy his parents relationship with the Logans or will it build a stronger bond; he hopes it will make the bond tighter.

Greg and Sandra decided to walk Wayne home as he decided to hold Sandra's hand as the three of the strolled along the road to his home. Once getting there, his mother walked outside on the porch to say to Sandra and Wayne. "I see you two are sharing your brother and sister's absence being away from each other by holding hands."

Greg said to Wayne's mother, "You just don't know how much the two of them made me sick of talking about their classes and their professors.

"Please don't listen to Greg, Mrs. Hunt, you know how he can take nothing and turn it into something worse than it seems. Sandra darling, you don't have to tell me about your little brother, because since you and Wayne has been away in college, all his mother and I could do is keep him fed so he would not be missing you two so much. All he talked about how he wished you two would hurry up and come home so he could be the life of the party."

Wayne said to Greg, "You didn't tell Sandra and me all about how you were missing us as we talked."

"Why would I bring that up Wayne? You two are here now. Come Thanksgiving the war will be on at the table because I know your mother is making one of her favorites, a banana pudding the old fashioned way and guess what, I bet you I will eat more than you my brother."

"Sandra if you and Greg like, you are more than welcome to come on in and have dinner with us because I promised Wayne I would prepare his favorite meal."

"No thank you Mrs. Hunt because we have to go home to have our dinner with our parents because our mother, like you, prepared my favorite meal and she wants the four of us to sit down together and enjoy it."

"You know Mrs. Hunt, I can have my fill of both dinners," Greg said to her laughing.

"That would be nice Greg but you better hightail it on home to get ready for your dinner as Wayne will soon have his."

"Thanks for walking me home and I will see you guys tomorrow."

Sandra said to him, "You know I will be busy helping mother in the kitchen with the Thanksgiving dinner which will be the day after tomorrow so I probably will not get a lot of time to interact with you and Greg."

"Don't worry because I am sure Greg and I will find things to do even if it is nothing but walking around the land scoping out the wild rabbits."

Wayne greeted the two of them a good afternoon and walked into his home while Sandra and Greg returned home to have their dinner. On their way home Greg opened up to Sandra to say, "Have you noticed anything strange about the way Wayne is acting?"

"Not really little brother, if he is acting a bit strange I guess he is trying to reestablish himself being back home for the first time away."

"Maybe that is all there is to it but I am beginning to get a vibe that it is more than that. Greg maybe he has found a girlfriend on campus and he is missing her," Sandra said to him.

"Believe me my little brother will be alright given time."

"Now listen, don't you go asking him into his personal business about whether or not he has met a nice girl and he is falling in love," Sandra reminded him.

"Hey, take it easy my sister, I will not do that and I will take your advice and not ask him but I still have this strange feeling that there is more going on with him than you and I know."

"Greg let it be a secret with you now and please don't do or say anything that will upset Wayne. Do I have your promise?"

"Of course, I will keep how and what I feel to myself. If I find out anything my sister, you will be the first to know because you and I can talk about anything."

"Greg I am going to hold you to that now," Sandra responded. Little did Sandra know about what Greg felt was right on key about how Wayne felt about her, but he could not put it all together for now. He just might ever find out because Wayne was making sure his secret about his feelings about Sandra would not come out until he was ready for it to be broken then he would be the one to expose himself to everyone.

Once the two of them had gotten home and were about ready to sit down to enjoy a fantastic meal their mother had prepared, their mother asked them why Wayne did not stay for dinner as she had hoped that he would because he likes what she had prepared.

"Mother," Sandra said to her. "He had to go home to have a nice dinner his mother also prepared for him too. He wanted to remain here but I told him that it would not be right to overlook the dinner his mother had prepared just to have dinner here with the four of us."

Sandra's daddy responded to say, "Baby girl you made an educated decision to encourage him to return home to have dinner with his parents. It's not that we would not have loved having him here to eat with us, but since coming home from school he should have a good meal with his parents as you two are with yours. Don't you agree Greg?"

"Now you know I agree because there will be more for me to eat."

"When Greg and I walked Wayne home, Mrs. Hunt invited Greg and me to remain there for dinner with them but I said we had to come home to enjoy what our mother have in store for us."

Their mother responded to say, "That was really nice of her to invite you two for dinner to enjoy it with their son."

"I don't know what she prepared for Wayne but I would have loved to help eat it all up," Greg said to his mother.

"Son, when it comes to eating I don't think there is nothing you will not eat and it doesn't matter who cooks it, you will eat it up because that is just who you are when it comes to food."

"Come on guys, enough talk of what you could have done and let us enjoy our delicious food where my wife and your mother have spent time in the hot kitchen making sure we have a good time just enjoying our daughter and you being home with us from college for a few days," their father let it be known. As everyone bowed their heads in grace and then noticed on the table in all bowls what was prepared, it was every bit of what excited Greg as he took each bowl to take what he wanted and then passing on to the next bowl.

"I know Wayne would love eating this Mother, not saying Mrs. Hunt's food is not as good as yours because you know that lady can cook too. I supposed she got it from watching how you cook."

"Come on Greg," his father said. "Enough of that is enough so I am sure Mrs. Hunt learned from her mother all that she know besides watching your mother do her thing. Just think, tonight we have our daughter home from college to spend the Thanksgiving with us. Sandra tell us how you really like being there at the university?" her father asked.

"To be honest with you all, it couldn't be better because I have met wonderful students who are there as I am to learn all they can to help change things in the future. It seem as if all the girls there Greg are only about getting a good education not about getting involved with every guy there on campus, I just want you to know," she said smiling.

"Now did I say anything about the girls there sister?:

"No you did not but I know how your mind works when it comes to girls."

Their mother responded in to say, "I don't know why Greg is so caught on those girls there in college because he has to do better with his studies than what he has been doing so far."

"Mother, I am doing quite well I think."

"Son, you know you can do better than bringing home a few B's and a couple of C's. I know you can do better and you definitely have seen what your sister did when she was in high school."

"Okay, I promise to do better and the next marking period, I will bring home all A's."

"I think you should Greg because if you are looking to enter college and your grades should be up to par."

"Alright, I hear what all of you are saying and believe you me, I will be ready Mother and Daddy, so you two will be proud of me as you are with Sandra.

As they enjoyed eating their dinner of roast beef with potatoes, carrots, green peas, and gravy, Sandra just had to mention whether or not Wayne was enjoying his mother's meal or would he rather have been here with them. "I think Wayne and his parents are sitting over there just laughing and enjoying their meal just as we are here," her father responded.

"Besides, he is home where he belongs this evening to enjoy his parents as you are enjoying yours Sandra. Listen you guys, after we have finished having our dinner, I do not want either of you to try and slip back over to Wayne's parents' home tonight because they need to be free of you two for a night. Besides, I know tomorrow the three of you will be hanging out together where neither I nor Wayne's mother will not be able to get either of you to help with anything," their mother said. "By the way Sandra since Florence and I will have our heads together tomorrow on deciding what each will make for Thanksgiving dinner, I thought maybe it would be nice of you to try to help out with the menu while Greg and Wayne are hanging out together. I think as a young lady, you don't need to hang with them."

"Mother, you are so right about that because the guys should have our time together so Sandra your job is with Mother and Mrs. Hunt."

"Hey, I don't mind and I will be happy to help out besides, there could be a lot I need to learn about cooking, brother."

"Now that has been solved, Elijah what will you and Samuel be doing while we do our things," asked his wife.

"I think Samuel and I will be checking out whether there are some rabbits around where he and I probably will be able to get some hunting in to kill a few for the winter time. Since Wayne is home for a few days from college I am sure he would like to catch up on old times with the guys who did not attend college to see what they are doing as he and I will go visiting them."

"Greg do you think that will be a good thing to do?" Sandra asked.

"Why not, they can see how Wayne has directed his life instead of hanging around doing nothing as most of them are doing. Besides, there are a lot of things I would love to ask him."

"Now little brother, I don't think you should be asking Wayne anything that is no concern of yours."

"Son, your sister is right," his daddy said. "If Wayne want to tell you anything about his business, I am sure he will if he so desires. It is none of your business to pry, so don't do it now. You hear me now son?"

"Since you put it that way Daddy, I will mind my own business."

"Good, you do just that," his sister reminded him.

Wayne and his parents were so busy enjoying a good meal because he had not had one of this type since being away from home and this one was surely a welcome sight. He said to his mother that she over did it this time with her roast chicken seasoned just right along with the vegetables to go along with it. "I am glad you are enjoying yourself son because I said to your father just the other day how I so much wanted to make sure you had a god dinner once getting home."

"Well Mother, you definitely out did yourself."

"Wait until you see the dessert she made especially for you, her banana pudding."

"Now mother, you know Greg would have rather ate over here because of your dessert."

"I know son, but he had to go home to have dinner with his family besides, his sister is also home from college just as you are and it would not be right for him to have dinner with us when his mother had prepared a good hot dinner for all of them you know. I know if I had not cooked this meal, you would have been right over there stuffing your guts too."

"What can I say, the two of you can really cook and I don't want to even ask anything about what will be on the menu for Thanksgiving. I know Greg and I will have to run down the road to exercise in order to fill up again."

"Wayne," his daddy said to him. "You said the right thing there. I guess Elijah and I will let our dinner settle by smoking on our pipes and talking about how good the food was, while you ladies remain in the kitchen cleaning to prepare for dessert to be served."

Episode Five

THE LONG AWAITED DAY HAS FINALLY ARRIVED WHERE THE TWO families will finally come together other than just meeting to talk and sit down to enjoy a welcome home from school dinner with two wonderful individuals, a black beautiful young girl, and a well-mannered young white man, as he has come to love this young girl from the time they were in school together as no one knew about it as it was kept in secrecy by him. The morning was starting off to be a very busy one over to the Hunt's home as Mrs. Hunt was up early in the morning before daybreak to start putting her last minute touches on the favorite foods she would be taking over to the Logan's home where everyone would sit down to enjoy themselves as one big family. In the meantime, both mothers had to prepare a short breakfast for their family members to hold them over until it would be time for their afternoon gathering.

Once Wayne has gotten up and walked into his mother's kitchen to get a bite of what she had prepared for he and his daddy so they would not be in her way while she continued to prepare her favorite dishes, she said to him after he had greeted her good morning by placing a kiss on her cheek, "Son, you are on your own this morning for you and your daddy to get your own breakfast as you can see, I have prepared it for you so you have to fix your own plates because I am so busy with other things."

Wayne turned to his mother to say, "No problem mother, I can do that and when daddy comes in he too can do the same for himself. Believe me, I wouldn't think about getting in your way today Mother, as I know this is going to be a special day when we as well as the Logans, sit down to have a wonderful

Thanksgiving dinner together like never before." The reason why Wayne said that was he would have the chance to sit next to Sandra his future wife to be as he had dreamed so many nights about it. He was so looking forward in seeing Sandra again and spending as much quality time with her before it was time for him as well as she to return back to college to begin their studies.

Wayne knew sooner or later his parents as well as Sandra's parents will come to know that there is something going on with him as he comes around them to force them to ask him exactly what is bothering him, because there has been a change in his attitude- not bad, but something in him has made his action viewed a little differently from all the times he had spent just hanging out with Sandra and Greg. Wayne's own parents also will notice a difference in the ways he responds to certain questions asked. It will get to the point that Catherine, Sandra's mother, and Florence, Wayne's mother, will come together to speak about what could be going on because this is not the Wayne they were used to seeing. "Florence, has something changed in your household that has made him act this way?" Catherine would ask.

Florence would respond by saying, "I don't know because Elijah and I have made sure that our communication with your family members has always been the same."

"Florence," Catherine said to her. "There is something going on but I just cannot figure it out but give me time I am sure I will come up with an answer." These thoughts of the two of them were before their big Thanksgiving feast. Of course Wayne in his mind had already sensed something was going on in the two of these mother's minds so he had to be very careful because this is not the time and it will be a while before the cats come out of their bags. Meanwhile, over at the Logan's home, the smell of good foods were in the oven and on top of the oven as Sandra and her mother had gotten up early to start off what they would be placing on the table. This morning it was no time before Greg, Sandra, and Wayne gathered together on the front porch swinging and talking while their mothers were busy in the kitchen.

Once when Greg and his daddy walked into the kitchen looking to have breakfast Sandra said to them, "Sorry fellows this morning as you know is a special time for this household so you two are on your own and you will have to defend for yourselves because mother and I are too busy with the afternoon's big dinner."

Sandra's daddy said to her, "No problem baby girl, you know I can get myself something to eat without having you and your mother get it for me. On the other hand I am quite sure your little brother will have mercy on the two of you and find it in his heart to do the same, right Greg?"

"What did you say Daddy, because I was just staring at mother's roast she is placing in the oven."

"You heard Daddy, Greg, so get your own food and please stay out of our way because we two girls are doing our thing this morning."

Elijah turned to look at Catherine to say, "Honey, I am so glad we all are bonding together today in this feast that will make a difference one day in other places to show that it does not matter who you are, we can come together in harmony to show love as a people and not look upon each other as being different."

"Elijah, you are so right and I am glad we are a living proof of that by sharing our lives together with the Hunts. Just think about it, if we had never moved here in this location then our children would not have met a wonderful kid as Wayne where the three of them have shed many good times together by eating in the kitchen of both homes."

Greg said to them with his comments, "Yes that is all well and good but there were times when I had to let Wayne know that I was in control of my sister's life and I decide who would be next to her."

"Oh Greg please be quiet because I had to step between you and Wayne many times to break up what would have been fights," Sandra replied to his crazy comments.

Big sister, I am not saying he was trying to get next to you, I was saying I had to protect you because he did not have a sister for me to protect so he just looked upon you as his sister and I was not going to have that you know."

"Okay you two guys, enough of that," said their mother. "Regardless of how you three guys got into arguments, you still shared love between the three and we as your parents as well as Wayne's parents are very satisfied so Greg finish your breakfast and get out of this kitchen and go see Wayne to spend time with him while foods are being cooked and you too Elijah, finish up your breakfast and go over to Samuel to do what you two have planned to do before this afternoon's dinner."

"Greg," his Daddy said to him. "You heard the boss lady, so let us get going." He was laughing as the two of them walked out.

By the time Greg and his father had gotten out on the front porch, who but Wayne and his daddy were walking over to meet them. As they walked up, Samuel said to Elijah, "I guess you two were thrown out of the house too?"

"How did you guess that because that is exactly what happened because these women did not want us around them as they prepared dinner as they said we would only be in the way."

Wayne asked Greg if Sandra would be joining the two of them as they go check out if there are a lot of rabbits and squirrels running all around their land. "Sorry to break your bubbles my dear friend, but Sandra is in the kitchen helping mother with dinner and don't you know, she too kicked daddy and me out."

"I was so sure she would want to hang with you and me today before it would be time for dinner."

Wayne's father said to him "Son, this is the day where all of the females stick together and we men have no control of it so I suppose it will just be you and Greg as Elijah and I head off into our direction."

"Elijah, why don't you and I get into my truck and ride around the lands to see what is needed to be done so after all of this excitement is over with, we can go on about our daily business to take care of things once again?"

"I think that will be a good idea at least we will not be around to hear the women yelling out to us to get out of their way."

"If you two are going to hang out together then I suppose Wayne and I will just jump on the back of the truck and ride with you two," Greg said.

"Why not the four of us just spend the day together before we return for the meal that is being planned?" Wayne said.

"My brother," Greg said to him. "Now that is a good idea at least you and I can keep our eyes on our fathers."

As the four of them loaded up and headed down the road toward the land Sandra looked out the kitchen window and said to her mother, "I see the four of them are in the truck going down the road so I wonder where they are going?"

"It doesn't matter Sandra just as long as they are together and about to spend a good day together, let them go at least you and I don't have to tell them to get out of the way. I know Florence is glad Samuel and Wayne are not around her to be asking for things which they could get themselves. She spoiled them you know."

"Mother, I hate to say it but just like you did with Daddy and Greg. You have spoiled the two of them by waiting on them so now they look for you to continue to wait on them," Sandra said to her. "As much as I hate to say it, yes you did and now they look toward you to continue doing it."

"Now that you have pointed all of it out to me, I guess I did but I did it to you as well you know."

"Yes you did, but being the person that I am, I did a lot on my own because being a female I want to not do the same things for my future husband if I get one as you mother."

"Sandra you know just the two of us are here in the kitchen and I would like to have a talk with you."

"What is it Mother?" Sandra asked her mother.

"I know once you finish college and hope to obtain a job here in the school system to teach English, but if you are not successful what other plans do you have in store?"

"Well Mother, I can always travel to New York where I understand the job opportunities are much greater there for college graduates, as told by Daddy's niece there so maybe I will wind up there."

"What about meeting someone to maybe one day get married?"

"Right now mother, I am not thinking about that because what I want to do first is to become self-sufficient to help Greg with his college expense."

"You don't have to worry about that because your father and I have already taken care of that since you two were small as we took out a college plan for you two so just like you when you were ready to enter college, your money was available to pay for your four years and Greg will also have his."

"Now that you and I are on that subject, what do you think will happen to Wayne once he completes his college education, Mother?"

"I do think he will return home as Florence has said to obtain a job working with the Agriculture Department to help and show farmers better ways to plant crops. As far as getting married, I just don't know yet because first he has to find someone to date and come to know. As it stands I just don't see that has happened so far. I know from talking with his mother, she and Samuel want him to get involved, but every time they approach him with the idea, she said he seems to go into another direction."

"Mother, they should just give him time to make up his mind. I do feel when he is ready the, he will go full force and find that special girl and get married."

"I sure hope so Sandra because Wayne is such a sweet young man and any mother would love to have him as a son-in-law to raise children with their daughter. I know when the time is right that will surely happen for him."

Sandra replied, "He is a good man and knowing him as Greg and I do, he will be a good father."

"You just make sure if you have to relocate to New York, the big city, there are a lot of young men up there and I don't want you to get involved with the first one you meet, but allow yourself to check them out before you leap."

"Mother, you are talking to your daughter who is very smart and you know I will not fall for the first available man that comes along offering me his likes. Besides, Betty, my first cousin, said that she will make sure of that."

"It seems as if you and Betty have already talked things over if you have to move there to find a job."

"Betty said I could get a job working in law firms there because I will have my secondary major to reflect that which will give me lots of experience in that field. I know I will be good at writing papers for lawyers. If that be the case then I will not have much time to date, Mother."

As the two of them talked girl talk, the phone rang and it was Florence wanting to know how things were going. "Things are going fine over here Florence," Catherine said to her.

"Girlfriend, there is peace over here because Wayne and Samuel have gone off with Elijah and Greg in the truck."

"Do you need any help there?" Catherine asked her.

"Oh no, because I am just fine and by the time they are back this afternoon, I will be over there with my foods to be placed on the dinner table alongside yours and then we can just watch those greedy men eat their hearts out as we three ladies watch."

"Okay Florence, I will see you when you have finished cooking. Let Sandra and me know so we can help bring the dishes of food from the car." As the two finished talking, Florence said to herself what a good day this will be to celebrate Thanksgiving. The two mothers wanted to make sure their two college kids will have enough to take back to their dorms with them.

Is Love Worth the Wait?

While the excitement weas being established in the kitchen of both homes, the men in the meantime were all busy enjoying themselves riding around the farm life checking on things that needed attention too once Thanksgiving was over with and the two college students were back in college to continue with their education preparation. Although Greg and Wayne were to be doing their own thing together but for some reason, all of was changed due to Greg's big mouth as Wayne alluded too. Maybe this was a good thing because that way the four of them could bond more together just know that the fathers of two sons decided to spend part of Thanksgiving day with them to show them how much the two of them appreciated their fathers. As they were riding from place to place checking out anything that seemed out of the norm, Wayne's father Samuel said, "Elijah, when they get back home in time to have dinner, you can bet your bottom dollar the foods would be worth the wait because as I think about it now, I am beginning to feel hungry as my breakfast has already left my body."

"Samuel, you know we will have to remain out from the house as long as possible due to the time dinner will be served as I was told my Catherine," Elijah reminded him. "But there's one thing you and I both have overlooked" he said.

"What is that?" Samuel asked of him.

"Those two boys of ours hanging out in the back of the truck. If they got wind of what you and I are speaking about, they will want to return to hang out bothering their mother and sister so it is our duty to keep them away from the house as long as possible so when it is time to return, they will be ready to chow down to fill their stomachs. Samuel, now that we are talking, what do you think about Wayne not dating any girls yet?" Elijah asked.

"Well to tell you the truth my friend, Florence and I both have tried to discuss the situation with him to see if he had found a girlfriend on campus, but we get no response from him only to say he is not thinking along that line at the moment, we both know that since he wants to be a good agricultural agent in trying to help farmers with their crops growth, we thought it would also help him to get interested in meeting a nice girl. I can surely say this much, he doesn't talk about them like Greg does you know and you would think the two of them would talk about dating all the time, but he never does as much as Greg pretends he is the Romeo with the girls."

"To tell you the truth, my Greg just be running off at his mouth because he knows that if his grades are not up to par then he will be put on punishment," Elijah said.

"Give him time Samuel, he will come around and when he does, oh you better look out. I have made myself to believe being away from home for the first time and surrounded by strange people of whom you never been around before will make you have a tendency to remain a little locked down in your own world guarding yourself. I do believe that is exactly what has happened to Wayne."

"Samuel, maybe I should not ask this of you because I don't know if you are ready to accept it or not, but if you tell me that you are not then I will understand."

"What is it Elijah, because you know as long as we have been friends just like family you can ask me anything."

"If you put it that way Samuel, I guess it will be alright to ask it. Knowing how guarded Wayne is, what would happen if he one day decided that he will do some changes with his life by marrying someone that out of his race?"

"Well I don't think I would have much of a decision to decide because he will be his own man and therefore, it will be his decision one which his mother and I will just have to accept it because as you and I both decided that in a few years things will be in the works of changing so we as parents will just have to go alone with whatever. In time, I think Florence and I would welcome who he marry and welcome his new wife into our family as one besides, we are looking and hoping to have some fine grandchildren one day."

"That is exactly what I wanted to hear Samuel," replied Elijah. "Now, how would you feel if either Sandra or Greg do the same thing by marrying someone that is out of your race"?

" I am sure Catherine and I will be so ever happy and we would not change a thing. You know all the changes that are soon to hit will be the best thing that ever happen to this country and world."

"Elijah, when those changes finally hit to stun everyone that have been so against people will definitely place a damper in their lives, they will either go along with all the decisions that will be made or else they will just have to pack up and leave the country," Samuel said to him. As the two fathers continued with their discussions, Wayne and Greg were busy in the back of the truck talking about things young people of their age talk about including school and girls. Greg asked Wayne if he would ever get involved with one of those fine girl that walks around on campus where he is in college or not.

Wayne said to him, "Little do you know I am already involved with one of the sweetest girls that I have ever known, I am just not ready to expose her yet to my parents and to her parents either."

"Come on brother man, tell me who she is/?" Greg asked Wayne but he dare not expose the girl he was speaking of was his sister and if he told him, he probably would jump right off the truck and hurt himself so that was all he would say.

"All this time, you had your mind set on this girl without even telling your brother?" Greg said to him.

Wayne said to Greg, "Listen to me very carefully why I just could not tell you or even my parents because it is not the right time to do it. First, I have to finish my college education and then get a job before I can even think about letting it out and I hope you will respect my wishes and repeat this to anyone, as my brother Greg since you said that you and I are brothers."

"Alright then my lips are shut tight although it will be hard for me to keep them closed, but since it is you, I will do as you ask of me. I know how you and Sandra share things together but please, when we get back home to get ready for our Thanksgiving dinner, let this be a secret around the dinner table. I had to really make myself to open up this much to you but I thought I better tell you since you and I have a lot in common."

"Greg if you came to me and trusted me to tell me that you yourself had gotten to know someone but you did not want anyone to know about it until you were sure things of the situation would work out, I would respect you and keep it to myself not to even say a thing to Sandra. You know how sisters feel about their brother's involvement with girls because they feel like a mother hen, although I don't have one, but from watching Sandra I can imagine it would be the same with me. Brother Greg you and I have shared many secrets but to me, this is the hardest one I had to tell you."

"Wayne can you just give me just a little bit information about this girl?" Greg asked him.

"No, I can't because if I did then the secret would be out of the bag and everyone would know. Until I am sure all things are in place and will work then it would be time to expose her." If Greg was able to read between Wayne's lines he then would understand that he was speaking about his sister Sandra.

"Tell me something Wayne is this why you have been acting sometimes strange when the three of us are together?"

"That's a possibility," he replied. Now, since I have gotten that much off my shoulders, tell me what is happening with you at school? Have you found a nice girl there to take to the prom?"

"No but I am not worrying because those fine girls are falling all over me."

"My dear brother Greg you are so full of yourself," Wayne replied laughing.

"So much for all of this talk and secrets, let us check out this place because I think if I set a trap there, I will be able to pull in a lot of rabbits in my box," Greg said to Wayne.

Soon his father slowed down and pulled over to the side of the road and he and Greg father got out to ask them, "Do you two guys want to take a walk with us to check out what is hanging around over there in that part of the field?"

"I think you two go ahead," Greg said. "Because Wayne and I will walk over to the other location where we placed our rabbits box to check them out. You know Daddy, I would like for Wayne to see what he has been missing since he has been away in college."

"Did you have to go there little brother about those silly boxes because you know I am the one who started this whole thing before I left for school you know?"

"You could have fooled me," Greg returned the answer with a smile.

As the two of them walked over to the location hoping to find something inside one of the boxes they learned that all of the lettuce that had been placed inside had been taken away and the hook was still in place so something outsmarted Greg. "I didn't catch anything this time but I will soon and I bet by tomorrow morning I will have a rabbit in all three boxes and guess what, you just might get the chance to have rabbit meat before you return back to school, Wayne." Wayne took a look at his watch to see what time it was because he really wanted to get back home- not to eat but he wanted to set his eyes on Sandra and maybe they could share a moment of delight together before dinner time.

"What is wrong with you my brother?" Greg asked.

"Nothing much except I don't know about you but I am ready to head home."

"I feel you because I too am ready to eat that is."

"Wayne can't you just smell all of that good food that is being cooked for us to share together this afternoon?"

"When we all sat at the table, why don't you and I place Sandra in the middle so we can bind her in while the adults sit together?" Greg said to Wayne.

"Wait a minute Greg we just cannot take over the table arrangements you know that will be the job of the females to place everyone."

"Wayne apparently you have not yet learned that I am the table controller and it is I who decides."

"Okay if you say so, but you know I know better and those are just words coming from out of your mouth wanting to be in charge, my brother," Wayne let him know.

"Exactly what time is it Wayne?" he asked.

"It is now two o'clock and we better call our fathers to let them know that dinner is being served at three o'clock."

By that time Elijah and Samuel were walking back toward the truck as Wayne and Greg met them there to get started back home. "Well guys, did you two check out the rabbit boxes?" asked Greg's father.

"We did and guess what?" Wayne responded that something had taken all of the lettuce that had been placed inside of them without bothering with the trap hook. Wayne's father said that it could have been a deer because when it comes to being careful they know exactly what to do without bothering hooks.

Both Elijah and Samuel said to Greg and Wayne that it was about time they return back home to prepare for a hearty Thanksgiving dinner, they know will be the highlight of the day once they dive into the turkey and roast surrounded by other good items.

"Come on then" said Greg. "Let us get started back down the road because I don't think my stomach can take much more not being filled. Why that little small amount of breakfast you and I had this morning daddy has left me. I don't know about how Wayne and Mr. Samuel fee but I can truly say, I know I will eat my share."

As Greg's father starred at him all he could say was this, "Boy, when will you ever get enough?"

Samuel said to Elijah, "I really cannot say too much about Greg but I do know my son Wayne isn't far behind him when food is mentioned."

"Okay, come on and let us get going by now I am sure the ladies are wondering when we are going to return."

As Wayne and Greg rode in the back of the truck, they found themselves wresting showing off their bonding effect. Elijah said to Samuel, "Would you just take a look through your rear view mirror to see what they are doing back there.?" As he looked, he yelled out to them that they better sit down and hold on because bumps were coming up and they were laughing.

"Elijah, I think that should get them to maintain themselves back there," he said as he continued on driving.

Soon, they arrived and almost before the truck came to a stopped, both Greg and Wayne jumped out and ran up on the front porch to be met by Sandra saying to them, "Oh no guys you cannot come in just yet because we are still placing the foods on the table." What Sandra said made Wayne happy because he finally got the chance to see her as he thought about her all night. As the four of them sat down out on the front porch because it was not time yet to be invited in by the ladies, Wayne thought in his mind that this would be the perfect time to not allow his action be different to give off any concern by the other ones, other than Greg.

As Wayne and Greg sat in the swing and talked, Elijah and Samuel just continued to make conversation concerning the crop of soybeans they were about to start taking care of to get them off to the market. "Wayne, my older brother," Greg said to him. "I wonder who will be the first to get through those doors once Sandra comes out to say now, you guys can enter to wash up to take your long awaited seat."

"It seems to me Greg you are calling out a bet, aren't you?" Wayne asked.

"Not really just making an observation to the fact if you will beat me or I will beat you."

"Listen you two," Mr. Hunt said to them. This is a wonderful day, and it is Thanksgiving where Catherine and your mother Wayne decided to put all this together and have both families to eat together so don't you two guys, and I speak for Elijah as well, get to the dinner table and act up like you never had food before. We all know how good everything will taste because there are two women cooking in there and to add Sandra who is learning a lot from them for one day she will be involved doing the same thing for her family, we hope."

Wayne's daddy should not have gone there because little did he know, one day the two of them just might be eating at his and Sandra's table with their grandchildren. As they all maintained themselves, soon Sandra walked out front to let them know, now it is time for the guys to come on in. Greg immediately jumped up but Sandra held the door so he would not rush in to allow both fathers enter first because that was the right thing to do and then the two sons would follow. Sandra said to Greg and Wayne, "I knew you two would try something like this so that is why I stood here. Now you two may enter and go directly to the bathroom and wash your nasty hands because I know being out there in the fields with Daddy, and Mr. Hunt, you picked up some dirt. Clean hands coming to my mother's table is a must you know. After washing their hands and walking into the dining room to take their seats, it was too good to be true as they all were directed to sit down as Wayne, Sandra, and Greg did sit on the same side as Mr. Logan and his wife Catherine took their seats at the head of the table, leaving Mr. and Mrs. Hunt to take their seats facing the children.

As Mrs. Logan made a shot speech saying what a joy it was just having both families to share in this Thanksgiving dinner together, which shows the love and bonding two set of people can have without looking at the complexion, but what's in the heart. "This is a honor and privilege to eat together. On that note, I think we should let one of the children say grace for us, don't you think Florence?"

"Catherine, since you, Sandra, and I sweat on the heat in preparing all of this, I would love for my son to open up with a thank you prayer. Do you mind son?" she asked.

"No mother, it will indeed be my honor to say prayer," he said because he wanted to sort of show off in front of Sandra to let her know in a few more years this will be what she would get use too, her husband saying the table prayer. After Wayne had finished, the food was started to be passed around for all to take what portions they wanted. For Greg being the person he was, he said to Wayne, "Brother, the next time please keep your prayer short because I could hardly wait until you had finished."

"Greg," his father asked him. "Is there a time when you can overlook your stomach and pay attention to something that is of importance like prayer?"

"I tried Daddy, but when my brother Wayne get on something to say, he doesn't know when to quit. He knows that he and I are really hungry as he said that while we were out with Daddy and Mr. Hunt." Wayne wasn't really paying any attention to Greg because he was just so very happy to be sitting next to Sandra watching her take her fork and place her food into her mouth.

"All I have to say to all these ladies that prepared this food is this: good oh so good," Greg said. "I would not change this day for any other day because look at all the various dishes sitting up here on this table. Can I eat all I want too mother?"

"Greg if you don't be quiet and eat, you better stop carrying on like you are."

Sandra said to Wayne and Greg, "I hate to burst their bubbles, but part of what you see on the table did have my help you know."

"And your help paid off a lot Sandra," Wayne replied to her. "Don't let Greg tell you any different." It seemed as if the table conversation was geared toward the three young people.

Mr. Hunt opened up to say, "This is a special day, because come Sunday, Florence and I will be driving Wayne back to his destination as well as you, Elijah and Catherine, will be on the road doing the same thing with Sandra."

"Hey, don't leave me out because I will be on that car to see my sister back to college," said Greg.

"Sandra are you ready to get back on campus to start your studies?" asked Mrs. Hunt.

"Yes, I suppose I am because it won't be long before Wayne and I will be home again for the Christmas holidays, you know."

"What about you Wayne?" asked Mrs. Logan. "Are you ready to depart and return back to college?"

"I think I am besides, I still have a lot to learn concerning agriculture affairs."

"I hope you two don't think you will pack up everything to take back with you to eat on campus because I have to have some of this food to eat myself."

"Greg, I swear you are the greedy young person I have ever met," said Sandra. Her mother said to her, "Please don't worry about what Greg says because there will be more than enough food left here for him to fill his stomach with you and Wayne will take all that you will need to get you through to keep you from eating that not so good cafeteria campus food."

Wayne said to Greg, "Right now you are making fun of Sandra and me, but just wait until you enter college then you will know and it won't be so funny because knowing you, you will expect your mother to send you a food box each week."

"What is wrong with getting a food box each week?"

"I can assure you this my little baby son, your mother will not be cooking like that because when you are out of here your Daddy, and I will have time to spend more time together along with Florence and Samuel to eat out. There will not be any use to cook a hot dinner each night especially when only the two of us will be here."

"You are so right about that," Florence chimed in to agree with Catherine. "Because the four of us will be just like when we first met. Greg when you finish your college studies, you will take on a wife as well as Wayne and Sandra. You won't be here to sit out on the front porch in the swing carrying on."

"Isn't it strange how time seems to have just flown by so fast?" Elijah said. "Our children will be no longer children, but they will be grown up and a possibility with children of their own we hope."

"The one thing that I will hate the most," Greg said. "It is that the three of us will not be together and who knows where we will settle down once we are married. I won't have my big brother to share things with and he won't have time to do the same. My big sister Sandra probably will marry someone with lots of money that will have her living in a big house up on top of the hill. You probably would have to have a ticket to get inside the gates."

"Now Greg why would you think I would want to live like that?" Sandra asked him.

"I don't know I guess it was something to say to get you back for choosing Wayne's side at dinner time," he said laughing. As they continued to eat, the conversation carried on to make things much easier for Wayne to deal with so no one would notice if there was something bothering him.

Of course he would have rather been all alone with Sandra just the two of them sitting on a river bank with a picnic basket having their dinner together and talking about how much he has always loved her. If this weas the case, what a difference a day would make. "Come Sunday, we will have to depart our ways again until we will come home again on break, but in the meantime, I better pretend to enjoy every moment of being here in her company along with all others. I really don't have a choice because if I slip then my secret will definitely be out and everyone would be stunned not to have given it a second thought about how I felt about the girl I have always viewed as my big sister. Lord god, help me to hold my strength until it is ready to be explored because if it comes out now then I would just have to leave this area as well as school and that too would just kill my parents. Not only my parents, but the relationship I have with Greg and Sandra would be destroyed. I could never face their parents again ever. Oh know, the time is just not right now because there are still so much to be understood by those that will be involved and surely this society. When it does happen, I want it to be right for Sandra as well as for me so we will live in peace and harmony."

As everyone sat continuing to enjoy the fine Thanksgiving dinner, it seemed as if everything that Wayne had ever wanted was truly paying off the way he had intended for it to. What better way to enjoy this special day than spending it in the company of the girl he loves and the fine surroundings. Why he already knew that this day will soon end and tomorrow will definitely shorten his time being home to be around Sandra so he was going to try and make the best of it. Little does Greg know that come tomorrow, Wayne has special time planned just for himself and Sandra not to include Greg, but something has to give and maybe not to make it seem to suspicious, he will rush right over to the Logan's home tomorrow morning right after breakfast to suggest the three of them just spend the day checking out the rabbit boxes placed around the farm land that way he could just walk close by Sandra's side.

If that was going to work as he plan it in his mind then he better be ready to accept all the smart comments Greg will surely make as he will about his sister. These were just Wayne's thoughts as he sat to enjoy his food saying to his mother as well as to Mrs. Logan how great this dinner is. "Why thank you son," replied his mother. "When Catherine and I decided to do this, we didn't know exactly how you kids would feel about everyone having dinner together."

"Why Mrs. Hunt," Sandra replied. "How could you ever think any different because you know how Greg and I enjoy eating up your good old dinners?"

"Yes Mrs. Hunt," Greg added his two cents' worth. "Why Mother and Daddy always fuss at Sandra and I about running over to your home at the time you are serving dinner to eat and believe me, we both can never repay you for welcoming the two of us in to your table just as we were your own children." Of course Elijah and Samuel both just sat there without a word to add enjoying their conversation not to add anything because what they said was the truth.

Once Greg had finished speaking, Wayne just had to add his two cents' worth by letting Mrs. Logan know as well how grateful he has been all these years for the nice and good hospitality that has been shown to him and his parents for allowing them to rest their feet under her table as well. The reason why he would say this because if he did it then his chances with their daughter would be even greater. "I don't think this day that we are enjoying right now over such a fine well cooked dinner would be any better if we were not together," said Mr. Hunt.

"I don't know about the other of you, but my best friend Elijah already knows what a blessing this is to come together as one to sit down and be so thankful."

"What about dessert?" asked Greg.

"Please little man," said Wayne.

"You have not finished eating what is on your plate yet before you can even think about dessert. Son, I think I have made myself clear to you many of times about bursting out about having dessert even before you have finished what you have placed on your plate before others have finished."

"Daddy, I just want to get into some of Mrs. Hunt's banana pudding so I can eat it all up from Wayne and I do eat it all up so he won't get any, my brother."

Greg's mother Catherine said to him, "Please cut it out now because we are all still much into our dinner and when the time comes, we will all be served dessert so you will have enough banana pudding as well as all other desserts to snack on son. Now, go ahead and act like you are supposed too. We are family you know."

"I know that mother that is why I think I can carry on like this, because that is what family members do. We all know just three more days our two college kids will be with us and then early on Sunday morning we will rise and prepare to pack them up in our cars to rush them back to school you know," said Mr. Hunt.

"Come next week at this time, there will once again be a void emptiness in our homes, not so much at yours Elijah and Catherine, because you still have your son to keep you busy. Florence and I will just have the two of us to keep each other company, because our only son will not be here."

"Oh Daddy, you and mother must know that it will only be just a few weeks before I am home again," Wayne said.

"Son, I am well aware of that, but it will not be as if you were here every day you know."

"Well, as I see it Mother and Daddy, this was exactly what you wanted. As long as I can remember, when you were growing up that was all you two talked about, sending your son off to college to make something out of himself."

Wayne's mother entered into the conversation to say to her husband Samuel, "Wayne is right and now the time has arrived so you and I have to accept it because it is not about you and I, but it is about our only child and we both want the best for him you know?"

"Wait a minute," Elijah and Catherine said. "I thought this was the day to be thankful and be blessed? Let none of us even think about Sunday morning on this Thanksgiving day to even worry about packing up our cars to hit the road to take them back to college. We already know that is going to happen so let us make this day a special day because we are together as one big family and Florence," Catherine said to her. "You and I have come together to make everything perfect in the food line for all to enjoy so not another word about our kids leaving us, let us eat and be merry."

After that, Wayne whispered into Sandra ear and said something which Greg being the brother he is wanted to know what was said. "If you must know Greg all Wayne said was this. Come tomorrow why don't the three of us just spend the whole day together in and around the location checking out the sights?"

"I think that will be a nice thing to do for the three of you," Catherine and Florence said. To Wayne it was not all about checking out the sights but it was his way of spending all the time he could being with Sandra although there was a problem, Greg hanging together with them.

"Maybe I will ask Greg whether or not he had a buddy somewhere around that he could visit and thus leaving Sandra and I to spend our time together throwing rocks in the water just like we have done in the past as sister and brother but this time, a little different feeling on my part to see each rock she would throw in the water would be a rock of love as I see as they fall. If Greg is not around maybe I would just grab hold of her hand to direct her from falling, not to allow her to feel that I am getting to close to her. This has been a very hard journey for me to deal with to keep everything about the way I feel for the one person I love from everyone. I feel as if I am caught up in a vacuum tube being sucked up by the wind ready to burst. Talking about stress, this is exactly what causes it, wanting to tell somebody but fear of backlash or not knowing what or how the one person you love will react. Why I cannot even say anything to the guy who is my roommate at college because he is from that part of society that see things as he were taught and if I mention anything to him about being in love with a beautiful black girl, this just might cause him to expose me on campus and everyone would just ignore me or cause me to be expelled from school by the college board members as they follows what has been set up long ago by society. No, I better keep it to myself for now until Sandra as well as I have completed our education and on our own so we both will be strong enough and smart enough to deal and fight. I won't be so worried about my parents because if at first they will be shocked, soon they too will come around to accept my decisions because I am their son and that they will not do anything to damage our relationship. Sandra's parents no doubt will just be over excited and welcome me as their son-in-law because I don't think they would rather have any other guy as I to be in their family. It would be easier for them to come to grip with it because their son Greg just might do the same thing one day as he finishes his schooling and be on his own. To me, I just don't see what the big problem is because we are God's children and surely he did not intend for this sort of thing to take place in the world he created for all. Once Sandra and I are out tomorrow just walking in and around the land which our parents own, it will be the beginning of something new that will soon happen whether she had thought about it or not. Who knows, while we are just walking maybe she will not pull away as I place my arm around her waist to keep her from falling as Greg, I hope, will run away and be with his friends, if that is possible for him. I don't blame him for being so overprotective of his beautiful sister, because if I had one as Sandra I guess I would be the same way too. Sitting here in the home of Sandra's parents at their dinner table along with my parents, it is a wonderful thing because we are just ordinary people as we look upon each other just as nice people. Nothing else. It doesn't matter what the other folks who live in this location think or feel, we are so totally different and our thoughts are good because we were brought up on good morals. I hate to say this, but society has been shifty to the effect why all of this racist, radical mess is happening. If God almighty is my witness I will do something about it once I am out of college and I will marry Sandra so all will see the color of a person's skin does not matter. Here I am sitting beside the girl that will be my wife one day, thinking all of these thoughts instead of just enjoying the day's moments and what is to come."

After everyone had almost finished eating, Sandra asked her mother and Mrs. Hunt if dessert will be served now or later on. "Honey," Mrs. Hunt said to her. "Since I am so full and I cannot eat another bite, I wouldn't care if we serve the dessert later on. Besides, we should give our stomachs time to setter down right Greg?" she said smiling.

"I guess so Mrs. Hunt because right now, I am really full so that way, if I wait I can eat more of your banana pudding." Catherine asked everyone if they had finish eating, "Please find your way into the living room or you two young fellows can do what you do best and that is go out on the front porch and fight over the swing. We three ladies will clear up the table and put the food away to prepare for dessert at a later time."

"Mother, you mean to tell Wayne and me that Sandra will not be joining us?"

"From the way I see it my sweet little son that is the way it is going to be for right now. She can join you two later once everything is cleared up in the kitchen where Florence and I can take a break to join our husbands in the living room to rest our feet. Greg we do need a break you know because we have been working real hard to make sure this day would be a good day. Did you see all of that food on the table for everyone to eat? It didn't get there by itself, it had help you know and all the help came from Florence, your sister, and your mother, Greg."

Episode Six

As Thanksgiving dinner was about to end and everyone had filled their stomachs to the height as they should be Wayne Greg Sandra decided to excuse themselves from the dinner table to make their way outside to let their food digest by sitting out on the front porch swinging to share a close togetherness before it would be the time for the two of them to pack up and be ready to make their way back to their dorms to start off come Monday morning with their classes. But in the meantime Wayne had something of important to say to Sandra although Greg would be included as he much rather he was not, but to keep everything on the downlow, he did not want anything out of the norm to jump out that Sandra would realize it was all about him. Wayne kept telling himself that he had to be very careful in how he chose his words not to give himself away about how he felt about Sandra.

Instead of just singing out what he had in mind, he slowly worked it into his motive as why they should do the next day together. Just as he started to sing out with what he would like for the three of them to do the next day, Sandra's mother walked to the door to ask her to please make her way back inside to help in the kitchen thus, leaving Wayne and Greg outside together until she finished her work inside. Right at that moment, it was a blow to Wayne's thoughts. Greg asked him about what he was about to say to Sandra before his mother interrupted. "Little brother, I was about to ask her if she would like to spend the day with you and I tomorrow messing around by checking out what was going on around the land."

"Do you really think my sister would want to do such a thing Wayne spending her day with you and me walking all over these lands?"

"I don't know, it was just a gesture I had and who knows, she might would agree to it you know Greg. Besides, you don't have her mind and you sure cannot regulate the way she thinks, although you would love to."

"To be honest with you, I rather think she would just might love it at least it would take her away from the house for the day. Just be up front Greg you know come Sunday, she and I will be leaving your butt again and returning back to college, leaving you here all alone to wait for our arrival for the Christmas holidays so you better enjoy the moments while you can now my brother," Wayne suggested to him.

"There's no doubt how I will be missing the two of you after you leave."

"Tell me one thing Greg I have never for one moment heard you say anything about your true friends while being in both Sandra's and my presence."

"Are you saying I really don't have any Wayne?"

"No I am not, but it seems to me being the young person that you are all you want to do is hang around Sandra and me. Do you have a problem with that Wayne?" he asked.

"I really don't and I do admire you for protecting your sister because I suppose if I had one, I would be and act the same way as you, but since I don't I have to accept your concerns. Finally, I am so glad that you are on my side. Now, you tell me something my big brother, why haven't you dated any girls here or in college?"

"Greg since you have gone there I have to tell you something and I hope you can accept what I am about to say. The reason why I have not dated any of these white girls around here even in college, because they have not turned me on that way. You see in order for me to be happy with them, I have to find something that stands out in them that will excite me and so far that has not happened yet."

"Wayne, I guess you and I are somewhat the same when it comes to girls, looking for that special someone."

"Greg you are on sixteen what on earth do you know about girls?" Wayne asked him.

"I know more than you think I know so don't let this little easy talking kid fool you.

By the time the two of them had finished with their conversation out walked Sandra again to rejoin the two of them to see what she had missed while she was inside. "Sister, you really haven't missed much since your absence. Wayne and I were just talking about girls."

"Greg knowing you like I do, I bet you took it to the limit didn't he Wayne?"

"Not really because he made some good valid points about dating."

"May I ask what type of points?" Sandra asked.

"Listen Sandra," said Greg. "That is between Wayne and me and I don't think you need to know because we have not asked you what you look for in a guy did we?"

"If you two would like to know what I look for in a guy, I will be more than happy to sing out," she said. Although Wayne was feeling a little uneasy because he wasn't sure what she would say, he would not meet any of her requirements as far as establishing a relationship with her one day. However, he was brave enough to ask her about what she looks for in a guy.

"First of all, if you two must know I first look to see how nice the guy is and then how smart he is, and his determination to want to do things that will make his life meaningful." So far, this was right down all the qualities of Wayne. And then she said, "He has to love me to make a good home for the family he and I will have one day." Bingo, Wayne felt as if he was already in that spot to do all the things she wanted, now he just has to wait for the opportune time for all of this to take place.

Getting off the subject, Wayne asked Sandra if she would like to spend the next day with him and Greg. "What do you two have planned that will take me away from home all day?" she asked.

"Well, we had thought about just spending time before you and I are ready to return back to college Sunday, enjoying all the free time we have together," Wayne said.

"You know, I think it would be nice just the three of us reliving the days over doing the things as we did while we were kids checking out the land and sights."

"Then it is a yes I suppose?" he asked.

"Only if Mother doesn't have anything for me to help her with," she said.

Greg said to the two of them, "I don't know if I want to do that, I just might go to my school buddy's house to do things with him. You and Sandra can have the whole day to yourselves. Besides, after Sunday morning once you load up in the cars to leave you won't see one another until Christmas holidays. I think you two should just hang out together to yourselves." What Greg said was exactly what Wayne had been waiting for all this time for him to say.

"What about it Sandra do you think you and I can hang out to spend time together checking out the scenes before we leave Sunday?"

"Why not because like Greg said, it will be a while before we can do this again."

"Then it is all settled," Wayne said to the two. "Come tomorrow morning Sandra why don't you make a few sandwiches so we will have to eat while we spend the day together down where we use to go as children and sit up under that old oak tree and just listen to the birds and talk about school, I will put a few water bottles in my cooler to have to drink our thirst away."

"You mean to tell me that for once Greg had decided not to share time with you and me?" Sandra asked.

"Big sister, I thought I better let you and Wayne spend your last day together because it is very important to let the two people I admire the most to be left alone without me tagging along. You two are now all grown up and you are college people making your preparations to change the way things are and heaven knowns, I don't think I need to be in your conversations as to how you purpose to work toward the changes. You two are my sister and brother and I think that is very important to let you two be all by yourselves," Greg said to them.

Of course Wayne wanted this to take place to get to know every in and out of Sandra and how he just might ease his arms around her to hope she would feel more than just the way she has seen him as a brother. "Well, I think it is now about time for the three of us to walk inside to take our seats at the table to have some dessert. Oh boy, here I go to have some of Mrs. Hunt's delicious banana pudding as I am sure I will try to eat it all up from you two," Greg responded with his greedy self. As they sat down and their parents placed the desserts on the table, Greg right away said to the others, "That pudding belongs to me because Mrs. Hunt promised it to me."

"No I did not my little one because it was made for everyone just as your mother made hers for all of us. I love you dearly Greg but it would not be fair if I did this only for you. Have you forgotten that this day is a family gathering?" she asked him.

"A good gathering it has been," he responded. "Because we are family and everything has been great."

Well, a new day has fallen after going through all the traditions that were celebrated on Thanksgiving day and now, two individuals who one day will become husband and wife are about to take this special day to be embraced by the one guy who holds all the secrets to what will one day be opened up for all to see and know. As Wayne hurried up to finish his breakfast with his parents to be able to meet Sandra to be ready to take their walk together this time, not being in the company of her little brother, Greg to spend the whole day together just the two of them, laughing and carrying on as two should as sister and brother, but only on the part of Sandra not Wayne because this was a way to finally get all of his future plans in perspective. Wayne's parents asked him why was he eating so fast.

"What are you and Greg up to this day and don't tell me nothing because I know the two of you son."

"Mother and Daddy, all I am going to do is just spend the whole day with Sandra because you know come Sunday morning she and I will be driven back to college so without Greg she has agreed that just the two of us spend the day down by that old oak tree, we used to spend time there while we were much young you know?"

His mother asked, "If you and Sandra are going to do that then what will Greg be doing?"

"Why Greg had agreed to just let Sandra and me have this last day before it is time to leave just the two of us."

"Why that is a nice thing for him to decide especially when the three of you are so close."

"Son?" his daddy asked. "What will he be doing while the two of you are enjoying yourselves down by that old oak tree?"

"Why Greg has decided that he would be entertaining one of his school buddies over at his place."

"So is that why you are placing those water bottles in the cooler?" his mother asked.

"Hey guys," Wayne said to them. "We all planned this yesterday afternoon after finishing dinner and we were sitting out of the front porch as to what we could do before we leave."

"Do Sandra's mother and father know of this?" his mother asked.

"I am quite sure she has explained it to them and if she did not, you know Greg has."

As Wayne was about to walk out the door with the cooler in his hand Sandra was walking toward his home with her bag of sandwiches in her hand to have to eat while they were enjoying their stay of their chosen place. As Sandra walked up she greeted Mrs. Hunt with a good morning and said, "This day Wayne and I are just going to go back in time when we were children, spending time under our favorite place that old oak tree down by the pond."

"I hope the two of you enjoy yourselves because after this day, it will be back to studying."

"Believe me, Mrs. Hunt, I know and I am ready to return back to get started."

As the two of them began to walk down the road toward the old oak tree Mrs. Hunt asked her if she had informed her parents about this. "Oh yes, I let her and Daddy know last night."

"How did Greg take it about not being included?"

"This time, it was a shocked to me because you and I both know how Greg is when it come down to being left out of the loop, but this time he took it all in stride. Besides, he planned to let Wayne and I spend the whole day together as he planned to enjoy his friend."

"Okay, since everything has been approved, I guess I will let you two guys go on your way and enjoy yourselves."

"Don't worry Mrs. Hunt if Wayne gets hungry I packed the two of us some turkey sandwiches and you know how good turkey is after it had been kept overnight."

"Wayne," his mother said to him. "Please look out for Sandra and do not let her fall into the pond now."

"Okay mother, you know I will take care of her not to allow anything to happen to her. Come on Sandra," Wayne said to her. "We better get going." As the two of them began to walk, Wayne decided to grab her hand as he did in their young days laughing and strolling on to their location. As they walked, Mrs. Hunt decided to walk over to the Logan's home to talk with Catherine. When she got there, she was met out on the front porch by Catherine, as the two of them looked in the direction as Sandra and Wayne to say, there our children go on their merry way to enjoy this day before we drive them back to college Sunday morning. As Florence and Catherine sat in the swing talking, they asked each other what are they going to do once they finish with their education.

Catherine, "I just don't know what Samuel and I will do once Wayne completes his studies and decides to take residence in the city to be near his employment. At least you will not be to lonely you and Elijah, because Greg will be close by in college so he will at least come home on some weekends to be with you. Our Wayne just might meet some nice girl to marry and live in the city forever."

"Florence," Catherine said to her. "Aren't you moving too fast right now on the situations that we will face?"

"I just might be Catherine but I think you and I should both prepare ourselves for what will and is coming down the pipe for us to face."

"Florence, I tell you what, let you and I think positive about the this whole situation to wish the best for the two of them and who they might wind up with. Look, the two of them are holding hands just as they did while they were small children, and Wayne is such a gentleman," Catherine reminded Florence. While they sat on the front porch watching and thinking all about what the two might just do once they finish college, Wayne mind was on other things.

Soon, Elijah and Greg walked out on the front porch after finishing eating their long breakfast to speak as Elijah asked where was Samuel. By the time he had finished with asking, Samuel was walking across the street to join them. When he got there, he greeted the Logans a good morning and asked Elijah if he was ready to go. Before Samuel could answer, Greg said to them, "Well, I better get going."

"Where are you on your way to son?" asked his mother.

"I am going to spend this day with my best buddy at school while Wayne and Sandra spend their day together," he said as he started walking on his way down the road.

"I suppose Florence, since everyone is leaving you and me, maybe you and I should think of something to do to amuse ourselves until everyone gets back for dinner."

"I know what we can do Catherine, we can go inside and pull out some of those plastic containers to fill them with leftovers for the kids to take back to school with them Sunday."

"Now that is a good idea because it will be less we will have to get rid of. You see, all is not lost by being left to ourselves."

"Come on Elijah," said Samuel. "You and I have a lot of checking to do on the land to see what needs to be taken care of before winter time."

After everyone had disappeared, Wayne and Sandra had arrived at their favorite place when they were children to take a seat on the grass. Wayne spread his blanket down on the ground so she would not get dirty. Wayne was in hog heaven because he never expected this day to turn out this way without Greg being in their presence. He was so overjoyed because he could feel free and not uptight being around Sandra. As they talked about old times and all the things they once did and how other kids at school would sometimes make fun of them because she was a black girl and he was a white boy hanging together and how they just blew it off and continued on being friends, they knew one day they would win and so far since that time, they have gotten over all of those hills, but he realizes there are many more hills he has to climb, but thinking with the positive mind as he has now will surely let him get to the top and look back down to say he made it.

As he and Sandra poked fun at one another while lying down on the blanket looking up into the skies, he wanted so much to turn over to her and plant a long sweet kiss on her lips, but to be safe at this particular time, he thought that he had better keep his composure to himself for a while and just continue to pretend they are just sister and brother. Sandra said to Wayne, "Before you and I leave Sunday morning, we have to give our dorm phone number to each other so we can call to see how things are going you know?"

"You know Sandra I never thought about that and since you have brought this to my attention, I think that's a wise thing to do."

"Then it is settled, when we get back I will give you my address and you do the same along with the phone number," Sandra said to him.

Wayne would sometimes grab hold of Sandra's hand to hold it up in the air to say, "My sweet and dear sister, this is a special moment for the two of us being here under this old oak tree once again to just bring back old times as if we were those two small children running all around hiding from our parents as they would sometime come to this place to get us. As you and I lay here spending old times together we can truly say all those times spent here were worth the wait."

"Wayne," Sandra said to him. "Sometimes listening to you say the things you say makes me wonder if you are not speaking about me."

"Why would you say that Sandra?" he asked.

"I don't know because you have a way with your words and you know exactly how and what to say to me."

"You are my sister you know," he responded but in his heart he knew he was lying to himself because she was right on key although she had not come to understand his motives, but in a few years she will know and then she will remember all the things he would say to know it was her he was speaking about.

"Wayne can I just ask you something about your school?"

"Why yes Sandra you should know that I will tell you anything you would like to know about Ole Mississippi University."

"Knowing how you, Greg and I grew up in a location that has not welcomed a lot of things that could be better although we were allowed to attend school together, how do you feel right now about these colleges not being on board to integrate to welcome all people in of color?"

"Sandra just as I would ask you the same about your university, I don't like it at all, but this state has not adhered to the government policies yet and therefore, I would rather be in the setting of all kinds of students because whether the world is ready for it or not, we are going to be tomorrow's leaders to carry on this society."

"How do you see things let me say in the next ten years Wayne?" she asked.

"My dear and lovely Sandra in the next ten years I see many changes for both you and me coming as one to share in all that everyone has to offer."

"Exactly what do you mean by that Wayne?"

"I mean there is a possibility that races of people will come together in marriages and other involvements."

"Now that will be something to see if I come home being married to a white guy to see what my parents would say or do," Sandra said laughing. "What about you Wayne how would you accept it if your sister winds up marrying another race?"

"Sandra what are you asking me to say, if I would approve of you marrying a white guy?"

"Yes, I think you and I should discuss this because as it is now, you and I think alike and we are into helping to change the world aren't we?"

"Now Sandra you know for yourself that I am all about wanting to help get rid of all these old established policies that were set forth by those ignorant people that have always said that races should be apart. But guess what Sandra if you marry a white guy you know you will have my blessing." Of course he was telling her all about himself as he planned to be her husband one day.

"Since we are on this subject Sandra if you did marry a white boy, how do you think your parents would deal with it?"

"I don't know, but in my heart, I would like to think they would accept him as part of the family because he will be their son-in-law you know and a possibility to have grandchildren. Look at the three of us, you, Greg and me all these years neither your parents nor mine have ever looked on us as being different."

"That is the best part of it all," Wayne responded to her. because if it had not been for the strong convictions between the two families, he would not be sharing this time her under this old oak tree with her being a black girl because that in many eyes would be totally not accepted.

"To come to the point whether you just might believe it or not but Wayne, I do believe we all were meant to be together."

"You could be right Sandra," he replied.

"With your roommate, do you discuss your involvement with a black family at all?"

"No, I do not because my roommate is a bigot and I really don't blame him for his action because that was the way he was brought up to be. I dare not mention to him that I am friends with you and Greg. I want to sometimes sit down with him to get his opinion on things and the way he feel about people but I am afraid if I did he just might do something to get me expelled from the university."

"Now Wayne that is a sad thing because the university I attend, the students can speak about anything even to wish there were some whites to be attending there within our studies because that is an awesome university and it does not keep any race of people from studying there. I think the barriers should be broken and just maybe other colleges would do the same. You know it has to start from someone. Let us have one of these good ole sandwiches I made," she said to him.

Is Love Worth the Wait?

As Wayne and Sandra ate on their sandwiches, it was quite evident that all this excitement of just being together just the two of them made all the difference in the world for Wayne because he can truly say he had the whole day enjoying being with the girl he had always loved without Greg's interference that would mess things up for him. It had gotten to the point with his feelings that he had thought for one moment to just open up and let the cat out of the bag by telling her just how he felt but then he knew it would not be wise to do that at this time so he continued maintaining himself pretending to be a big brother to her. The two of them exchanged many secrets within their conversation because of the trust they had built up since their youth. As the two of them continued to talk and share with each other, time was moving fast before it would be time for them to make their way back home to answer everyone's questions of how did things go while they spent the day together.

Sandra finally said to Wayne what would inspire him the most as he thought what she had to tell him was how she had always looked upon him more than just a brother as he was hoping that would be, but she let him know that once she get back to college, she would be sure to contact him at least twice a week to keep a check on him to see how he was handling things being there in that all white college knowing he did not want to be there at all. He said to her, "Why thanks a lot because I am sure every time you call or write to me will indeed help me to sustain myself there being around all those self-centered students thinking they were better than other races of people. Sandra?" he asked her. "Do you think the college you are enrolled will let me transfer there if I ask for it?"

"Wayne it is not the point whether or not the school would reject you, it would be whether your parents would let you. In my heart I really think the school board just might welcome you in at least you would be the first to integrate our college" Sandra did not know the reason why he wanted too was all because of her.

Wayne realized if he could be next to her or close by then his chances of making sure he would have a future in her life without her involving herself with someone else on campus, as he thought about all possibilities, he knew he had to be very careful not to open himself up too fast but rather, let nature take its course to allow Sandra make up her mind on deciding what she wanted to do after graduation, whether remaining in the location if she was lucky enough to gain employment or make her way off to New York to live with family members there to obtain a good paying job. This he knows will all be her decision and hopefully one day she would get enough of being there in that big city and decide to return back home where she started from to be his wife and the mother of his children.

Just at an instance, Sandra said to Wayne, "I think it is time for the two of us to start our way back home before it gets too late and once again just like when we were small children, our parents will come looking for us.

"I guess you are right because we wouldn't want that would we?" he responded. As he began to roll up the blanket the two of them spent almost all their time together on, just talking, eating their sandwiches, and drinking water, he wanted to just grab her around her waist and pull her over into his arms to give her the kiss on her beautiful sweet lips as he had always wanted to so she would know all these years it was only her he always did craved to be with. This was a very important thought of his, but he knew he dare not to do that because he was so afraid she would go running home to tell her parents as well as his of what he tried to do with her.

"No not yet Wayne," he imagined in his mind because the time is just not right just yet. "Okay Sandra we have everything so let's you and I make our way home before they get suspicious."

"Wayne," she said to him. "I don't think either your parents or mine would ever think of such a thing, so stop thinking like that."

"Hey," Wayne said to her. "Look around at that old oak tree for the last time as we get ready to say goodbye to it because you know this precious time we have spent here just might never happen again you know?"

"I have to agree with you on that Wayne," Sandra replied.

"Because things in school will get harder for the two of us and we probably will not have as much time to be around one another when we are home on break. We know time like this we will not have due to all of our studying to make sure we are prepared to graduate without having to attend summer school. I think we will have time to spend just a little time together, not as much, as I will be learning all I need to know about agriculture. I will need to prepare myself with every detail that will be thrown out to me by those tough professors," he said to her.

"It will be hard you know Wayne not to spend time with you as well as Greg as he too will be in college so when the three of us are home on break, we will be busy in our books. There will come a period once we have placed our books aside and spend a little time together but not like we are doing now Wayne."

"In that case, I will have to make time to spend at least some quality time with the two of you to keep things the way they are now. Just think Sandra come next year, Greg himself will be in college. Do you know if he plans to attend the same university as you?"

"I don't know because you know my brother as well as I do when it comes to keeping secrets. He waits until the last minute before he open up to let anyone know of his intentions."

"I think he should at least discuss it with your parents so they will know in advance. I am not to worry about that because I know he has chosen the college he plans to attend. Think about it Wayne," Sandra replied to him.

"What is it Sandra?" he asked.

"The three of us as the amigos will be away in college and who would have ever thought that our time spent as childhood would turn out to be this way, isn't it a wondeful thing Sandra?" Wayne replied.

"Only if the whole world could just take a look at all we have achieved from our childhood days, remaining together as one and to be able to go on to college to prepare to change the world in years to come to help make things better for everyone."

"Sandra it will not surprise me if you graduate with honors when you graduate as I can see you now walking up on the stage to receive your degree and being dedicated the top graduate student by the college president," he said laughing as they walked home.

"Hey Wayne please don't sell yourself short because you know where there is one top individual with success on her mind then there is another young man with the same thing on his mind that will also follow in her footsteps. Do you think that is what I plan to do?" Sandra asked Wayne. "To follow in your footsteps?"

"Well, from taking all the conversations you and I have had over the past few years, I would say so and do not get me wrong, I think it is a wonderful thing, at least we know we are on the same guidelines to work toward a suitable goal in bringing changes. Since you put it that way, I have to agree with you," he said as they continued to walk home holding hands as sister and brother, sharing their innermost moments. Wayne knew that his day has truly made a reflection on his life to know without a shadow of doubt, there would be no one to stop him from seeking the girl he has always loved. If this was going to be a mission, then this would be the one for him to fulfill. As the two of them reached Wayne's home Sandra said to him, "Brother I have made sure you got home safe and sound, as I am sure your mother more so than your father, will be thrilled."

"Sandra I want you to know this day has been the best thing that I can remember happening in such a very long time." He leaned over and kissed her on her cheek to say, "This is your goodbye kiss because I probably will not see you tomorrow."

"Why thank you Wayne," Sandra said as she too leaned toward him. She placed her kiss on his cheek to say, "That should keep you in good spirits until the next holiday. You have a good afternoon and please let your mother know that you and I only spent time rediscovering old times while we introduced ourselves to that old oak tree that might had forgotten us as we played under it when we were children. I know I will be busy packing up things tomorrow to be ready to check out from here Sunday morning to head back. At least we both know that we spent quality time just sharing things together about our likes and dislikes. Alright Wayne enough is enough so I am moving on to my home to be asked a million questions by you know who, little brother Greg."

"Don't forget what you said about staying in touch with me," Wayne reminded her.

"How can I forget not to do it besides, I wouldn't want you to get so lonely and up and walk away from campus to head my way," she said laughing. As Wayne disappeared inside his home, Sandra made her way to her location. As he walked inside with his blanket and water cooler, his parents were sitting in the kitchen at the table having some dinner as she asked him if the two of them enjoyed their day together down under that old oak tree.

Samuel said to Florence, "For heaven sake let the boy settle down and come to the dinner table before you start asking him a thousand questions."

"Thanks Daddy, because I think mother wants to know every detail of how Sandra and I spent our time."e

"Yes I do and I am quite sure Catherine and Elijah will want to know the same thing."

"Daddy, did you see Greg any more today since this morning when he left home to visit his buddy?"

"Son, Greg came home right after I dropped his daddy off from checking out the farm land. I am sure he is home preparing to ask Sandra a lot of questions."

"Now Samuel, what is wrong with that?" Florence asked him.

As Wayne took a seat to have some dinner, he said to his mother as well as his daddy how they spent their day. "All we did was visit that old oak tree, the one where you guys would always come looking for us when we were children to bring us home before it got dark. I took the blanket so we could just sit down on the ground and talk about all old times without getting dirty. We had a good time going back into time. This was a good day not only for me, but also for Sandra as well because she was glad we decided to spend time there. We talked about college, things in the world, people, and how we want to help make a lot of changes in the world. She agreed to call me sometime in the week after classes to make sure I am alright and not lonely."

"Son, I think you and Sandra deserved spending the day together because come tomorrow the two of you will be so busy packing to make sure you are ready to leave come Sunday morning to return back to college. It is nice to have someone that is doing the same thing as you for moral support," his daddy agreed. His mother was busy making a dish of food for him to eat as she too agreed with his father.

"I feel much better now since Sandra plans to call you."

Episode Seven

THIS IS THE DAY THAT EVERYONE HAS BEEN WAITING FOR TO MAKE sure the two love birds return back to their destination of the colleges they were attending. Wayne had been up and wandering around in his room looking our his bedroom window as he hope he would get a catch of Sandra placing her things into her parent's car with the help of her little brother Greg to possibly raise his window to yell out to say hello to her. After he did not, there came a knock on his bedroom door which was his mother to let him know that breakfast was ready and he should hurry up and come out so the three of them could have a nice breakfast together before it was time to leave to return him to the university. After Wayne made his way out of his room looking all sad as he walked into the kitchen to take a seat at the table to start eating a delicious breakfast, his father looked toward his direction to ask, "Son, you seem a little down this morning, what is the problem?"

"There's nothing really wrong except, I will once again be leaving you and mother here all alone until it is time for me to come home on break again."

The reason why he said that to his father was because he did not want him to get the idea that he was sad because he was going to be away from Sandra as she would be in another part of the state attending college so he let it be if he would be missing the two of them. In a way he would miss them because they were his parents and who would not miss from being around parents knowing how they stood by you all the way until you have grown up. He had to let the two of them know how much he loved them and he wanted them to know how much he appreciates their concerns about his future. In so many ways he realized that parents are supposed to be that way, caring and motivating their children for a better tomorrow. He has long prepared himself that once all of how he feel about Sandra comes out, there just might be some downfalls.

As far as he was concerned, the heat would be on as he sat there enjoying the last good breakfast he would have being with his parents until he returns back home to enjoy the Christmas holidays break. Wayne knew in the next three years of his life, this would be something he would just have to deal with and that is being silent about his love for the girl he had always viewed as a big sister he never had. "Now the thought of this I think just might be an all-out war between the two families that has held friendship ties all the years and now, I come along and spoiled everything for them. The most important concern I have when it come to the light is will Sandra change from the way she feels about me now, being a big brother or not?" he asked himself. "Will Greg, my little brother, change his mind toward me and start hating me for doing this to both families? I sure hope nothing of this sort will ever destroy our families."

Wayne ate real fast as his mother said to him, "Son, you don't have to swallow your food so fast because we still have time before we leave as your father and I have placed all of your things in the car while we decided to let you sleep a little while longer before disturbing you."

"Do I have time to run over to the Logans home to say goodbye to Sandra and Greg?" he asked.

"Yes," his father said. "And I tell you what, since all of your things are already in the car and you have on what you plan to wear back, you can go and spend time with them. We will stop off to get you just as the Logans prepare to leave with Sandra."

"I think that will be a good idea," his mother said to him. "At least the three of you can enjoy your last moments together." After that, Wayne just pushed his chair back from the table and out the door he ran over to the Logan, because he really did want to see Sandra as they will go off in their separate ways.

Wayne's daddy said to his wife, "Gee that boy could have jumped straight across the road onto the Logan's front yard if his legs were long enough."

"Well, you know those two kids of the Logans, are all that he has and by him being away from Sandra and Greg has put a damper on him," his mother responded. "I am sure those two kids are feeling the same way as he does this morning knowing it will be sometime before they see each other."

As Wayne reached the Logans home, Greg walked out on the front porch to greet him to say, "My brother, this is the day that I once again lose my two favorite people until next time I want you to know."

"Greg things will still be here and the same once I am back on winter break." By that time Sandra walked out to join the two of them to greet him with a good morning hello big hug as he placed his arms around her as well. Now, this was exactly what he wanted before leaving to be able to show his affection toward her with a deep feel without her knowing anything about that much. Wayne said to Sandra, "Jere we are about to depart and return back to college to get started once again with our studies."

"You know Wayne, Sandra said to him. "I am sort of looking forward in going back because these few days away from class has seemed like a long time which I know were only a few days."

"Are you really looking to return back to your professors' classes?" he said to her.

"Oh yes," Sandra replied, "because remaining completely in my studies, time will fly by fast and before you and I know it, we will be graduating and out there preparing to challenge the word to help change things."

As the three of them stood there talking and waiting to leave, Greg asked Wayne if he felt the same way as Sandra about his studies? "Why of course my little brother because little do you know right now once Sandra and I graduate, we will be a part of that group that will be fighting to change society rules and policies as who can and who cannot be together. You should know that Greg because when we graduate, you will be in your third year of college, coming on up behind Sandra and me. Neither Greg nor Sandra caught on to what he meant when he said he and Sandra would be fighting to change things. Marrying her was exactly what he was speaking about.

Soon, Wayne's parents had backed out of their driveway headed toward the Logan's home and stopped by to get him, as Catherine and Elijah walked outside to greet them to say, "This is the big day where we dump off our son and daughter."

"Florence," Catherine said to her. "Please don't start crying once you drop off Wayne as you did when you and Samuel took him there."

"I will try not to, but it is hard Catherine you know, with your only child."

"Okay son," Wayne's father said to him. "Hug, shake hands, and load up so we can get going before it gets late."

"Okay guys, I think I better get into the car before my parents have a fit. Sandra you make sure to call me like you said you would do to keep a check on me so I will keep up on my studies."

"Okay Wayne as if you really need for someone to see that you are lacking in your studies," Sandra replied, "but I will."

"Greg you too behave yourself and stay the course in your classes so you too will be taken off to college just as Sandra and me." They loaded up and the Logans pulled off right behind the Hunt's car headed toward the interstate, but they would go in separate directions as they waved out the windows as they were splitting up.

Greg said to his sister, "This is it, you going back to your location and big brother Wayne on his way back to Ole Mississippi university." Wayne's mother had packed him enough food to last him for a few days as he would place it inside the refrigerator in his room for he and his roommate to eat.

While Sandra's mother unbeknownst to her packed more food than she thought to share with her roommate and maybe a few friends since she loved being on campus there. In one moment Greg asked his mother if she left him some food home since it looked as if everything was packed in the big box for Sandra. "Son, you know your mother left you and me some food so I don't know why you would even ask that question," his father said to him.

"It is not like your sister will be gone forever, I just wanted her to have good home cooking you know son," his mother responded to him. "Now you should know that we will never forget to take care of you when food is mentioned. Isn't this ride is a very exciting ride as the four of us are driving once again to take our daughter your sister back to college Greg?" his mother asked.

"I have to agree with you mother, this is a very exciting ride because once I get back home I will have everything that was left there will be mine to eat you know sister dear well come tomorrow will be back as the same before you left," Elijah said to them.

Catherine said to him, "Honey, come first light you and Samuel will be up standing outside before Florence and I can even get breakfast."

Is Love Worth the Wait?

Sure enough, just as Catherine had mentioned to her husband Elijah, the day before about him and Samuel, Greg's father would be standing out in front of the house just talking and speaking about their day's duties while breakfast from both wives was being prepared for them to eat. Soon, Wayne's mother Florence telephone Catherine to tell her husband Samuel to come home because she had prepared his breakfast which gave would give her a chance to speak about their son Wayne as she had sensed something of important going on with him that she felt that he was about ready to break the news to them. This Catherine had some time ago held a conversation about their children, but when it was to come would definitely be a great shock to everyone and then too, it just might be a joy to hear at least the two families will finally realize that things in our society were about to be changed for the good of all people. Anyway that anyone viewed it, Wayne was a good person as he did not look upon a person just because he was a different skin tone, but from the time he was a little boy playing and running around with Greg and Sandra he saw them as his sister and brother to later on in life began to accept those feelings that came upon him as she grew into a teenager about Sandra.

There came times when he tried to shake those feelings off but to no avail as he soon accepted the fact that just maybe it was mean to be because in life no one has all the understanding of whom they one day just might fall in love with. As he grew up to become a fine teenager, his mother often wondered why he never wanted to date any of the girls at his high school, as she once sked him. He would always answer to her that none of them excite him enough to want to be involved with. He didn't tell her at the time because he was afraid if he told her, it would mess up the friendship the two families had together as it had been all those years so he decided to keep it to himself just a little longer until the time was right then he would break it all down to them this way, he hoped that both families would accept it and move forward to wish Sandra and him the best, but the first thing of all he would have to let Sandra know all about this in hoping she would accept him now the two of them had all grown up to become a part of his life where the two of them could grow so the whole world will see the color of a person's skin does not matter when love is involved. Wayne knew that pill would be hard to swallow because there will be those narrow minded individuals who will not accept his crossing over, but for the love he holds for Sandra will not make any difference in his life and he hoped that when all of this finally come together, it won't matter with their parents and brother Greg as he knew it wouldn't then it was time for the two of them to graduate from the colleges they were attending to head out to their destinations. Sandra knew that it would be hard for her to be the best English teacher there in her location because since high schools were still divided, the state board would not give her an assignment to either one of the white schools there as parents wouldn't want a black teacher teaching their children because of that old myth about black teachers are not educated enough to spend time with their children in classrooms teaching about something they knew little of.

Sandra knew if she was going to be a successful English teacher, she would have to take a job at an all-black high school to teach her own, but that was in Sandra's agenda because she knew in her heart that things could change and it would only take just one person to do it so that person had to be her. Wayne knew how bad Sandra wanted to teach at an all-white school to break that bond between the race of people to let everyone see that changes can be made and by George it would be right now as he himself will do all he could within his little power to make sure that happen. He knew since he was in the agriculture field, he would not have any problem because that field was all sold out to white guys who majored in agriculture so once they graduated they would not have any problems finding a job because they were already set aside for them thus causing the blacks who majored in the same field would have to leave and go elsewhere to find work. As Wayne and Sandra geared up to be marching in less than a month to go, he became so excited to know the two of them had grown up as small children together and now, the two of them will be graduating from college holding their degree in the field of agriculture and English with both honors as if the two of them had been competing through their whole four years of college. It was something that Wayne had thought about more so than Sandra because she had nothing on her mind but how good she would be teaching all students the way they could write correctly to make it their everlasting thing not to forget. About the time for Sandra to graduate, she began to send out her resumes highly recommended by all of her deans and professors that taught her to let school and businesses know just what they would be getting if they hired her. Of course Wayne being a white young man did not have to do all the things that Sandra had to do because he knew just how unfair things were, as it really bothered him a lot because he knew that Sandra was just as smart or even smarter than he and she should be given the same opportunity to reap some benefits as well.

As the two of them finally graduated and headed back home to rejoice into their success, Wayne would often come over to the Logan's home to see if Sandra heard anything from any of her resumes to find, not a single one had responded once they found out that she was a young black graduate trying to penetrate her way into an all-white life to teach their kids. This made Wayne very upset as he announced it to his parents and they too agreed with him as they said to him, "Son, you know how this state is about how things should be and I don't think it will ever change in our life time, maybe it will in yours."

His mother asked him, "What will Sandra do since she had not received any leads from any of ther resumes son?"

"Right now mother, I just don't know but I do know one thing, it is not fair for me to have a job offered and she has not." After his short and direct conversation to his parents, he said to them, "I don't think I will be staying here at home with you two to travel back and forth to work but I rather be living in town having my own place. Being here and seeing how Sandra is suffering from all she had placed emphasis on will just destroy me. I think I will walk over to her parents' home to sit and talk with her to get her take on what will be the next steps she will be looking to involve herself in." Little did Wayne know that Sandra had a cousin living in New York who had asked her to come live with her there to seek employment because her chances there would be greater than where she was at the moment. Once Wayne walked onto the porch, Sandra met him and the three of them sat outside as her brother Greg was always around because as he had stated before that he and Wayne were brothers to the end, and therefore, he wanted to know everything that was going on. Wayne alluded to Sandra that he thinks that he would be taking an apartment in town that way he would be close to his job not having to drive back and forth each day for work.

He said, "Sandra I am just so mystified of the bad treatments you have received not wanting to offer you a job just because of the color of your skin which I feel it is a disgrace upon all humanity."

Sandra said to him, "I really appreciated all that you have said but I plan to leave next week and go to New York to live with my cousin because she said that I would not have any problems obtaining a teaching position there because teachers are in great demand."

This Wayne did not want to hear because if he did not move fast it was a possibility that he just might lose the love of his life so in his mind he asked himself, "What do I do or what should I say?" By hearing this information it surely had weakened him to open up because of his fear that Greg as well as Sandra would reject him, not to speak about both of their parents.

Before all of this will take place, Wayne will just have to put a lot of thoughts into all what he will get up enough nerve to say. He is hoping that there will not be any conflicts between the two families because it would really tear him up completely if this did happen because of all the years they have spent together as one family. Will he be willing to wait until a later date to spill his beans or will it be wise for him to go on and let the cat out of the bag before Sandra leaves for New York or will it be safe for him to wait until she had left before he tells it? Wayne knew he will have many nights to sleep on this issue to come up with the right decision to express himself to all while Sandra is away in New York.

Come the following week Sandra will be saying her goodbyes and traveling to New York City on that long train ride to seek employment there where here in the county where she lived all of her young life could not obtain any progress just because of the color of her skin to show the outright evil that had been a part of the control government for years not wanting to change things to suit everyone who lived there. How so much Sandra had looked to change things there, but as it was set in stone, there was little hope there for her to show narrow minded people so it would be to her best interest to not intensify the situation that just might cause harm to her parents and brother, even to Wayne and his parents as well because of the closeness they had with each other. Wayne and Sandra sat talking about how the two of them had wanted things to change is why he encouraged her to seek her most desire in becoming a good English teacher, as she had encouraged him to go into the field he wanted to and love so much because he felt in his heart that he could make the way farmers use their lands for production to be better if he suggested and show them how ther soil could be treated that would give them more yields of corn, soybeans, and other items that would fulfill the needs of communities.

Sandra told Wayne regardless how she felt about not getting any response back from all of the resumes she had submitted should not have any bearing on his luck because she understood now more than ever and she wished the best for him. Right at that moment, Wayne wanted to break down to tell Sandra just how much he loved her and how bad he wanted her to be his wife didn't matter what anyone would say, because he had loved her from the time they grew up together and he just could not take it any longer because his love was only for her and the color of her skin did not matter to him because when you love someone and truly from your heart then what does color have to do with it he asked himself. He realized that was a question being asked by individuals who live for the outer appearance and not from within one's heart.

Neither Sandra, Greg, nor their parents had ever given a thought about Wayne being in love with their daughter because to them, he was another son to help the son they had Greg to grow, nothing about even considering the fact that this little skinny white boy who lived just a few yards from them who came to put his feet under their table and ate as much as their own son Greg to be in love with their daughter. How could Wayne's parents have known or Sandra's parents because there was no indications between the two of them that would have given them any idea? The three of them were always in the company of each other out on the front porch at his parents' home or on the front porch of Sandra parents' home so there were no indications, of course both of the parents knew the situations there in Mississippi during that time and knew the two of them would not be attending the same university, but separate ones because of the hate in and around there about mixing. It would have been nice if the two of them could have attended the same university to graduate together with honors to really make a difference. As such that just did not happened. In time Wayne knew something good would come out of all of this and things will be changed for the best where all would live together in harmony.

Since Wayne wanted to burst out to tell the whole world just how hard it has been not only for him, but with other young minds that in many ways felt the same way as he did about how thing should be he decided that he would wait as long as it would take and when the time is really right then he will let the whole state of that mixed up Mississippi know that life is very special and no judgement should be passed on any person because of the color of one's skin. After Wayne had accepted Sandra leaving to head to New York, he began to feel a little better because although she would not be in his presence, he definitely could shower her with letters to keep her spirits up as if she was still home to share laughter with him and her brother Greg. He knew she would make it there where she would be able to use and exercise her education where she had worked so hard to obtain to present it to others. After spending time with Sandra and Greg, Wayne then returned home to sit down with his parents to let them enjoy him since he had given Sandra and Greg his four one four about taking his own apartment into the city where he would be close to his job as Sandra and Greg did congratulate him. Greg did ask Greg, "Does that mean it will all be over with the two of us as brothers? You moving away from here then there will not be anyone for me to spend time with since my darling sister Sandra will be leaving tomorrow for New York, which will be hard enough for me and now you taking residence up in town. What am I to do?" Greg asked.

"Greg," Wayne responded back to him. "My dear brother, I can come on weekends to spend time with you as you know I just will not give up on your mother's cooking as well as my own."

"Now that you have put it that way," Greg responded. "Then I guess I will be able to make it through the week without you and Sandra being here."

"Are you now satisfied my little brother?" Wayne asked.

"Now wait a minute Wayne do I really have a choice as you know I still have a year to complete high school so I am stuck here without the two of you being here to cover my back."

"Well guys," Wayne said. "I think I will walk home to see what my parents have to say about this whole moving affairs."

After Wayne had left, and Sandra and Greg remained out on the porch for a while until being called in to have lunch, Greg said to Sandra, "I don't know but I have a feeling about that young man that I just cannot put my finger on."

"What are you talking about my brother?" Sandra asked.

"I don't know but I do feel that time will tell as I know it will because this feeling just won't let go of me."

"Greg are you saying there is something that is unusual about Wayne that he needs to let go of?"

"I can't say that my dear sister but I do know that time will tell." After talking about Wayne maybe is hiding something, their mother called out to them to come to prepare for lunch. Just as Wayne walked into the house, his mother and father were had taken a seat at their table waiting for him to get there so the three of them could have a good family lunch time together. Just as Wayne sat down to begin to eat, his mother asked him about his move into town maintaining his own apartment, not knowing how to prepare his meals.

"What are you going to do son, you know nothing about cooking as I should have taught you to learn how to do some cooking?"

Wayne's father said to his wife Florence, "There comes a time when every young man will have to learn to do things on his own without their mother interfering because it is the only way they are going to learn without being mothered all the time. Son, you will be just fine and I think by moving away into your own place will give you more of the responsibilities that you will have to face that way, you will be able to meet them head on with your determination."

"Samuel," Florence said to him. "You act like you want our son to get out and move on his own."

"No I am not saying that Florence, I am merely stating the fact that he would have to make a move one day sooner or later because he has finished college and did all the things we have wanted him to do so now is his time to decide what he wants to do with his life. Like you my dear wife, I would love for our son to remain here with you and me, but we must face the fact that maybe one day he will want to take a wife to have children that is what you want as much as I do, isn't it Florence, grandchildren running around the house playing?"

"Honey, nothing would suit me any finer to have a couple of grandchildren running in and out of this house yelling grandma or grandpa. Wayne?" his mother asked. "What is your take on what your father and I just talked about?"

"Listen you guys, it all sounds good as I want the best for you two guys because that is what I want as well to get married and have a couple of children, but right now I have to get started with my career and then see what will happen. First of all I have to marry a girl that I love and hope she will love and see me as I see her," he said to them. His mother responded by asking him did he meet someone while in college and has fallen in love with to one day ask her for her hands in marriage.

Samuel said to Florence, "Please let him be because when the time is right and he feels as if he has met the right young lady then things will happen. Let us remain silent because Wayne is now a grown up man and he will know when it is time."

"I know," Florence responded. "But I just can't wait because I want a good daughter-in – law to sit and talk and do things together." Just then and there while the conversation was going on about his life, it was his perfect time to tell them, but something said to him, not just yet because the time isn't right just yet.

To get their opinion on something to see just how they would respond to his about to be asked question, he said to them, "Dad and Mother, how would you feel if the girl I did choose was not white, but she could be a Japanese, Korean, German, French, black, Mexican, or any other race for my wife, how would you feel about having mixed grandchildren?"

Well! That big question surely did get their attention more so his mother rather than his father. His father answered and said, "You know son, I have not been exposed to many races of people and since you are a young man of your own convictions, I have to respect your decisions and welcome whomever you decide on having as a wife."

"What about you mother?" he asked.

"Son, you have thrown me for a loop because like your father, I wasn't ready for that type of question. To be honest with you son, your father and I have always taught you to treat all who you come in contact with the same because in this world we all are one in the spirits of God almighty, and I must follow those guidelines what will make you happy." Those were the things that Wayne had wanted to hear from his parents to accept the girl he would marry was Sandra, but they don't know that yet. His parents asked if he had found that someone to spend his life with.

"Hey guys, not so fast because I have to get my life established first before I open up the whole can of worms. Once things I feel will happen then I hope to let you know who it will be. Until then you two guys will just have to be patient. After they had finished with their lunch, Wayne's father said to him to come go with him to help him do something outside that he needed assistance with.

As Wayne and his father walked together outside to get started on what he needed help with, Wayne said to his father, "Daddy, come Monday morning you know that I will be starting out with my job that I had been given."

"I know son, and I will truly miss you from being around here until I get used to it. What about Greg?" his father asked. "I know you were over there talking with Sandra and Greg so tell me about how he took it about you moving into town and he won't be seeing you except on Sundays when you come to have dinner with the two households?"

"He didn't take it too well, but he could accept all the changes that are about to take place, his sister Sandra leaving tomorrow for New York, and me moving into town. He feel like his world has ended until I told him that I will be home on weekends to spend time with him to eat up everything his mother and my mother cooks so he began to feel better."

"You know Wayne, I am so very proud at the way you three have taken to one another as a family and never once looked upon each other as different but rather as one. Not only did your mother and I teach you well, but Catherine and Elijah taught their two children the same. I know Sandra will probably meet such a nice young man there in New York, and it just might be a possibility she will marry." What Wayne's father had just said did not go off well with him because this is not what he hoped to face about whether or not Sandra just might meet an individual there in New York, fall in love, and marry him. Surely, this was not in the plan for Wayne as he has always wanted to let the cat out of the bag to tell everyone just how he feels and care for the love of his life in hopes that one day she will become his wife and the mother of his children. Whatever his mother and father had talked about has become at this time a shut closed door in his mind, after the three of them had finished having their lunch time and talk together, Wayne decided to go to his room to make sure that nothing had been missed as he packed to move into his own place come the following week to live and work there in the city. With the new job that had been offered him, a state agriculture car would be finished to him for work purposes and that way he will save on the cost to operate his own vehicle while out on his business runs. This made everything all well and good with Wayne because something good had come out of his ordeal, but not so good for Sandra because she would be a hundred miles away from him as he would not be able to see her, only to write.

Wayne would ask himself why does life appear to be so hard and the one thing that you love has to suffer? He realizes that it would only be just a short while before things in his life would look up and he will have joy and peace to fulfill his meaning being here on earth with the one person who he thinks was destined to be his. As Wayne sat on his bed thinking about all the things he envisioned to be bright in his life, he wondered what the thoughts of Sandra were having going through her mind knowing that she had no ideas about the situation with Wayne. For now, all Sandra was thinking about was going to New York to obtain a good job with a possibility to reach English to underprivileged kids to make them better prepared for society. Nothing of the thing called marriage was on her mind and surely getting involved with anyone was not on her list now at this time in her life as she had just finished college with her degree to teach.

If anything of how Wayne had been feeling about her ever came forth right at this time, she just might lose it and make other arrangements to go into other directions. This is why Wayne had to be so protected in presenting himself to his parents, her parents, and especially her little brother Greg, because all the years that they have been in the presence of each other, they viewed themselves as brothers and now, if Wayne came forth with this would surely tear things apart so his work had to be safe to break it to them gently so everyone would be able to accept what will come forth, especially in Sandra's case once she learned of it. There was one thing for sure as Wayne already had prepared himself for it, as his mother Florence will definitely speak to Sandra's mother Catherine, about the conversation they had with their son about his one day marriage. Knowing his mother as he does, he know she will make it seem as if he had already found the young lady that he wanted to share his life with and he will be ready to get married real soon, the way his mother Florence will make it seem as she and Catherine speak about it. Wayne was glad that he did not mention anything about Sandra as he asked them if it made a difference to whom he would married that way his mother could not run over to her mother and let the cat out of the bag, as she would and he knew it too.

As Wayne looked out his bedroom window, he saw his mother making her way over to Sandra's home to speak with her mother as she just could not keep what he had said to she and his father about his future plans, because news about his future she just could not keep anything to herself if she did she would burst. "One good thing about it, she would not tell her that it was Sandra because I have made sure to guard her well so neither one of them will know just yet until the time is right and then I will hit them with a big bang. Besides, once Sandra comes to know it, she will have plenty of time to know all about what has taken place with me, she will either accept it or she will not. It will be her decision to make up her mind whether she wants to be with me for life or she will go another route. Right now, I have to let the chips fall where they may and with the hopes that they will fall into my space."

Once Florence reached Catherine's home she said to her, "Girl let me sit right down here beside you because do I have news to tell you." Catherine asked Florence if she wanted a cup of hot tea.

Florence replied to her "Yes, I think that will help me to spill the beans so you will know just what Wayne, his father, and I talked about while having lunch to our surprise to hear it from him, because you know for yourself just how quiet he is when you ask him certain things because he like to remain secret."

In the meantime, Sandra had walked into the kitchen to speak with her to say, "I wouldn't mind sitting her with you and mother Mrs. Florence to hear what you have to tell Mother about Wayne."

"I don't think it involves you daughter," her mother said.

Florence said, "Let her stay maybe she can say something of importance that might be useful." At that moment Sandra took a seat to listen to what Wayne's mother had to tell. It was taking her so long to bring it out as she sipped on her tea.

Catherine said to her, "Florence will you get to the point because the day isn't getting any younger you know, and I do have to make sure my daughter has packed everything she will need for her trip to New York next week."

"Catherine?" Florence asked her. "Do you think it is right for me to repeat what my son had spoken to us about?"

"Florence, it never stopped you before so let's have it."

"Well to start, and I don't know why he would say this to me and his father."

"Please Florence, is this some big government secret you want to tell, but you are afraid to?"

"Not at all as he asked his father and I would it matter to us if he married a young lady that is not white, as you know by now Catherine, color doesn't matter to Samuel and me. At first we did not know where he was going with this because how it got started, his father and I were saying to him that we would like to have some grandchildren one day to run all around the house calling us Grandma and Granddad, as we looked to Wayne and that is when he asked if it would matter if he married an Indian, a Japanese girl, a Korean girl, a Mexican girl, a Spanish girl, or a black girl? It happened so fast until his father as well as I were caught off guard, blindsided as our mouths just dropped opened before we spoke."

"I guess once the sudden shock passed over, his father said to him, 'Son, I feel like in this life and especially your life, you will meet people from all walks of life and if you meet a nice lady that shows you compassion with understanding, it doesn't matter to me where she comes from just as long as she makes you happy and you make her happy as well. We are all God's creatures as he developed each person as he wanted to love and carry on so what race she might be, I know I will be thrilled as well as your mother also to give us some grandchildren.'"

Sandra asked Wayne's mother how she felt. "Sandra," she said. "Let me express myself to you because you and Greg have been just like my two children as well as Wayne and there is nothing that I wouldn't do for you guys the way your mother Catherine wouldn't do for Wayne so I am with his father all the way as I know if you tell your mother you have met a nice white boy and the two of you have talked about marriage, you would hope that she and your daddy Elijah will feel the same way."

"So, this is the information that was so stressing you had to run over her to tell me about what Wayne had said?"

"Yes, it is and I hope that you are happy for Samuel and I hoping one day we will get some grandchildren."

"Florence," Catherine said to her, "don't go counting your chicks before they hatch because I am sure Wayne just wanted to see what you and Samuel would say. Besides, he has to build on a career as he is now just getting started in the work field. Give himself some time and you two just keep on with your lives until this thing finally happens and then you can become overjoyed. My God Florence the young man has not even started dating anyone yet."

"I know Catherine, and once he move into the city maybe being around a lot of girls, he will meet someone to date to see where it will go."

"Florence, I guess I can also hope the best for Sandra once she moves to New York to work and maybe she too will meet someone whom she will become to enjoy to married, but for right now, I just want her to be the best with what is given to her in her job to make a good future for herself. You know, once Sandra leaves, Elijah and I still have to think about our son Greg."

After Florence has spoken her peace about her son Wayne, she said, "I better get back to my family before the day ends to spend as much time with Wayne as possible because the house will be lonesome come Monday night because he will be living in his own place to get used to being alone for how long he decides."

Sandra opened up and said to her, M"rs. Florence, I don't think you should worry too much about whether Wayne is going to be alright because I know he will and I will give him my best wishes before he and I get ready to leave each other's space for how long it takes."

"I know you and Greg will for I will still be able to see him come weekends as he promised Greg that he would still be available to spend time with him on weekends as he come home for some good old meals here at Catherine's home as well as mine." As Florence prepared to leave she said to her best friend Catherine how great it is to be able to just come over and share important things with her to be reassured that everything will be alright.

Little did the two mothers know that their whole conversation they had was geared around Sandra which neither one of them picked up on anything that would draw Wayne's conversation to Sandra. If they found out that he was speaking about marrying Sandra everything would surely fall apart and it would be a possibility that Sandra would not be traveling to New York to start off her career so it had to be this way for at least now until things could be worked out by Wayne to get everyone on one accord with why he did what he had to do give them the time to accept his hidden secrets, as he was afraid that things would not be as he had planned. Wayne knew that his plan he had mapped out would not be happening just yet because it would have to take a while, a few years before the wheel will start to be put into the grinding motion to open up a whole new world not only for the two of them and their family members, but also to the whole state of Mississippi to change old laws into new laws where it will not matter if people of color would not be able to be together and when Wayne and Sandra tie the knot and the biracial children appear that old divided pandemic of people will be gone and changed forever because all children will finally be as one.

As Sandra and her mother continued to make sure she was going to take with her to New York had been packed so once she arrives there, she would have no reason to call back home to tell her mother to send her what she had forgotten to pack as she now needed those things. Sandra's mother said to her, "What do you think Florence was going on about when she came running over ther to tell us about what Wayne had said to them about whether they would have a problem if he decided to marry a girl not of his race?"

"Mother," Sandra replied. "I think Mrs. Florence just wanted to get your take on how you would feel if I decided to marry a white boy. Even if Wayne should decide to marry someone not of his race, it wouldn't make any difference to him because that would be exactly what he would want. In this life mother, you just cannot decide what would be good for some people as everyone has his or her own mind to decide what will be best for them in whatever they decide to do and it will be their decision not anyone else's. Mother, just how would you or Daddy feel if I decide to marry a white boy or another race?"

"Daughter, you know just how much we accept things although we had hoped that you could have gone off to college the same place as Wayne but it wasn't meant to be so I think your father and brother would welcome whoever you decide to marry into this household and in this family to love him as we love you. Knowing your brother as we do, he would not have a problem because who knows when he finishes high school and goes off to college who he just might fall in love with and decide one day to marry."

By that time as Sandra and her mother had finished talking, in walked Elijah and brother Greg to ask them what were they talking about to cut it short. "Hello Daddy," Sandra said to him. "I see you and Greg are back from what you two had set out to do."

Daughter, don't try to evade my question because I know you two when you get together. I think your brother and I as the head of this household should hear and know what the conversation was all about between you and your mother."

Catherine spoke up and said, "Elijah, all Sandra and I were talking about was this to add to what Florence came over to share with the two of us this morning. Florence came flying over here to get my feelings on how I would handle things if Sandra would marry a white boy as Wayne had alluded to her and Samuel that one day, he just might want to marry a girl not of his race."

"Catherine, what did you tell her about how you or I would feel if our daughter decided to marry a white boy?"

"I said to her that you and I would take him in and treat him with love and respect knowing that he will be our son-in-law to possibly be the father of our grandchildren."

"Well! How did Florence say how the two of them would feel about Wayne might marry another race?"

"She said she and Samuel would do as you and I would, take her in and love her as a daughter-in-law who they hoped would be the mother of their grandchildren."

At that moment as Elijah looked around at Greg. He said, "Catherine, standing here next to me is our son to think about because you know after this last year of his schooling, he will be going off to college and who knows what he will do once he finishes and goes his separate way, different from his sister to marry who knows. Like I said about Sandra and Wayne we all will just have to accept come what may. You do know that things are changing as we are in the midst of a renewing living atmosphere. Soon as years come and go, it won't really matter about a person's complexion just as long as they find love to live a fruitful life with their children."

"There's one thing for sure," Elijah said to Catherine. "Come next week this location will sort of be lonely because we will only have our son here to make us feel good not like Florence and Samuel having just the two of them to sit down together and enjoy their meals minus Wayne. I guess you and I can still count our blessings to be able to sit down and have our son Greg to share our meals with as the voyage of his sister will be empty. I guess this is telling us that we have reached a point in our lives that the change has arrived and we must let the door fly open so the kids can walk out into a world of their own which they have chosen or will choose."

"I know for sure, I am going to miss my son when he leaves," Elijah said.

While Elijah stood speaking with his wife Catherine and daughter Sandra Greg was just standing there listening to all of it before he finally spoke to say to his daddy, "Hey there big guy, I am still here as you know you and others will not be able to get rid of me that easy by rushing me off to college once I graduate because I am sure you will make preparations for me to have my own vehicle so I will be able to come home on most weekends to eat and fill my car with foods to take back to share with some of my roommates." Sandra reminded her little brother that he will not be able to have his vehicle on campus for his first year because the president there want all of the freshmen students to get a sense of responsibility by remaining totally dependent on the campus transportation to ride here and there.

Greg said to Sandra, "Is that a fact my dear sister?"

"Yes my dear brother that is a fact."

"You know son, while your sister was a student at the university, she never once said a thing about having her own transportation because she was there only to prove a point in her life and that was to make herself believe what she enrolled there for a good cause and look my son, it surely paid off," his father Elijah reminded him. "Now that is exactly what your mother and I expect out of you, nothing but the best. You wouldn't want to one day come to the realization that you wasted your time not living up to your expectations that you set out to do, but other things you placed before you caused you not to follow into your sister's footsteps would you?"

"Daddy, as you now put it that way, I don't think I would want my sister to throw it in my face every chance she got to say Greg you see how hard Mother and Daddy worked to prepare a better life for you and me and look what you have done, nothing but messed around when all the time you could have prepared yourself to make them proud as parents."

Greg responded to his sister to say, "Hold on one minute there my sister, I am not going to do that nor will I let them down so when I enter college once I graduate, I will make sure they will not have to worry."

Good that is exactly what I want to hear and expect of you little brother because there will come a day since you are the one in line to take over and run this land which our parents have developed, you must have the mindset to carry on keeping the property in the family name."

"Okay Sandra," he said. "That is all well and good, but tell me, what will your plans be as keeping the family name with this property after it is turned you and me? Do you plan to return back here or do you plan to remain in the big city of New York forever?"

"Right now, things have not been shaped for me just yet, it is still a possibility that I will not remain there in New York but return home to obtain a teaching career once things open up here in this state, and then I will be around to assist you in certain details, but don't expect me to work on it." Their father and mother just stood silently listening to the two of them talk about the future which was all well and good to hear, but they opened up to let them know that they still had a long ways to go besides, they were still young enough and able to run the farm as is so the two make sure when the time come, they will be able to do all the things they are speaking about now.

"Daddy and Mother, you two know that I have always said that I though since Greg was your only son, he should be the held to run things because as a girl, I know nothing at all about running a farm."

Soon their mother Catherine spoke to say, "All we both want from you two guys is this: make sure you continue to care for one another as you are doing now and if the two of you get married and have children, we want your children to be close and continue to carry on the family traditions."

Greg said to his mother, "Hey I am not even out of high school yet and I have a long ways to go before I even think about marriage, maybe Sandra will get married before too long."

"Listen Greg I beg your pardon, but that is not in my mind because I am on my way to get myself established in my career, not in a marriage."

"Have we four finished talking about what is to come and what is expected of each of you? their father asked. "If so maybe your mother can make some sandwiches for Greg and me to eat because we still have work outside to do."

"Now, I can agree to that because you know ladies, there are still two heavy working men that need to be fed and I am sure over to the Hunt home, Mrs. Florence has put food on the table for Mr. Samuel and my brother Wayne to eat because they know come tomorrow he will disappear into the city setting up his apartment with their help. I am hoping that he will let me go with him too."

As Catherine rushed into the kitchen to get some sandwiches made, as Sandra assist her, she said, "Do you think it would be right for you to want to go along with Wayne and his parents tomorrow to help him set his own place up?"

"I don't see anything wrong with it. Besides, he probably would want me to see where he will be living."

Sandra said to Greg, "I don't know brother. Besides, he will need to get used to living alone and surely he want need you to trying to come over to be so noisy as you will be."

"My sister, you are just jealous because he will be here you will be heading off to New York come Monday morning so he will not be here to greet you goodbye."

"I know that Greg that is why he is coming over tomorrow just before he and his parents leave to wish me good luck. "

As the four of them sat down to eat the sandwiches made by Catherine, Greg opened up to say, "You guys know one thing, come next week I am going to be all alone because not only will my sister be gone, but my brother Wayne will be gone too so where does that leave me? I will be here all alone to go back and forth from this house to the Hunt's house to eat up everything that will be available since Sandra and Wayne will not be around to share."

"Come on you guys, we don't want your mother to start crying now before your Sandra leave now. Let us make this time we all have before her departure good. This is no surprise to your mother and I because we have talked about this day long ago as we knew it would come because we could not keep you two little kids always. Besides, with all the hurt you and Wayne will cause because you will be just like eagles being pushed from your nests to make waves for your own lives to be something which you have always wanted to do or be. It will be tears of sadness and yet tears of joys because you will be making a mark in your life."

"Greg very soon it will be your time to leave your nest and boy, I just can see all of the tears being shed by your mother because her little baby boy is finally leaving home to take on life journeys, which will be a good thing just as long as things are going in the right direction for you son. Yes, we will be so sad about Sandra leaving home for the first time in her life, but please try to understand it is not like she is going to someplace where she doesn't know anyone. She have her first cousins there to help see her through and protect her so that makes your mother and me very happy, in your case my dear son, you will still be in our presence because although you will be away at college, she and I can jump into the car and take a drive there to see you and to invite the Hunts to come along to see you as well because you feel just like their son too. Since Wayne will be away living in the city doing his thing, they will look

Is Love Worth the Wait?

to you as their son to help the get through all the lonely times that will surely come upon their household. I am not worrying to much about whether Wayne will not be checking on them because he will because he will miss them as much as they will miss him."

After those devoted moments at the table, Sandra father turned to her to ask if she had made contact with her cousin who will be meeting her once she arrive to take her to her place where she will be staying. "I have called her and everything has been set and I have my ticket as well as my spending money and all the clothing I will need to get on board in the work place."

"Do you have your resumes written and a copy of your degree because we don't want you to take the original copy?"

"Don't worry Daddy, because I have thought about everything with mother's help so I am ready to roll out."

"Yes my sister," Greg responded how it was easier for her to say that, but leaving him would be a hole in his life because he want have anyone to sit out on the front porch to talk about certain things along with Wayne. "Things are happening so fast until it doesn't seem real especially when the two people I have grown up with are now going on their separate ways as what we once had may never be that way again."

"I know how you feel right now my darling son," his mother said, "but life is a challenge to all of us. Let me tell you two something about the time your father and I met, we were so hurt to the mere fact that we knew if we were to make a go of it, the family members that we loved so dearly would make or break us because we knew we just could not remain with them forever if we wanted to make a life for ourselves to raise a family to grow so it didn't matter how hurtful it was, we moved away to face the good as well as the bad, but we knew if we stood together, we would be alright so moving here in this location working hard and establishing ourselves, something good would come out of it, look what came forth out of all what we faced, a beautiful daughter and a handsome son. This is what life is all about son, Sandra is moving on but she will never forget what she left behind, a good brother and parents who love her dearly as they will always be there when needed, as the same for you Greg."

"Come Monday morning when I wake up to know that Sandra will have to gone down to the train station to ride away to New York, my eyes will be full of tears as yours and your father's too because we are sending our only daughter off to a big city to find her own way in life to wish her well. After she has departed and the three of us remain still in silence on our way back home, the house will not be the same, but it will still be intact because your presence, my son, will still be there. Just wait until you have all grown up and take on a family of your own and then all of what is happening to you right now because you sister has left will be the same with you and your wife when your children have all grown up to decide to leave home and just then all what your father and I have been saying to you and Sandra will come face to face with you and just then you will understand."

Greg said to his father, "Come on let us get out of this house because the more Mother keeps talking about the absence of Sandra, the more it is about to make me start crying before time."

"Okay son, I think you and I should go out back and finish up with that part of the fence we were preparing before coming in to get a bite of food."

"For your information Sandra, while Daddy and I were working outside, I looked in the direction of the Hunt house to see Mr. Samuel and Wayne out back sitting out on the bench under that old big oak tree talking and laughing. I am sure the two of them are spending some quality time together as father and son before he departs come tomorrow. I yelled over to them and he said that he will be over this afternoon to say his goodbyes."

While Greg and his father were about to walk out the back door, the phone rang and wouldn't you know it, it was Mrs. Florence calling Mother to let her know that all of them were coming over this afternoon to spend time together as one big family to give Sandra and Wayne a going away dinner. After Catherine had finished speaking with Florence, she said to them, "The night will be here this afternoon. Florence is busy cooking a roast with potatoes, carrots, and onions with gravy and I will make the other vegetables with my favorite dinner rolls, some of my potato salad, and top it off with a chocolate cake."

"Daddy," Greg said. "With all of that cooking going on are you sure you want to continue preparing that fence because right now I have developed this hungry appetite," he said laughing.

"Sandra!" he yelled. "I guess all is not lost yet because by you and Wayne leaving, I will have all I want to eat starting tonight," he said laughing.

Catherine said to Sandra, "Come on let us get busy with our cooking before it is time."

As the two of them starting working in taking care of what they needed, Sandra said to her mother just how much she will be missing all of them especially getting up on Saturday morning sitting down to have breakfast together to fuss with her brother not to eat up all the bacon before anyone else can get some. "I know Mrs. Florence will be missing Wayne as she and Mr. Samuel wait until he comes to the table share their breakfast together."

"I don't know Mother," Sandra said to her about how long she might be able to stand being in New York, away from them although she will be with family members, she still will be missing them, especially her brother Greg as her, Wayne, and Greg would spend time out front talking and having a good old time.

As much as Greg wanted to be in the kitchen with his mother and sister, picking up what would be left after they prepare the dinner that would be served later on in the afternoon once when Florence, bring over all of her prepared meal, Elijah, said to Greg, "I don't think it will be a good thing for you to be in the way there in the kitchen while your mother and sister Sandra getting thing all set up so all of us will have a joyful time as you know this big dinner is geared around your sister as well as Wayne's departure."

"I know Daddy, as Greg said, but it would be nice just to be able to taste some of the crumbs that had fallen on the table especially as mother put the finishing touch on that peach pie, she is making."

"Come on let us get our job finished besides, you will have plenty of time to eat the leftovers as I know there will be quite a bit left."

It look as if both households were busy with big going away party dinner for two special individuals that will be missed from the families gathering on weekends, as things will look dark as far as having the laughter heard out on the front porch as well as seeing the running back and forth from house to house tasting both mother's good old meals which always consist of blueberry pies, strawberry pies, apple pies, you name it, they were always available for three hungry mouthed children. Although Florence was busy in her kitchen cooking and making sure her delicious roast was perfect, she tried not to feel the way she was feeling just knowing that come tomorrow her only child would be on his way to a new life, a new start by obtaining a place finally of his own where he would not have his mother to come in to make up his bed or wash his clothes. These things he would have to attend too himself unless he waits until he come home on Saturdays to have his mother to take care of washing his clothes for him. While Samuel and his son Wayne continue to sit outside under that big old oak tree just laughing and sharing all old times, she could not help but look out the kitchen window to see them together to know Samuel was trying to show his son that he would not miss him, but deep down in his soul, it was tearing him up, but he had to show face value to keep Wayne lifted up.

As Florence continued with her cooking, she said, "I think this big roast should be enough besides, Catherine is making other dishes that will fulfill everyone's stomach and what will be left, I know my second son, Greg will have a field day finishing everything off. My poor Greg because I don't know if he will be able to stand the fact that his only sister to whom he had always looked up to will no longer be around in his presence come Monday night to talk with him to get her opinion on some of his ways of doing thing especially his lessons. I guess the five of us will be crying our eyes out in missing our son and daughter. The only difference it will be is my son Wayne will still be close by where Samuel and me can drive into the city to visit him from time to time, but in Sandra's case, Elijah, and Catherine along with Greg will not be able to because she will be hundreds of miles away in a big unknown city only to see her when it will be a time when she can get off and come home. My heart goes out to them because I know I as well as Samuel will be just as sad as they will be not because we will be missing our son, but also we will be missing our daughter as well as she grew up with our son and has been a part of our family as well as our son has been a part of theirs."

To make Samuel and Wayne think that she was enjoying herself being in her kitchen cooking, as it was sad to her, she decided to hum a song to throw them off the way she was really feeling so it would not be too hard on Wayne as he pack up and drive away tomorrow headed down the road headed out to the city to his already obtained living apartment. Wayne had decided that it would be best if his parents did not help him move in because it would only make his mother cry even more as if her crying would not be enough once he kissed her goodbye to hug his daddy's neck as he too will be sad, but he knew this had to be if he ever was going to set roots for himself to try and win Sandra over in his life one day to be his wife, Wayne knew there would be a lot of things he had to work out and by being away from his parents living out on his own would be the perfect time to work toward it. Samuel asked Wayne as the two of them set outside just talking about his new responsibilities, if he thought that this was the right thing.

Wayne in turn asked his father exactly what did he mean. "I mean son, do you think the move you are making will make a difference in your life by being out on your own now since you just finished college, living away from home where you want have the expenses to face?"

"Daddy, if I am ever going to find my own way in life, I have to take many as many chances in life as I possibly can because just think about it. Things have really changed since the time you were a young man where you had to do what you thought was right because you and mother had to work together to make things work for the two of you because there were not the availabilities back there but now look what has changed, a whole new world has come forth opening up to a new generation of people to make their own decisions without being housed in their parents' homes."

"Since you have put it that way my son, I guess I should be satisfied with your decisions as I know you have given it many thoughts about what it is that you seek and you have made up your mind to go get it. Wayne, unlike your mother, I want you to feel good about yourself and do what you think is right for you. You have my blessings and if you decide to meet that girl in your life that you have possibly dreamed about well, go get her when it is time and rejoice in each other."

Wayne asked his daddy, "Do you really mean what you just said?"

"Yes I do my son because since your mother and I were blessed with only you, some grandchildren running around on all this land which not only will be yours one day, but it will be theirs as well."

Soon Florence just could not take what was going on outside with her husband and son, so she decided to walk to the kitchen door to ask if there were anything the two of them wanted or needed. "No Florence," Samuel returned with an answer to let her know the two of them were fine just sitting having a man one on one talk. Samuel knew that Florence wanted to know all about their conversation because she just did not walk to the door just to offer them something, but she was dying to find out what their long discussion was all about.

Since Florence was not applied with what the two men were talking about she made it a point to return back to her duties in her kitchen to check on her roast and her pies she had placed in the oven as she said, those two are being very secretly not to let me in on their conversation. "That is perfectly alright maybe it's a good thing as I don't need to know because it's men talk." As she continued to try and make a conversation, she yelled out the window to ask them if they smelled the aroma of her roast.

"We smell it mother," Greg said to her. "And we are sure when we all get together this afternoon, it will be up to Greg and I to eat it up. Her fabulous cooked roast, as she could cook it like no other was to be served with her dry cooked rice to have gravy to pour over it that would make you want to slap someone's face because it is so good the way she cooks it. It's no wonder why Greg and Wayne race among themselves eating at the tabl to see who could eat the most because they are eating the foods of two women with a gift for cooking anything to be enjoyed by all that come into their presence.

Soon Samuel and Wayne noticed Elijah and Greg working on the fence they were preparing to keep his animals inside so they would not get out to destroy Samuel's crop. They walked over to see what they could do to help as Greg said to Wayne, "Brother, I am having a little hard time trying to stretch this piece of wire so can you please give me a little assistance here?"

Once Wayne walked over to him ,Greg said to him, "Man we are about to have a big delicious afternoon dinner in your and Sandra's honor as you guys will be leaving me here all alone to deal with these four grownups."

Wayne said to him, "My little brother, maybe that is just exactly what you need because having Sandra and me around, you have someone to run to when you are being chastised and now you will not have the two of us to bail you out when you do something wrong."

"Brother, you are turning on me as I thought you had my back."

"Greg I do have your back, but sometimes you have to face the music on your own because that is the only way you will learn by not having me to run to all the time. Come tomorrow you know, I will be moving in to the city away from you."

"What will I do Wayne?" Greg asked.

As the day moved forward and after Wayne and his daddy Samuel had spent time with Elijah and Greg, it was time for the two of them to walk back over to their home front to see if his wife Florence had finished preparing everything that needed to be brought over to the Logan home for a combined dinner which was set to be served at around the time as always, when the whole group got together to entertain each family, at exactly at five o'clock. That way it would give everyone time enough to get all washed up and set their minds of enjoying all the festivities prepared for two wonderful children that have shown their abilities to brighten up both families homes with their great and wonderful accomplishments they set out to do. While Wayne and his father had come back home, Florence asked them to make sure all the prepared dishes were placed in the boxes she had gotten for them to carry over to the Logans to be set on the table next to what Catherine and Sandra had prepared for the glorious time they all would be having once they had taken their seats at the dinner table.

Wayne asked his mother, "Do you think that roast you cooked will be enough because you know exactly how much Greg and I can swallow?"

"Listen son," she said. "If that roast along with all the other things Catherine and Sandra had prepared won't be enough for everyone and if you think you and Greg will not have enough then I guess we will just have to send out for some pizzas to be ordered to fulfill your needs. I am quite sure son there will be well enough for you and Greg to partake to fill up your two stomachs.

After that brief conversation and he and his daddy had placed all the hot cooked foods in the boxes, Florence said to them, "Now guys, go and change your clothes so you will look presentable in a nice atmosphere setting because you know this affair is geared toward you and Sandra, Wayne." Samuel said to the two of them how this occasion will mean a lot after it is all over with because neither Greg Wayne nor Sandra will be here for a long time to take in such an affair like this, once it gets started this afternoon other than when Greg packs up his bags to head off to college come this fall after his graduation.

"I think we all sure make the best of this gathering because come tomorrow as well as the time Sandra makes her way down to the train station Monday morning to prepare to board the train headed for New York, there truly will be a change in the atmosphere in our households because neither one of you will be present. It will definitely be much easier for your mother and me Wayne because we already know that you will have the option to drive home on weekends to spend dinner time with us, but for Elijah, Greg, and

Catherine, things will not be so good because their only daughter will be miles away from them."

"That is true Daddy," Wayne responded, "but you have to look at it from Sandra's point of view, she is only stepping out into a new surrounding because of the way things here in this state are that has forced her to relocate to use her education. During the whole time Sandra, Greg, and I were growing up, I never expected something of this sort would still be around because I was hoping that all old ideas among all of those old evil folks would have died by now but I suppose I never thought about how they instilled into their narrow minded children the same rituals to continue to be carried on even through their children. I must say, after spending my childhood years with two wonderful individuals and their parents seeing me as their own child, I can't say I blame her because she had worked so hard to bring out her talents to share with everyone not because of their skin tone, but because they are children and they deserve to know about all cultures. Now, can you and Daddy understand just why I have not been eager to fall in love with a white girl? I was so afraid if I did, she would be full of hate and would not understand the importance of all people. I have a lot to consider and to think about which road I will take or which way I will go so that is why I decided to move into the city since I have been given this job to learn and see what it is that make one race of people to think they are better than the next. Mother and Daddy, since I am moving into the city, please do not think I will go running around looking for a white girl to marry because right now, the confusion lies in my heart to be able to work out a lot to whom I will marry."

Right at that moment Wayne just wanted to tell them that he had found the girl of his dreams, but she has been forced to move away from him because of the situation here in the south that would prevent them to get together so in a few years as time goes forward, he knew in his heart that this will happen and there will not be anything that anyone will be able to do to stop it. Wayne did not want to hurt his parents if he told them now nor did he want to hurt Sandra's parents and brother because this was just not the right time. So he will join in with the evening feast pretending that he was happy for Sandra knowing deep down inside his heart it was killing him, but what else could he do but to put on a false face and live through it knowing as he looked toward Sandra there sat his future wife, but he dare not let on not just yet? Soon the three of them had changed their clothing and were about to leave to meet up with the Logans for a fabulous going away dinner for their two children at hand.

In the meantime there in the Logan household, Greg, his father Elijah, Sandra, and the mother of the house Catherine had already changed into their clothing with the table set just awaiting for the Hunts to arrive with their dishes as Greg kept going to the front door checking to see if they were coming because his stomach was telling him it was time to get the ball on the road because he just would not be able to hold out much longer as he just might walk around the set table to stick his fingers in the already made dishes to taste, but his sister kept an eye on him because she knew him to well when food had been placed on the table. Greg kept saying, "What in the world is taking those guys so long to get over here because I am about to get to the end of my wit?"

"Wait one minute son," his father said to him. "You know this evening affair is a special occasion and I want you to act accordingly because this dinner we all will be engaged in will be to the achievements of your sister and your adopted brother, Wayne to send them off into the world as we wish them much success."

"Daddy, will I too have the same send off?" Greg asked.

"I can't see why not because in a few more months to come you too will be leaving your nest off to the college of your choosing my son."

"Oh boy," Wayne said as he walked back to the front door to see if the Hunts were coming as he noticed the two large boxes being carried by Mr. Samuel and Wayne with all that food inside. He ran back into the dining room to let everyone know that the crew is on the way with more good eating and laughing.

Sandra said to him, "Go open the front door for them to come in little brother."

"With pleasure my big sister because this day I will do as you ask because this is your day today, and Wayne's as well."

As the Hunts walked inside the dining room, she greeted everyone and said, "Come on ladies," as the guys placed the two boxes down. "Let us place everything on the table alongside of all what you have prepared Catherine so we all can say grace and sit down to start the most important dinner evening we have had for a long time with this special one being a grand one. As you know my adopted daughter is leaving me as well as her mother, and my son is now going to leave his adopted family as well."

"Catherine," Florence asked her. "What are we going to do?"

Catherine, being the strong woman that she is, says to Florence, "We two will be alright because think about it, we have each other, as we have spent many years in the presence of one another alongside our family giving advice and sharing food in each other's home so everything will be alright. It is not that they will be gone forever and we will not see them again."

"You know we still have this greedy Greg here with us still so whatever you cook for you and Samuel, you know nothing will be wasted because this garbage disposal will clean up everything, as he is the cleanup man," he said laughing.

After all the food from the two boxes had been placed on the table, Catherine said to all, "Can we all gather around the table behind our seats to say grace led by no other than my dear sweet son, Greg?"

Wayne said to all, "And he does it so well." After the grace was said, everyone took their seats and began to exchange dishes as they passed from one to another. Wayne did make sure he took a seat next to Sandra as Greg sat on the other side of him thus making him sit between the two of them as the grownups took their seat with Elijah as the head of his household and Samuel at the other end.

Since the two men decided to be the head of the dinner table that left Catherine and Florence to take their seats on the following side facing their children which made it much easier for everyone to exchange conversations. Although Wayne was sitting in the mist of Sandra and Greg he considered himself as well as Sandra the queen and the king of the road, knowing one day she would be his queen, as they ate Greg just had to comment on how good the roast was because it was cooked to his perfection which is nothing new as all foods are cooked to his perfection. There was a lot of laughter and just having a great time as Sandra asked Wayne if he was ready to move into his new home for the week before coming home each weekend to see his parents. "I think Sandra that I need this time to be on my own because there are a lot of things that I need to get control of in my life. What about you? Are you ready to catch that locomotive come Monday morning to head off to New York leaving Greg behind?"

"Yes, I am ready to go but not because of Greg as I will deeply miss him for aggravating me but I am going there to get my career in order and hopefully one day when things here in this state has been changed and cleared up, I will be able to come back to regain what I have set out to do right here."

Wayne returned his comments by saying, "I sure hope so because a person of your caliber should not have to travel hundreds of miles to be noticed by your accomplishments. I am so ashamed of this state on the ways it has treated black people, because this should be all about growing together."

"Well Wayne," Sandra said. "Maybe one day all of this hate will soon fade away and everyone will be able to live in harmony. Believe me, people like you, Greg, and I will have to make that change and in time, I do believe something good will come out of all of this to see how changes will take place because not all of the new generation will continue to live in the past because they want changes as well as we do," Sandra said.

After listening to that speech by Sandra Florence, Catherine, Samuel, Elijah, and Greg said, "Amen sister." Although Greg did speak, but all of them knew his mind was on all that food on the table needed to be eaten.

As the evening wore on and everyone were having the best time of their lives, there was still a stillness with Wayne as he held himself together as he sat next to his future wife everyone would soon know and things will surely be brighter and there would not be any more surprises within the two families. Wayne could hardly wait until all the day's excitements were over with the celebration of a well-planned meal for him and Sandra so they could have some time together out front on the porch swinging as they always did together with Greg sitting not far away looking not because he thought there was a thing going on between his sister and Wayne, but because he saw it as a good time with three family members as a sister and two brother being one as the adopted one. After about an hours when all had had enough to eat to include all the wonderful deserts, everyone excused themselves from the table as Elijah said to Samuel to come on out side to walk some of that food down as Catherine and Florence had agreed to clear the table and wash all the dishes as they placed leftovers in containers to be had at a later time.

Sandra agreed to remain inside to help clean too, but her mother said to her, "Why don't you three children let us do this and since you and Wayne had been given this great treat, why not go out front as you guys always have and just enjoy yourselves? Besides, you two won't have this chance again to get together for a very long time."

"Greg why don't you join them?" his mother said to him. "Because you will have lots of left over to eat that is if Florence decides not to take her roast what left of it back home so she and Samuel will have for their dinner tomorrow."

"Oh no Catherine," Florence said. "I am going to leave what is left of it right here so Elijah and Greg will have for their dinner tomorrow. You know Samuel and I plan to follow Wayne in town to his new place as I am sure Greg and Sandra will want to go along to say her finally goodbye."

"Okay, if that is what you want to do Florence," Catherine said. "Greg you go out front anyway with Sandra and Wayne to enjoy their time together." As Greg walked out front, he did notice Sandra giving Wayne her address on a piece of paper to keep in touch.

"My, my, what are we doing now passing notes to each other?" Greg said.

"No silly," Sandra said to him. "I was only giving Wayne my address where I will be living in New York so he could write to me or call me besides Greg he is our brother you know and we all grew up together so he has a right to write or call me anytime he so desires."

"Wayne when I leave from here to enter college will you do the same for me?"

"Little brother Greg I don't know we will just have to see if you will be worthy to receive a letter or even a call from me."

"You are being funny this afternoon since you and Sandra were blessed to have two wonderful mothers to prepare a delicious dinner in your honor because it has come the time for you two to just walk out on me and leaving me to hold the ball of both families," Greg responded with a laugh. As the three of them sat talking about all the times they had just being together, Wayne wanted to burst out to tell Sandra all of his smiles were killing him, because those smiles were love smiles for her as he loved her, even though she had no clue.

"Well my brother Greg come tomorrow, the two of us will ride into town with your parents to see your new apartment where you will be residing to be close to your work each day, free of me and your parents during the whole week until the weekend as I am sure you will come to visit that is, if you don't find yourself one of those little pretty filly there in the city to hang out with thus forgetting all about me or to visit your parents much," Greg said to him.

Wayne sort of smiled and said to Greg, "Listen my brother, I am moving to be closer to my work so I will not have to get up so early in the morning to travel so far. I have not even thought about running into that filly as you said."

"So Wayne will your car be so full of your things tomorrow morning until Sandra and I want have any space in it to ride with you or will we have to ride with your mother and father?" Greg asked.

"I will make room for Sandra and let you ride on the back of daddy's truck if you like. I am just kidding because yes, you will be able to ride in my car."

"You know, you were lucky to receive as a graduation gift a new car to let you know just how much your parents love you my brother," Greg alluded to him.

"I am not going to argue with you on that because when I first found out that I had been offered the position, I started to wonder just what would I do without any transportation to take me to and from and then I heard Mother and Daddy talking about how it would be hard for me to get back and forth to see them on weekends only if they would travel to pick me up and that I didn't want them to be do because that meant they would have to do it every weekend and with Mother, she would just worry Daddy to death so the two of them left home one morning to tell me that they were going into town to do grocery shopping, which I had always seen Mother driving off to the store to shop but I really did not think much of it until I was sitting in my room and I heard a noise to see Daddy driving his truck and no sight of Mother to soon notice a car driving up into the driveway and guess what, it was Mother. The two of them had gone out shopping for groceries to learn the car was what they went to get. Daddy got out of this truck and called out to me to come outside because he had seen something coming into his driveway that had not been there before. I suppose he never gave it a thought that I was looking because when they left, I was still in bed so I guess he assumed that I was still sleeping. When I walked outside and saw the car, he and my mother were standing beside it with the keys in her hand holding them out to me to say, 'Son, your daddy and I really wish you a happy graduation with this gift of your own car to have to drive since you will be living away from the two of us.' At first, all I could do was to stand still in shock because I never expected this of them. 'Come son, and take your keys because this is your car to know just how much you are loved by the two of us.' To be honest, I had tears in my eyes of excitement."

Greg said to him, "Since I am the only son, I sure hope Mother and Daddy do the same thing for me when I get ready to be on my own starting out for my first beginning. How touching my brother, but that still doesn't keep you from coming back home on weekends maybe not all weekends, but most to see me and to go riding around checking out what your job consists of."

Sandra sitting still listening to her brother and Wayne carry on about his car and all the wonderful things he hope will happen to him while he is on his own, she advised them what a wonderful gift she received for graduation. "Tell Wayne," Greg said to her.

"Well, you got a car from your parents and me, being the only girl in my family I was given the best gifts I could ever receive."

"Do tell my sister," Greg said.

"Wait just a minute little brother, don't rush me little brother because I am sure Wayne will enjoy hearing it without you forcing me to hurry up and tell."

"You tell him Sandra," Wayne said to her because Greg can be so pushy at times.

"Since I could not obtain a position right here in this state as it is, I was given a trip to New York to pursue a career there with a large sum of money to hold me over until I land a job, which was something I never expected to receive because I thought Mother and Daddy did not have the money to find out that they had been in a saving mode for years making sure Greg and I would have what we needed to start off a life of our own with having to ask for help. Greg and I never thought for one minute what our parents had set up for the two of us with a saving insurance that had grown over all of our years to be paid off as the two of us matured into adulthood which at such time the policies would be paid up and then the full indemnities would mature to be paid in full over one hundred thousand dollars for each of us. Now, I think that is the nicest graduation gift anyone can ever give to set their kids up."

"I guess Greg when you graduate you will be given the same as your sister, right?"

"Yes, but mother and daddy will not turn it over into my hands but rathe, hold it until they think I am mature enough to handle my own. Wayne do you think I will be mature enough too when the time comes," he asked.

Wayne look toward Sandra to get her opinion as the two of them said, "We don't think so. At least the one things we can say is this, having to two of us around to guide to direct you, you will be great our brother."

Greg asked them, "Why is it that I am always placed under yours and my sister's control?"

"I suppose it's the love we both hold dear in our hearts for you and we don't want you to turn out bad, but to keep you as we are, strong."

"I don't know about all that jive you and Sandra are talking about because you two are strong so therefore I have to maintain myself as you two but I can assure you that I will be fine and when I go off to college you can bet your bottom dollar that I will be a popular guy on campus, because all the girls will have to stand in line to get to me."

"Is that what you are going to college for my little brother?" Sandra asked him.

Wayne did respond to say, "I thought you were going to get an education to be able to make your mark in society to help change things, is that not true?"

"Alright so you two have gotten me over a barrel as I was just making comments. Sandra you know that I do a lot of my talking, but there is nothing that I will do to embarrassed Mother and Daddy, as they have held you and I up high and for me to follow in your footsteps."

Wayne and Sandra said out loud, "Boy are we glad you came up with that because we were starting to worry all about you and I was thinking whether or not I should travel to New York or to remain here to keep an eye on you my brother."

"Let me assure you two that I will be alright because I have already made up my mind as to what my plans are once I leave home and enter into college. I will be there for one thing and one thing only to graduate and to make you two guys as well as our parents very proud of me as well. I fooled you guys didn't I with all of my crazy talk?"

"Not really," Wayne said, "because that is just who you are at times."

Soon, Wayne's mother Florence and Catherine had finished in the kitchen so the two of them walked out on the front porch where their children were to spend some quality time sitting talking with them since this would be Wayne's last day to be sitting on this porch with Sandra and Greg together so there was a lot of laughter out there as tomorrow night, it will be quiet because his absence will be felt to be spending the night in town in his own place probably being lonely because Sandra's presence will not be available. Florence did ask if they all get enough to eat because there's plenty more left in there.

Sandra said, "I just could not eat another bit."

Greg said, "When I feel like getting up in the middle of the night to look for something to snack on, I know exactly what to do."

"Yes, you are so right my dear bother, you definitely know what to do when it comes to finding food," Sandra said laughing.

"Now children," their mother said, let that go and just enjoy Wayne's last night here with us and you yourself Sandra as you too will be a void her as well come Monday morning. I don't want to cry now, but Florence I know our eyes will be filled come tomorrow morning when Wayne hugs me goodbye and Sandra hugs you goodbye Monday morning."

"Florence, what are you and I going to do with our children gone?"

" I can tell you Catherine, I just don't know but shut myself up in the room and cry all day," Florence said.

"Now ladies," Sandra said to them. "There is no reason why you should do that because you will have someone here to really keep you busy with an empty stomach Greg running back and forth from house to house seeing what he can get to eat on so that will keep the two of you busy all day until you won't have time to cry."

"Mother," Wayne asked her. "If you plan on keeping yourself shut up in your bedroom all day crying then what is Daddy to do? When he comes in from working, he will want to eat and if you are spending your day crying because I am not around, it will make him think that something serious is going on with you, don't you agree? After Sandra and I have left and everything settles down then it will be normal again so you will not have a lot of empty time on your hands to cry. Just think, if you guys are acting this way now as the two of us are preparing to leave then what will you do when you find out that the two of us are planning on getting married?" Wayne didn't mean to put it in content that way as he realized that he had made a mistake hoping no one caught on to what he was say that would associate his action toward Sandra.

Florence and Catherine didn't read into it that way as they said, "I guess the two of us just have to prepare ourselves because we already know that it will be soon to face it."

Catherine said to Wayne, "By you being there in the city and it will be a possibility that you will meet some girl there and one day fall in love to marry her, as my daughter being in New York in the presence of all those high power professional guys just might meet a nice person and she too will bring him home to meet her family."

In Wayne's mind, he knew if he had anything to say about what was just said, it will not be happening because before Sandra even thinks about falling in love with someone there in New York, the cat will be let out of the bag and then everyone will be shocked. Catherine said to Florence, "Why are you and I sitting here in the presence of our dear children talking about all the possibilities that are far away from their minds?"

Wayne said to her, "Mrs. Catherine, my mother started it because she can't accept my leaving tomorrow morning moving into my own place that way, she won't be able to baby me any longer."

"Now Wayne," Catherine answered and said, "I somewhat have to agree with you on that and I can understand because you are all that she and Samuel have so why would she do what she does for you maybe she goes overboard just a tad bit."

"Okay Catherine," Florence spoke out and said. "Now come Monday morning when Sandra says goodbye and boards the train don't come running to me with your eyes full of tears because I am going to remind you exactly what you said about me carrying on about Wayne. Just think about this whole ordeal, the men are out in back making plans on how to continue on with their work and here we are as their wives sitting out her among our children talking in the midst of their conversations as we should be out back with our husbands involved in their conversations."

"I have to agree with you mother, because I am sure Mr. Samuel and Daddy would love for the two of you be out there with them sitting on the bench out back as Greg checked on them. They made a point not to get involved with our conversation because this was the time to allow the children to hang out."

"So what are you saying to Florence and me, daughter that we should leave from out here and go out back to join our husbands?"

"As a good daughter mother, I don't think I need to answer that," she said smiling.

"Come on Florence, can't you see that our presence is not wanted out here among our children?"

"Mother, don't be upset," said Greg. "This is our time you know to enjoy our last day being together with Wayne before he departs so don't feel that we don't want you out here. Besides, I am quite sure Mr. Samuel and Daddy would just love to have you two guys out there with them to just sit and enjoy the moment."

Florence said to them, "Alright you know it doesn't take a rocket scientist to tell us to leave, right Catherine? We are on leaving you guys now so we will see you later."

Once they had left Wayne said to Sandra, "I thought they would never leave so we could still share our moments together. Just think, this is the last afternoon the three of us will be spending time out here swinging and talking together because the time has come where the rooster and the hen have to leave their nests and go in other directions to begin anew."

"Is that a true saying Wayne?" Sandra asked him.

"As long as I have heard that saying, it has come true with all whom I have known. While in college, all the students that I met were dying to get away from their parents' home because they felt like they were being smothered by their over action where they could not breathe. So they were so looking to get away after graduation."

"I guess that is exactly what you and I think of our mothers because you know they are too overprotective and they hang around us just like mother hens with their chicks. By breaking away I think will reorganize their minds to see things a little clearer."

"You're forgetting one thing Sandra. Greg is still much a part of that where your mother will guard him in every way she knows how to since you won't be here in her presence to take up the space of Greg."

"I know Wayne and I think a break from her more so than my Daddy will be good for her to realizes that just as she and Daddy came up the same way as Greg and me, as they pledged not to be the same with their children for some reasons fell into the same situation because knowing how they were overprotected by their parents they fell into the same realm of protecting their children, nothing with them was intended it was just that they don't feel like letting go just yet. I guess life has that way with everyone when they become parents."

"You know Wayne once you and I get married one day and have children of our own, although we say this now about how we will not be like our parents over our children, but to be honest with you, we will do the same thing. I suppose there's no exception to life rules."

As the evening was getting to its final stage and Wayne and Sandra along with Greg were about to complete their final time together as a group, it was time for Wayne and his future wife to bring it to a close for this would be the last time the three of them to be sitting out on the porch together laughing and talking about the times when they were all small children running around the two houses playing hide and seek, as now they have met their requirements to prepare for the path of their fate. As Wayne was about to say to Sandra along with Greg because he just could not leave him out of their conversations because this might start him thinking about something that just might bring to his attention he had a feeling about, but just could not put it all into perspective so Wayne was very careful not to give Greg anything to go on this way he would not have anything to tell both parents. Sandra was just so happy that this dinner for the two of them came off without a hitch and everyone seemed to really enjoy themselves just knowing this would be the last night something like this will take place again.

Now, everyone is aware that it will not be for long before Greg parents as well as Wayne parents will have to do the same for him as Greg was also like a son to his own mother and father as they too held him in high esteem. Wayne knew without a doubt that he would be present when the time came, but he was not quite sure of Sandra as whatever position she will be holding in New York would allow her the time to travel to see her brother's graduation. Wayne had already made up in his mind that he guessed he would have to replace Sandra by standing in for her. There would be nothing better than to have Sandra come home to be in his presence but not to tell her exactly how he felt about her because the time just would not be right, as it would not have been long enough for him to prep himself. Just about time for Wayne to leave to go home to make sure he had packed everything, he grabbed hold of Sandra's hand to say to her, "Well, this will be our last night together and come tomorrow you and Greg will ride with me as I move into my own place to take up my own responsibilities."

"I know," Sandra said with a smile not know anything still yet as Wayne was telling her through so many lines about just how bad he wanted her, but since she was focused on her own journey, nothing what he had said gave light to any romantic feeling. As the three of them started walking together down the road to Wayne's home to let him know the two of them would be ready to ride off into the sunset with him, they headed into town to help him unpack and get settle in as his parents would be following him close behind with other things on the truck.

Wayne continued to hold on to Sandra's hand as they kept walking as Greg said to him, "Turn my sister's hand loose because you are holding on to her hand like she is your girlfriend or something my brother."

Sandra said to Greg, "Oh my little brother, Wayne and I will not be seeing each other for a very long time and we are enjoying the moments."

Wayne asked Greg, "My little brother do you have a problem with me holding Sandra's hand?"

"No I do not, but if someone else who did not know how we roll would think something else."

"So let them think whatever they want to because I am sick and tired of this stuffed state setting policies and procedurals for people to follow and live by according to their standards of life," Wayne said.

"Why Wayne, I have never heard you talk that way about this state policies before like that," Sandra responded.

"You know my dear sister, I think our white brother has had enough of this old south, and he just might be ready to leave it, but for now he has to make sure he remain close to his parents. Wayne?" Greg asked him. "Is there something you would like to get off your chest before Sandra departs for New York come Monday morning?"

"Why did you ask me that Greg?"

"I don't know because here lately I have watched you being in a slump as if something is making you sad."

Wayne thought for a moment how to come back to Greg with an answer making sure he doesn't spoil all his plans he has for Sandra. "Greg, it's just that we three have shared many days and nights together ever since we were small children and now, since we have all grown up and Sandra and I have graduated from college, she will be in New York and I will still be here, but living in the city has and is making me sad because we will not be a close family any longer."

"Hey my brother man," as Greg responded. "How do you think I will be feeling know as I come home from school each afternoon to find that my only sister is away living in a big city, which she doesn't know anything about, but having to depend on our first cousin there to make sure she learns her way around? Besides that, when I run into a problem with some of my school work, I will have to try and figure it out by myself because the brains of the family won't be present. If anyone should be so depressed, it should be me, but as a brother I am holding my own for her to keep her strong in that way she will be alright and I suggest you do the same as I my white brother as you and I both know that we will get together again one of these old days." The thing that Greg did not even think about was the white boy he has always called his brother would become a part of the family and everyone will be happy. As they reached Wayne's house, they stood out in the middle of the street talking and having a joyful time as this excitement will not be that way for a very long time if ever it should take place again so they were making the best of it.

Soon out came walking out of the Logan's home were his mother and father greeting Catherine and Elijah good night and thanking them for the gathering. As the two of them got closer to where the three were laughing and carrying on, Wayne's mother asked them, "Are you guys having a goodtime since this is Wayne's last night here on this hill?"

Greg, laughed and said, "Mrs. Florence, did you leave that leftover roast beef behind so I will be filling my hungry stomach at night as I wake up?"

She answered him to say, "Why yes Greg, I didn't bring anything home with me because Samuel and I thought it would be best if I left it there as we know it would not be a waste having to throw it out. Wayne's father asked him if he had everything already for him to get up early to load on the truck to be ready to leave whenever he was ready.

"Yes daddy, I don't think I have forgotten anything; if so then when I come home on weekends I can be sure to take it back with me after I leave." As his parents walked inside, the three of continue laughing and carrying on like small children.

Finally, Wayne said to Sandra and Greg, "Guys, I better go inside to entertain Mother and Daddy because if I continue to remain out here knowing my mother she just might get a little jealous and come back out to join us. Now, we don't want that do we?"

"Oh no," Greg said, "because we would be standing out here all night." As they were about to depart Greg said to Wayne, "Listen white boy you turn my sister's hand loose for we will see you tomorrow morning as we take that ride with you. By the way Wayne, I just want to let you know that I will be riding in the front with you and my sister will be sitting in the back seat because that is how it is here in this state where a black girl will ride in the back seat of a white person's car and a black man riding up front so these people down here want get the wrong idea."

"Wayne said to Greg, "Who really cares what they think? Maybe something like this should wake them up to know that this world does not belong to them."

As Sandra and Greg were about to depart and go home, Wayne said to them, "Hey guys you know the one thing that I am so blessed to have been given?"

"What is it now my brother?" Greg asked.

"Wait a minute little brother," said Sandra. "Let Wayne tell us before you open up your big mouth with some crazy stuff coming out."

"Okay Wayne, Greg said. Go ahead and give Sandra and me the four-one-one so we can believe you."

"What I am about to say guys is this, I think it was meant for the two families to come together as one to grow and learn each one's differences to understand that we are all the same just the outside and if we are truly honest with ourselves, the color of a person's skin doesn't matter. I know Greg, you are going to say something crazy, but you know it is true and just look how much of my mother's cooking you eat and I on the hand am always eating your mother's good old food. Not once have you, Sandra, or I have ever had a fallen out to call each other out of our name. This is what I mean about this state still caught up in a world of wrong among people, but let me tell you this that good old boy network will soon be broken and when it does take place, there will be a new life for all to enjoy being together."

"Wayne?" Sandra asked him. "If you are going to break that cycle, just how you do you plan on doing it?" He could have said to her right them and now by marrying her, but he will have to let it be a surprised to her in that way, when he decides to pop the question to her then all what he had been talking about from all the times they sat and had conversations would register in her mind that it was exactly his plans along when the three of them would sit and have long talks about the color of people skin tone. Once it come to light into Sandra's mind she then will realize it was there all along it was just that she did not see it coming because she had viewed him all those years as a brother. All the time he was madly in love with her, but she had to appreciate him because he had carried himself so well.

"Come on Greg before our Mother and Daddy will be sticking their heads out the front door requesting that you and I come on in because it was getting dark and being outside in the dark made our father a little leery as he wanted the two of us inside with him and Mother. Overprotected I guess you would call it."

Greg said to Wayne, "Hold on my brother because come tomorrow morning after we all have had breakfast and you pull up in front of our house, Sandra and I will be ready to ride with you in the wind. Good night our dear brother man, try to sleep good because come tomorrow night you will be in your own place preparing for your work day on your new job."

"I have to mention this to the two of you about my job, as I will not be turned loose on my own for the first couple of weeks because I will be under the wings of a trainer teaching me the ropes as what to do and what to look for in this field."

"I am not worrying about you at all Wayne," Sandra said to him. "Because you are a quick learner and you are smart and pay close attention to details."

"Are you telling me you yourself doesn't have those qualifications?" Wayne asked Sandra.

"No, I am not as I know myself and I am sure I too will be a little nervous at first that is, until I get my feet wet. Wayne come Monday morning, I will be at the train station preparing to get on board as you will be in the agricultural head office waiting for your assignments."

"Isn't it funny Wayne," Sandra said to him, "just how funny life is and how it can take you around about way to what is good for you and then bring you back to reality?"

"I know and that was exactly what I had been talking about as I spoke of all the changes that are to come to change the way this state government is working. Although you will be in New York, you will hear about it as I write to you often. Now Sandra when I send you letters are you going to find time to return letters to me to let me know exactly what is happening there?"

"Wayne, I promise I will and when you get your telephone and send me your number, we can communicate at times by calling instead of a lot writing."

That was what he wanted to hear as he was laughing under his breath. Wayne did ask Sandra had she thought about what type of position she might want to hold that is if she was not able to obtain a teaching position at first. "Well, my first cousin had related to me that the city is in dire need of teachers especially ones that are in the English field or math field because there they lost a lot of teachers because they have gone elsewhere to teach."

"I am quite sure I won't have a problem finding a job if not then I will just have to see what other field I can go into. Of course my cousin said that I would be good at working with attorneys because they really need good writers who can put their court cases together."

"You see Sandra you want have any problems getting job offer there because you are smart in every way. Who knows, you just might be back here in no time once things begin to open up and the situation here changes where it won't matter who you are to teach in any school."

"If that did happen Wayne you know I will be the first to come home to apply because this is truly where my heart lies being here around my parents and brother if he will still be here after he too graduates from college. I don't think Greg will wander of too far from here because he too has a certain protection for his parents as you do. I think that brother of mine just might meet a girl and fall madly head over in love with her and they get married."

"You really think so Wayne?" Sandra asked.

Wayne responded back to Sandra's question asking if he really thought that her little brother Greg would wind up getting married before she does. "Who knows, he just might beat you to the punch since you will be up there in that big city of New York as you just might get into the habit of waiting for that Mr. Right to come along to sweep you off your feet to bring home to let him meet your parents as well as my parents too."

"Wayne," she said to him. "I can assure you that something like that will not be happening because I first have to gain the opportunity to find myself a good paying job and then I will think about other things like meeting a good guy to fall in love with." That was exactly what he had been waiting for those correct words to fall out of her mouth to know his chances were much greater to establish a lasting relationship with her. He thought for a moment to say in his mind that once Sandra relocated to New York, and he communicated with her via letters or phone calls he just might let some of his secrets come known to her about the way he has always felt toward her.

It just might be a possibility that if he did that, she would refuse him because she never had anything for him but brotherly love and therefore the possibility of anything other than that would just not come to life. Regardless of just how hopeful he looked into all the possibilities, the whole situation could fail and it would probably put him into bad state of shock so this was crucial and he had to move slowly. Wayne knew if any of what he wanted did happen how would this affect his parents relationship to Sandra's parents relationship being together as good neighbors all these years. Wayne knew all of this has become a battle for him to fight and if he did win his battle, there would be a lot of things to consider as far as his job was concerned whether his coworkers would be willing to continue to work with him knowing that he had stepped across the line to marry a person of a different color. Once he decided that it was time to open up and tell Sandra about his lifelong love story and she was willing to accept it then if things there were not pleasant for him therefore deciding to do what he felt was right in his heart to do then he would take his wife and relocate.

The only thing that he would have to be worried about were the kickbacks some of the closed minded people there in Mississippi would give his parents as well as to Sandra's parents as well, at least this would be the start of something new that just might see other young people to come on board to defy what their parents had always taught them and marry whoever they wanted too. However they see it, there will be a great change because there is Greg who will be facing that opposition and heaven knows who he too will wind up marrying. "I just don't care about what people think, I am just so glad I came up with a girl that I have loved all my life and I am willing to live my life with and to have children with so this whole confused country as well as this state of Mississippi, which is so hurtful and backward to all people, will finally come to its senses to welcome people as they are so everyone would have a life of harmony. I am not even ashamed because I am just so glad I had good parents who taught me the good values of life and how to share with others just as Sandra and Greg parents taught them too."

"I know our roads will be rocky if we got married and decided to remain here to fight our battles each day as people with closed minds will look upon us as evil, but we will not care because she and I will know that the love we hold dear for one another will sustain and keep us together. I just cannot believe people are this way because they think they were given the authority to rule on everyone's live telling them who they should or who they are not to marry because what they say is the law of the land. I will have all the time in the world to think and decide what will be good for Sandra and me, while she is living in New York, and I am sure she too will have plenty of time in her spare time to dwell on what is good or will be good for her. When I feel that I am really to let her know about what I feel, I hope that she will be woman enough to accept it and make up her own mind know just maybe being involved with me would be the best thing that could have ever happened to her. Maybe she will even say, why didn't I tell her all of this early on?"

Maybe she would even say to me, why did I keep the feelings I held for her kept in the dark so long or were you afraid to let your parents or my parents, even my little brother Greg know because you might have started a hold world of trouble? I think that would be my return answer to her. Anyway, I would tell her that I thought this way would be better if I kept it a secret so when the letter had been opened up, my changes would be better received where it would not hurt so much. I guess I could go even further by telling her all of this as she doesn't know or cannot imagine how many nights I laid awake at night just thinking about she and I and how our lives would be a turning point to better things as our love for each other grew. I suppose this is good therapy for me because it helps to unclog my minds of a lot of things otherwise would stay locked up."

"Oh well, it was nice to have this whole conversation to myself on exactly what I have been felling and going through all by myself without anyone knowing so now, I think I can rest assured come Monday when Sandra boards the train for New York, I will have some peace at night while I am sleeping just knowing that I want have to wonder about anything as to how she is doing because my love will help her to remain herself until she is given the go ahead at the stop sign which has held her there for a signal that real signal from this conductor, her secret future husband." After all of Wayne's thinking as he was about to turn into a deep sleep knowing come Sunday morning he would have a very busy enchanting day as the three of them hit the road and drive into the city where he would be living until such time his whole situation would be changing. Wayne just could not believe there could or would be anything better to happen to him than what is on the horizon for his upcoming future that had been planned out only by him. These plans were already in the making many years ago when the three of them played as children as he had a different view about Sandra as their parents announced them as sister and brothers. Wayne continued to go along with it as it had been tearing him apart to hold fast because he knew there would be the time to speak his mind. While Wayne was busy pondering over his events, over at the Logan household all were asleep except Greg because he waits until he thinks everyone is fast asleep when he creeps into the kitchen to raid the refrigerator for leftovers because he said that he was a growing boy and he needed to eat as much as possible because he knows once he had graduated and gone off to college, there will not be food at night for him to get up to eat unless what he will be able to keep in his dorm room refrigerator, hoping his roommate or roommates would not eat it up from him. As he made his way into the kitchen and pulled out that leftover roast beef left by Wayne's mother, she made him a roast beef sandwich and he sat down with a glass of milk to enjoy all alone before Sandra decided to join him not disturbing their parents. "Big sister, why are you up because you never get up in the middle of the night to have a bite?"

"I know, but this time, I just could not sleep just know come tomorrow Wayne will be leaving us and we won't have him around."

"Wait one minute my dear sister, you too will not be around for me to see so at least Wayne and I will still be connected because he will still be able to come home on weekends, on the other hand you will not be able to because you will be in New York."

"What are you trying to say little brother she asked him?"

"All I said was this, you say our brother Wayne will not be around here but I think you meant to say that you yourself will not be around to see him on weekends as he comes back from the city to see his parents as well as ours. Be honest with yourself my sister, you'd rather be here with all of us instead of living there in that big old lonely city of New York, am I right?"

"Little brother, I can't disagree with you anymore, but you know all the situations here in this state about hiring educated black females as English teachers to teach in an all-white school that is not yet mixed. That is the reason why I have to make a move and maybe one day soon I will return to make a stand. You are so right about missing Wayne because he has been a part of your life as well as my life and it doesn't seem right for the three of us have to go through this terrible situation."

"Big sister, you would have thought after all of these years, things would have gotten better where these narrow minded people would come to the reality that they will no longer have control over this generation of young minded individuals who will be stepping out making decisions of their own. If things were the way they are supposed to be then I would not had to go out of this state to the University in Louisiana. I could have enrolled in the University of Mississippi as Wayne did and everything would be alright my brother. Greg I know you will be graduating this year and off to college you too will go as I know you will be attending the same university as me."

"Big sister, I am looking forward to it because there, I will see a lot of fine black girls there from all walks of life."

"May I encourage you to concentrate only on the field of study you have enrolled to study." You know wanting to become a mathematics teacher is hard as there are a lot of formulas you will have to learn to make you successful. I suggest you dive head over first into your studies and afterward concentrate on those beautiful women. I hope by the time you finish with your college education, things will be better and you want have to leave this location but will have the opportunity to work in this state in a school that will be mixed where you will be able to serve all students regardless of their skin tones. You know my dear little brother, I feel good about your college education because in my heart, I know that things will work out and you have the time of your life."

"Sandra I feel the same way and now, are you going to have a roast beef sandwich too?"

"I think that I will have a small helping of that left potato salad left. Boy, I bet if Mother and Daddy knew you and I were up sitting in the kitchen talking about things, they too would join us, but since they are asleep let them remain there. What they don't know will not hurt them. This will be just our little secret talk. Now you know that come tomorrow morning when you and I take that ride in Wayne's new car to help him move into his apartment, it is going to be hard not only on you, but also on his parents as well because not only will you be crying, but his mother will too so the two of you will be wet from sharing tears."

After spending time together while their parents continue to sleep, Sandra and her little brother Greg as she called him finished having their conversation together as they talked about good times as well as the bad times spent with Wayne and helped him go through his growing up period without any siblings of his own, stepping in to let him become a part of their lives, and they decided that the night was not getting any younger knowing they were going to be riding with Wayne come in the morning when he will take his responsibility to having his own place in town as they were going to help him move in and unpack his things, before they would have to greet him goodbye for now as the two of them would hitch a ride back home with his parents on their truck used to bring all of his things to put into his apartment. As they were about to depart out of the kitchen, their mother appeared to ask them what were they spending time here in the kitchen.

"Please," she said. "Don't tell me that brother of yours got hungry as he get the urge to get up to eat and he knocked on your bedroom door and got you up to join him, am I right?"

"No Mother," Sandra said. "It was not like that. As a matter of fact I heard something making noise in the kitchen so I got up to investigate and behold I found a live rat in here eating up everything without cheese, my little brother Greg eating a cold roast beef sandwich and having a class of milk so he invited me to come join him and I decided to have myself something as well. He and I were sitting here enjoying our bite to eat and discussing all the good times we have had with the presence of Wayne and now to know that he will no longer be around to harass Greg because just a few more hours, he will stop by here to retrieve Greg and me to greet you and Daddy so long for now as the three of us will drive away."

Sandra and Greg's mother Catherine responded not too favorably to say, "I am truly going to miss that young man, but not as much as his parents will. To put the icing on the cake, why come Monday morning not only will your brother be in that same fix as you leave to board the train to new York, but your father and I will be saddened too. The only positive outcome of it will be your brother will still be here with us to help ease the absence of you, but Wayne's parents will have no one with them to fill that voyage, only having to wait until he comes home on weekends to have dinner with them and spend a few hours with them before it would be his time to get back to his place to prepare for a new work week."

"Mother," Sandra said to her about how this could work for them as well as for the Hunts because Wayne will be coming over to spend time with Greg so he will have something to look forward to in my absence.

"Yeah, I guess you just might be right as I never looked into the situation that way at all daughter," she said.

Greg finally said to the two of them how touching what they said was, "But don't you think this should be between Wayne and me? Of course my sister, I will be lonely once you have gone and then too, I will be happy to know that you will be away in New York, a place where you have never been before learning to get use to all of the surroundings where you nor even I have been accustomed too here in this state of Mississippi, why you will have a lot to share once you come home so I will at least be up on things if ever I had to face the same situation."

The moment came when their mother said to them, "Guys, it is getting on in the night and if you guys are going to be ready to go with Wayne tomorrow morning, don't you think you should get some sleep?"

"We hear you loud and clear Mother," they said as the two of them left to join their beds in their rooms. After the two of them had left, Catherine said quiet for a few minutes just thinking about her best friend Florence and her husband Samuel on how they will handle this moving out situation by their only child. Also she thought to herself how she too would handle her only daughter leaving come Monday morning to head for New York, a city where she had visited to hopefully get a job there as the opportunity was not given to her here because of how things are. Catherine was so happy for Sandra in one way but then she was very sad and concerned for her in other ways to think of all the hard work her daughter had lived up to her own standards and to get to the end of her college graduation to be let down because of the laws.

There has to be an ending to all of this madness preventing smart minded children of all race to be denied the opportunities to help to make this a batter place for everyone to live in by working together on one accord for the growth of our nation. Catherine even let her mind go back into time when she and her husband Elijah wanted to involve themselves into several projects that would benefit everyone, but they had to remain on the other side of the tracks because they were not smart enough or white enough. What silly laws man has developed. Elijah and her thought by now since their children have the opportunity to grow in obtaining a higher learning, a lot of that old southern white pride would have resolved itself and new ideas would have come forth.

"I guess in so many ways, I had fooled myself or disappointed myself to think changes had finally arrived once and for all, but still in so many places the pride of the south still want to hold on to the old traditions. Regardless of how many of those old hillbillies continue on with their ideas, these young people will definitely change things and the best part of it all my two children and Wayne will be the ones to be a part of all the changes that will soon take place as I see the coming of all of it just around the corner. I am proud when I sit in the midst of my son and daughter to hear them speak about the things they want to do to help make this country better for all people. Being black and living across the street from three wonderful white people, has been the joys of anyone life because neither one of us as parents looked upon the next because of their color, but looked inside of their spirits of treating people the ways they should be treated. There has been a loving bond with both parents as well as our children because they grew up to see the goods of each one and shared. Wayne being the best friend my two children ever had as they grew up together, they learned to love and share things together not only the many dinners we have had together, but the giving of each other to one another what has made life so pleasant. Florence, Wayne's mother is so caring until she seem just like my own sister to whom I could go too and share my secrets with and she saw me the same way."

"Soon," Catherine said to herself. "Enough of this as I too better get back to bed before Samuel reached over and I am not there for him to come looking to find me in here and then I won't get any sleep."

Catherine returned back to bed and soon the morning had appeared as it was time for her to drag herself out of bed as she was tired due to her two children Sandra and Greg up having a conversation as she joined in with them. She did not have to knock on either child's door because they were already up and were having their light breakfast of cereal and milk, as their mother walked into the kitchen they said to her, "Good morning. Sandra and I just could not wait for you to get our breakfast ready because we decided to have what we are eating to hold us over until such time when we return home from spending the day with Wayne."

"I see, and if that is the case then maybe I should have allowed you two to prepare your own breakfast all along that way, I would only been responsible for just your daddy and mine."

"Now that is a good idea Mother, but you know I couldn't eat Sandra's bad cooking because I would be as skinny as a bird."

"What time will Wayne be stopping by?" she asked Greg.

"I looked across to their house to see his daddy, Mr. Samuel bringing things out of the house to put on the back of his truck. I am sure it will be about an hour or two. I better give Florence a call Catherine said to them to see if she needs anything. Elijah, had not joined them just yet because he was still in the bathroom dressing. Catherine called Florence to ask if she was alright and needed anything or if she need me to make some sandwiches for all of them? She said to Catherine, thank you so much but I did all of that last night before I turned in to bed because I wanted Wayne to have plenty of cooked foods to last him all week until he had sufficiently established himself in the kitchen. I think Catherine that I have packed enough to last him. Now you know I don't mind jumping right on in and do my part you know Catherine, said to her. Florence said to Catherine, I don't think I would or could have made it if I didn't have you working close by myside, making me to accept the fact that my son, is moving on as you yourself have set your own boundaries.:

"You and I are two mothers who are in the same fix, losing our child because they feel a need to be on their own which we thought that day would never come or we just did not want to see it come. Now that it has finally landed Catherine, it is so hard for me as well as you to accept the fact that we have lost in so many ways but I suppose we must see it as all is not yet lost because there will come a day when big surprises will come to us if we wait to see the outcome of what will take place in their lives to give us some grandchildren to fulfill our final days."

"Florence, I better get breakfast ready because Elijah will surely be ready to eat as he want to be ready to see Wayne off too. I understand he wanted to help Samuel to pack and go with you guys as he said he and I could drive in together to help unload but Samuel, said to him that it would be alright. Listen Florence, don't let on to Samuel, but Elijah and I will be on the road to following because we just could not stay behind to not go to help as you know Wayne is our as well so there won't be anything that will keep he and I from going."

"Now that will be great having everyone there together moving our son into his own place showing our love for him and wishing him the best. That will make me feel so much better Catherine, just knowing you will be there standing by me as we watch each of them take in his belonging to place them where he want them. I know Samuel will be shocked that Elijah, showed up especially when he said that he could do it all by himself because that is just what most fathers think, they can do it all on their own. Come tomorrow, things will be a little dull around the house but then too, I know we will have Greg to fill in the lonely time as he come over and place his feet under our table to take Wayne's spot."

"Catherine, you and I better get used to it now because very soon, this will again hit you and me when Greg goes off to college to prepare to make his way into society. You, Elijah, Samuel, and I will once again be just as we were when we got married alone just the two of us without any children."

"Florence, as you see it now that is the way I suppose life is meant to be for all as we live it to the fullest."

After all the conversations back and forth between Catherine and Florence, soon Elijah walked into the kitchen to take a seat to enjoy his breakfast when Sandra and Greg greeted him a good morning as they were about to leave from the kitchen table to go to prepare themselves to meet Wayne as he would soon drive up to blow his car horn for them to come on out. "Where are you two guys speeding off to?" asked their father.

"Not much time to talk this morning Daddy," Greg said. "Sandra and I have a job to do."

"What type of job is there for you two to do?" he asked.

"Didn't you know that it is time to help Wayne get settled into his new home?" Sandra replied.

"Oh that," he said. "But why are you two rushing because your mother and I will also be there although his daddy suggested that my help was not needed."

"I suppose it was because Mr. Samuel did not want you to see a grown man cry Daddy," Greg answered.

"Will someone around here tell me what is so secretive about a father shedding a few tears when the only child, a son, is leaving home to settle in to someplace else?" Elijah asked.

"Come on Elijah, eat your breakfast because the kids were only expressing themselves. Soon, you know you and I will be in the same position as the Hunts are when our only son packs up to depart from this house as well and tell me, will you or will you not be shedding some tears of joy as well as sadness too?" Catherine responded.

" Right now, all I would like to do is to enjoy my breakfast while you Catherine, go to get ready for our trip there with the others and then I think I will be alright and I will accept what is to come my way as a daddy when my son, Greg is ready to leave. Catherine, you know it is hard right now for you and I to know that come tomorrow morning our only little girl who have all grown up will be boarding the train to take her first ride away from home to head to New York to make way for herself, a place where she had never visited before."

"Elijah, Sandra will be just fine because you know your niece Delores will look after her."

"She had better because I will definitely let her father, my brother, know just how disappointed I will be if anything go wrong there."

"Elijah, stop worrying so much because our little girl is now a fully grown woman and she must find her way."

"Why, you and I both knew this day would be coming soon or later and now that it has, let us prepare ourself for the same with our son too. Before you go Catherine, I want to say one thing and that is: isn't it funny just how time slips away when you are the least expecting it?"

"So well-spoken my dear husband and now I have to go to get dressed if we are going to be ready to leave when Samuel, Florence, and Wayne with our two children are leaving". As Catherine departed the kitchen, Elijah sat and continued to eat and enjoy his breakfast think about how it is going to be once Greg leave to go on to college. In his mind he kept thinking that maybe this was a good time to reorganize their priorities and spend quality time together since he and Catherine will soon be as one again to do a bit of traveling to see those relatives whom they have not seen in many years. He thought if they did that then the lonely of missing their children just might not be so bad.

After Elijah had finished his breakfast and Catherine came out of the bedroom after changing into something more appropriate for the trip into town, she said to Elijah not to worry about washing his dish just place it in the sink and she would clean up the kitchen upon their return because just because Wayne would have departed, there still was a need to prepare a dinner meal maybe to invite the Hunt over so they won't be alone to feel their loss. "Yes, I think I will let Florence and Samuel know once we are there to let them know to come on over to share in our dinner together. I think this will be some good therapy for them to not sit around and think about their son not being in their presence."

"Okay Catherine, I heard the kids out front making noise so that mean they are ready to move out so we better load up too. How are you going to not let Samuel see you as he said to you that he rather you didn't come? What you and I will do is this: once they have driven off, you and I will get into the car and drive slow behind them so he want see us and when they get there we will drive up next to them to say, do you think we were going to let this happen without my helping hands Samuel? No way was I going to allow this to happen when Wayne is a part of my family too."

"Come on Elijah, they have pulled off so if we are going to keep them in sight, don't you think we better get a move on?" Catherine asked him.

Wayne, Sandra and Greg were the leaders of the pack because Wayne had to lead because he knew where he was going to the location where he would be living. While the three of them were driving forward and Sandra was sitting in the back seat looking at the beautiful scenes, Greg opened up to say, "Now my sister how important it is for you to ride in the back seat especially when a car driven by skinny white boy with a black guy and a black girl on board would look to all narrow minded white people?"

"No offense my brother because at least you know and understand the situations down here that is why you can attest to what I am saying."

"Greg don't you have something else to say that will make this trip more enjoyable and not so full of your drama?" Sandra asked him.

Wayne didn't have too much to say to what Greg was talking about because his mind was on the girl who was sitting in the back of his car hoping that one day, she would be in riding in the front with him and just maybe a couple of their kids would be in the back singing and carrying on. Sandra did ask Wayne why he was so silent. All he said was he wanted to make sure he wasn't driving too fast so his parents wouldn't be able to keep up thus missing their turn off to his apartment. Wayne said that to throw off Greg so he wouldn't suspect anything nor did he want Sandra to think otherwise of his actions that had been shown a couple of days.

Soon they arrived at the apartment dwelling and when they drove up Sandra said to Wayne, "This is a nice complex as it is so neatly kept as it seem everyone is inside minding their own business. Greg asked Wayne about whether he had noticed any black people living there in those apartments? "I

" truly can say at this time I have not seen any, but that does not mean there won't be any as I am sure in the near future things will be changed and blacks will be able to enjoy some of the luxury that is around, but until now, we have to try and make that happen my brother," Wayne said to Greg.

"Now words are so well spoken by a believing young man!" Sandra shouted out to what Wayne had said. As they pulled up, Wayne had already received his apartment keys so all he had to do was open the doors and walk right on in. Sandra said to him just look at this nice place as everything are on the same level, no upstairs just every apartment has its own private level. The three of them got out and when they walked inside, Greg and Sandra just could not believe what they were seeing. Wayne had one bedroom, a living area, a nice bathroom, a lovely kitchen space with a breakfast nook, and a closed in patio where he could sit out in without any interference from neighbors.

Greg being as silly as he sometimes gets, asked Wayne, "Hey brother man how much will this place cost you each month because it doesn't look cheap?"

"Now Greg that is none of your business because you won't be paying for it," Sandra said to him.

"You never know my sister, our brother just might have to call on me to ask me to rob my piggy bank."

Wayne said to him and Sandra about what it would be costing him each month will only be just five hundred dollars. "With all of this space, I don't think that is too much." Soon his mother and father walked in with her mouths wide open to see such a nice safe place where her son will be living. As they looked around in walked Catherine and Elijah too as they said, "Now, I don't think you guys didn't expect for Catherine and me not to be here as well."

"Now don't start with me Samuel for telling me you didn't need my help because I am here and now that we are all here, come on and let the unpacking begin so we grownups can get out of the way of these children." Catherine and Florence found themselves in their favorite place in the nice small kitchen placing things away.

"Look Florence," Catherine said to her. "What a nice layout where Wayne can have his breakfast right here in this nice kitchen nook."

"I have to say to you Catherine," Florence said. "They don't build places now as they built when we came up." Sandra and Greg were so busy with helping Wayne to decide where he wanted his things place as the two grownups brought them in off the truck. Samuel said to his best pal Elijah, "I am so glad you decided to disobey me and come anyway because the need for help would have been appreciated."

"Now all the time you thought you would be able to pull this off with just your own hands. Samuel, our children have made a good career for themselves wouldn't you say?" Elijah asked.

"I don't think you and I could have done anything any different because they have been good children and they all got along so well throughout their periods of growing up together. I have to consider everything you have said about them Samuel, because it seemed as if those years flew by. One day you and I were sitting out on our front porch watching them as they ran around the house playing, laughing and having the time of their lives and now look, they are all grown up preparing to make their way in life. You and I surely can say, we have no regrets." As they talked, they were busy with removing everything they had brought to furnish Wayne's apartment so he would be very comfortable in his first night alone in his new home. As everything were placed in it prospected places and everyone took a breather, Florence opened up the box of what she had made to offer everyone sandwiches she had made.

Catherine said to her, "There is no need to offer up what you had made for Wayne to have to last him for the week before he come back home to get a real meal, because we will be alright."

Greg said to her, "Mrs. Florence, you know I would love to have a couple of those sandwiches to hold me over until I get back home to eat my mother's dinner."

"Little brother, why you have to be so greedy all the time eating up food that was made for our brother Wayne to have to eat because he will not be able to do any cooking as of yet until his feel has gotten wet with his new position. Do you always have to spoil everything when it come to your stomach?"

Wayne said to her, "That doesn't matter because I am sure I won't be able to eat all what mother had prepared so I want to share with you as well as Greg. This so far has been a good day because we are all here once more together as you know Sandra after you leave from here this afternoon, it will be the last time before I see you again."

"I know Wayne, but you know we will be in touch with each other that way, it will seem as if we are still around one another Sandra said to share in all of our laughter."

"Wayne," Sandra alluded to him. "Isn't it funny just how life can throw a curve in your life and cause you to meet things that are waiting for you out there?"

"Sandra I think about that all the times because just look what has happened to the three of us. You and I have finished college and now, preparing to enter our careers as our little love brother Greg will soon be entering into his own destiny of life to head into his own direction where we three will might not be in the company of one another for a very long time. I find that there will be something good coming out of this whole thing in the near future that will open up hearts and minds and just then we all within this stiff society as well as the whole world will then see just how foolish the whole way of life set for everyone has been so very foolish to see and understand just what has been lost because of so much hate. Sandra I do believe deep within my heart that you as well as Greg and I will break that mold."

Wayne stood before everyone as they were sitting down resting from all the lifting and putting things together so he will be sufficient and said, "I am truly thankful for all things that have come upon these two families and above all, I am so grateful to have been a part of everyone lives. I didn't have any sibling to grow with, but for some reason Sandra and Greg, came into my life as a true sister and brother to love and to know what love is to share. Come tomorrow morning, my dear sister Sandra will not be around any longer for me to pick a fight with but I will hold her dear to my hear while she is up there in New York, missing this place to hope one day she will be returning back for good to teach in a school that will not see any discrimination with hopes that she will find her destiny here with the one she will love forever." Wayne was very sharp and careful of how he put his words because if he slipped up then Sandra as well as Greg would know he was speaking about his own self to understand that was the reasons why he had been so quiet in their presence many of times. Right now, Wayne could not let that happen because it would spoil the whole layout of what he had planned for the love of his life Sandra.

"Now, I have said my peace, I salute all of you for showing your love for me this day as I will be living here all alone in my new home but mother and daddy, don't you dare to rent out my bedroom to anyone because you already know that I will be coming home on weekends and I will still need a place to sleep. Mr. And Mrs. Logan, just because I am not around to run back and forth over to your house to stick my feet under your table when I smell food to fight with my little brother Greg it will not go away because I will still be around to eat some of your special pies. Besides, I want Greg to be able to hang with me on weekends until it is time for me to return back to my residence. Too bad Sandra you will be away from Greg and me, but we will have you in our hearts each time he and I take a bite of your mother's banana pudding, hoping that you can visualize tasting it."

Mr. Elijah spoke to let Wayne know how glad he had made him and Catherine as the relationship built between him and Sandra and Greg could not have made them any happier.

Soon hear came the tears from his mother eyes, Catherine, Sandra, his father, and a few from Elijah as they prepared to say goodbye but Greg thought if anyone had to remain strong enough for Wayne because he didn't need to shed a tear, it had to be him holding the light bright. As all of them were about to depart and his mother and father placed their arms around him as if it would be the last time ever, Greg said, "Hey wait a minute you guys, it is only going to be a week before you see him come driving down the road toward your home so dry up those tears, it's not like he will be leaving the state you know."

While they were crying, Sandra and Wayne had walked out onto the patio to say their goodbyes as he was cautious enough not to grab and hold her in his arms as if she was his girlfriend for all to finally know so he held her hands so everyone could hear exactly what he was saying to her. "Sandra my darling sister, this is it at least for a long time before we hook up again to spend qualities time together, as I am wishing you all the best while you are there in the city and above all, be very careful because if anything go wrong there, Greg and I will have to come there to rescue you and bring you home."

Soon, it was time for everyone to depart to return home thus leaving Wayne there in his new place to defend for himself as well as start to get used to being all alone away from his parents and his buddy Greg because Sandra would not be present because come tomorrow morning, she will soon be on her way to New York to gain a fruitful life trying to establish herself meaningful before she would return back to her location once she find out that what she thought was glamorous in New York did not give her a sense of confinement. As all of them walked out to get into their vehicles, Greg and his sister decided to ride home with their parents thus leaving Wayne's parents to make the return trip all by themselves, just before they pulled off, Wayne said to all of them to come and let him give them a hug as Greg indicated that he hope he was included to get one also laughing. After hugging and saying goodbyes, Wayne said to Sandra, "I guess it is the end for now as you will also depart from this old place come tomorrow."

"You are so right," Sandra responded back to Wayne as she said that she really hoped that everything will go well for her there.

"I really hope so myself," he responded back to her.

Wayne didn't want to let go of Sandra's hand until Greg said to him, "Hey my brother don't you think turning your sister's hand loose will be a good thing?"

"Oh yeah, I forgot as she and I have so much in common not only growing up together, but attending college and graduating together only from different universities."

"I know Wayne," her mother said to him. "So I can understand how hard it is to let go of someone that has been a part of your life all these years."

At that moment Sandra started to cry as Greg said to her, "Now come my sister, dry up those tears because tomorrow we all will have a lot of them to pass around. Wayne will still be here for me to run around but you, it will be hard too because you will be miles away only to call or write to check the two brothers." Leaving Wayne behind was hard for his mother more so than his father because it wasn't like they would not see him for such a long time as it would be for Sandra because his presence each weekend at home will be as if he was just away on vacation.

Wayne's father walked over to him to say to him, "Now son, I know all of this is new to you but I encourage you to be very careful of the people you will meet around here trying to get to know because although you are in a safe place, you still have to be very careful and wonder how people are especially when they see that you have a good job and you live alone. Worry about you being here all alone, sure I will, but to keep your mother from going stir crazy, I will have to assure her that you are a young man and you will be able to take care of yourself. I am holding you high my son because I know in my heart that you will do the right thing, now, it is time to say so long for now because saying goodbye doesn't seem right because you will be home each weekend to be with your mother and me, as well as with the Logans."

Florence said to her son, "Do not take any wooden nickels from anyone and if the going gets too tough for you to handle, you know where your home is." The two of them finally pulled off as they thank Elijah, Catherine, Greg and Sandra for being with them to enjoy this time with their son.

Soon, after all greetings were said, Mr. Logan said to his crew, "Gang I think we will get started as well because I know Wayne would like to go inside and just sit for a while before he decide how he will place his things in the right places where he will finally have some quiet time to think out all what he has been thinking about all this time. Am I right Wayne?" Mr. Logan asked him.

"You hit the nail on the head there Mr. Logan, "Wayne said. "Because I have so many thoughts you can't imagine to work out hoping one day it will all play out as I have planned over and over in my head."

As Greg and Sandra got themselves into the back seat, his mother Catherine said, "Greg why not come and ride in front with your daddy so Sandra and I can share the back seat together because I know that is exactly what you would like."

"Mother, you took the words right out of my mouth because I was about to allude to that but your daughter pushed in in first." As they too pulled off, Wayne stood there watching all of them drive away to finally realizes that this is something like being in a storybook where the end has come and all characters had been abandoned.

As Wayne still stood watching and hoping that this could have been a better way as the way he felt about Sandra wishing she could have been lucky enough to have been given the opportunity to obtain a teaching job right here in this state so she would not have to leave to find work especially away from him, as his heart was so heavy because the love he held for her was just making it so hard for him to breathe at times. After he realized that they were out of sight, he decided to walk back into his now home to take a long hard look around to know that this is where he is to live if he is to take on the position he had been offered to make a life better for him and hopefully for Sandra as well. The one good thing about Wayne was that he had patience and he was willing to wait as long as it would take because he was determine to have Sandra one day as his future wife to be the mother of his children to make both grandparents happy. Once back inside Wayne sat down and thought about all the possibilities that would surely come his way as he intend to work hard in his job position to be able to accomplish all that will be beneficial for him to support a family.

It is true, Wayne will be lonely many of days, but within those lonely hours missing the love of his life will give him something positive to keep his mind sharp thinking about how safe he hopes Sandra will be there in New York. "Come tomorrow, I have to report early to work to meet all of my counter partners to get use to them and Lord, I hope that they are not racist because if they are, I don't know for sure if I will be able to stand the things they just might be saying. If that does take place through their silly conversations, I will just blow it off to hope they don't ask me why I don't agree with them. Know the ways I was taught by my parents and all the time I spent growing up with two wonderful black brother and sister, how could I allow myself to be changed to agree with them? To be honest with myself, I wouldn't know how to respond to such outrageous comments. I find that people are really sick in their minds when they have been taught such unnecessary ways. Those ways are not supposed to exist, but due to the evil of man, those ways has existed for many of years and it hurts."

All through the night as Wayne tried to get a good night sleep in order to be ready to first time meeting his boss with his new job was such a hard time for him because he kept thinking about Sandra and knowing that come morning she will be up preparing to catch the train to head off to New York, which would be her home there for a while until she feel as if she was ready to return back home. "This is truly something I will just have to accept and deal with because if I don't then everyone will know that I had been talking about Sandra all along when I got into the mood where I didn't want to be around anyone, it would have been nice to let all of them know while they were here but then too, it just might had spoiled the whole thing for she and I so it will have to remain in my mind daily until such time I need to release it. This place is going to be a very difficult way of living and maintaining this place because to be honest with myself, none of this was planned by me, as I can blame the whole situation of this state and its policies concerning people. If everything were on the up and up here in this sad state of Mississippi, Sandra would not be catching the train come tomorrow heading off to that big lonesome city where she knows nothing about except in reading about all the highlights the city has to see. This I know within my heart that it is a sad state of mind. If only the power to be could just come to grips and get a handle on the hate they carry around each day then I do believe Sandra would have been given a English teaching job right here not having to travel so far to gain employment and then she would be here with me and we could move into a quiet relationship to prepare for our future. It will not matter who I meet and how many girls here that I meet there will not be one that will take the place in my heart to become my wife other than Sandra. I know my parents are desperately waiting to one have grandchildren and because they have not given Sandra a second thought as being my wife, they think it will be a white girl as has been the norm, but not this time because look out Mr. and Mrs. Florence and Samuel Hunt, your son is in love with a black girl and she will be my wife regardless of all the racism that just might still be."

"I know it will take a very long time before things become quite clear that in this life, colors will not matter and just then in all of these bigot minds down here in this old south will realize that they had been wrong all these years and now seeing their own children jump over the fence to grab something that is so beautiful will definitely blow their minds to the point they will not have a choice but to accept or continue to live without the company of their grandchildren of color. It's going to happen and it will take place very soon even if Sandra and I are not the first to peel the potato first. There is one thing about love, when two people fall head heel over in love with a person not the color of then there is very little anyone can do to make them change how they feel. I know this whole thing will be a shock to my parents as well as with Sandra's own parents, as well as her bother but then too, I really believe Greg will accept it more so than the others because he and I have always had a close connection not to say, my parents or Sandra's parents want welcome it after the shock wears off. Once Sandra has fully gained knowledge of this whole parade, I think she will do the right thing and begin to love me not as a brother, but as her future husband because she will realize that the whole time she spent in New York hoping to maybe connect with a wonderful guy was all a waste because they had different aspects of how they wanted their lives to be. Sandra, on the other hand, would like to have a very quiet genuine life with a good man who will accept her for who she is to grow with great priorities. How I wished this was a nightmare and I would wake up from it to say that all of my thinking was a long dream but unfortunately it is not and it is as real as can be. I think I better turn over and stop thinking about my relationship with Sandra in my mind for now since she doesn't have a clue to get some sleep because come in the morning I will receive my first big responsibility as I am brief all day on certain things I will have to look for and put in place that is, if I plan on becoming a good agricultural provider to these farmers and their crops. Sandra my darling dear, I am going to shut you off from my mind and say goodnight because I have to face our future very soon."

As Wayne finally fell asleep in his own apartment, Sandra and Greg were busy in her bedroom chanting all about the do's and don'ts there in New York when she arrived not to appraise herself with them. "Now I want you to listen me big sister, as Greg caller her. I know you will be on your own, but don't forget you still have a responsibility back here with Wayne and me."

"May I ask you something little brother?" Sandra responded to him, tell me what will be my responsibilities back here with you and Wayne? I don't know it sounds good. You have to understand this Greg, didn't we help Wayne to move into his own place just this afternoon? That is now his responsibility to ensure that he do the right things because he is the one who went off to college to attend that old racist Mississippi University to major in agricultural because that is exactly what that university turn out, white men being agricultural agents to help these white farmers to control all the farming land they possibly can to keep the black farmers from making a living with their land."

Believe me, if Wayne had the opportunity to attend a black university, he would have as he would not have been discriminated against because that is not what our established universities does, but to welcome all individuals who care to attend for a much wider and prosperous field of education. Right now Wayne seemed to be happy with his new given job as that is exactly what the good old boys' network run to these while universities her in this state and pump funds in their programs to turn out smart while guys to fulfill the shoes they had set into stone to keep the heat on. Sandra Greg asked her, "Are you telling me that Wayne isn't happy with his job?

"No, he is not, but since that was his major, he has to let his parents think that he is so happy but I know different because he and I talked long and hard about it. Although the three of us grew up together, he much rather be involved with something else that would definitely benefit him the way he wants to be."

"Are you going to tell him later that you think he should try to find something else that he would enjoy working in?"

"I don't think so because if I did, and he took my advice, it just might send his mother more so that his father over the bend."

"Greg I am telling you, no, I am ordering you to keep quiet on this matter because I know exactly how you are when it comes to Wayne as you feel you just have to tell him all of your business and if you did, then he will know that I told you so promise me this, keep quiet on this because when he gets tired, he will work something out. Right now, he seems to be happy because he is away from his mother, always looking over his shoulders to be able to grow intro a man."

"Sandra you know that is exactly what our mother will be doing with me since you won't be around. Guess what, I will get all the attention finally around this house because you will no longer be here to be in the middle of it all as I will be treated like a king."

"Don't hold your breath little brother, because you might be treated like a king in the eyes of our mother, but let me assure you not our father. I will have Wayne all to myself come weekends so he and I can ride around to yell at all the girls we see walking down the streets."

"Do you really believe that my brother?" she asked him.

"I guess I was just making conversation because I don't believe it myself knowing how stiff necked Wayne can be. You know Sandra you and I both love him as our brother, but there is still something I have been feeling a very long time that I just cannot seem to shake off about Wayne."

"Do tell little brother so I will know before I leave tomorrow and when all that you have been thinking about will not be any surprises to me you know."

"Please give me some time and I will have it all figured out."

'You better hurry up because in a few months you will be graduating from high school and off to college so you better make it a point to come up with an answer to your solution. To be honest with you Greg I just don't think you have anything that bothers you about Wayne it's just that you can't figure out some of his moods. You know, we all do have some strange ways at time where we get into our own world not wanting to be in the company of anyone."

"You just might be right, but I don't think so my sister."

"Once when you find out please write or call me in New York. Right now, Wayne is there in his own place probably sleeping by now to prepare himself for a new beginning in his life."

While Sandra and Greg continued to talk about things which they shared with Wayne growing up, their mother Catherine walked into the room to say to the two of them, "Hey guys, if we are going to be at the train station in a timely manner so Sandra won't miss her train, don't you think getting some sleep will be the most appropriate thing to do?"

"I guess you just might be right Mother dear," Greg said to her as he got up to go to his bedroom because he knew once the four of them got up to have their last morning breakfast together, things would definitely be a whole lot different once they had dropped Sandra off and she had boarded the train headed to New York to return home. Once Greg got into his bedroom he said to himself, "What a difference a day will make when I come home from school not seeing my sister here waiting for me to go over some of my school work with me. Now I understand all what one of my teacher said to the class about trying to stand on your own feet once you are doing your homework, only to ask for help when you feel that you have ran in a situation that you just don't understand. I truly believe she was speaking to me because that was just what I did, when I came a matter in my assignment that I just couldn't seem to figure out so I would run to my darling smart sister to help. Not to say that I didn't have the smarts too, but it always seem as if Sandra knew it all."

As Greg took a look into his mirror, he said, "Well partner, it is all up to you now to figure out your own solutions because the resource you had to depend on to help you out will no longer be here. What a shame this had to happen to a smart person having to leave from this stupid state to travel hundreds of miles to seek employment when it could been right here, the place where she grew up, but thanks to these hateful individuals living here who have made things work for them and not for everyone especially people of color." As Greg continued to admire himself in his mirror he said, "That is alright because not only will some changes be implemented by both Sandra and Wayne, but by my generation as well because we will not stand for all of this nonsense. Once all the young people have all grown up and ready to tackle this world, they will not allow their radical parents to tell them who they can and cannot married because they will not follow their old traditions, but make new traditions that will sustain all to live according to how things are supposed to be. Once this old backward south finally realizes what is happening, just then maybe they will come alive and get on board with the flow of things. Come this fall I will be entering into college to make a stand not only in my education which will be the most important thing in my life but I will be making a serious change in our society to fight for what is right and should be taught. Listen old southern bells and old taken land owners prepare yourselves to fight as the war of the south is going to be fought by your white children to whom you have bedded into their minds that they are better than the average black or other race of people out there because we all are going to band together and show everyone that the heat is on and love has no separation when it comes to finding the one that you love. You see, the government here in this old state thought they had control over who they should let teach because they did not want any black smart teachers into their classrooms to teach their children, but they are in for a rule of awaking because not only am I going to fight to change things so my sister Sandra came return back home to do what she set out to do, teaching English to any race of students and to be able to walk into any classroom down here whether black or white and be appreciated. Now, since I have said my peach in front of my mirror, I better get my behind in bed to get some sleep so I will be ready to get up have breakfast with my sister for the last time and ride to the train station with Mother and Daddy to release her into the hands of the train conductor telling him to make sure she gets there alright." After Catherine had left out of Sandra's room she knocked on Greg's door to see if he had turned in to hear him say, "Yes mother dear I am in bed. Good night as I will see you at breakfast in the morning."

"You know Florence and Samuel will be going to see Sandra off as well you know Greg. There will be more tears to share by Mrs. Hunt and your mother as if we needed more crying."

Once when Greg's mother left his door, he said to himself, "I just don't know why that woman cries so much, just like a river of running water. I know she will be lonely because Wayne won't be there, but she will have her husband Mr. Samuel to make a fuss over to come over here to make me think that I am hers. I truly can say that all of it is worth the fuss. I miss my brother Wayne already and we just left from his place not being three hours ago. I have his number and I should give him a call but I think it can wait until he is full settled and then he and I can chat all night about his work and to hear if he had met some fine girls. I have to make myself believe that things around here will not be the same like before when Sandra he, and I would hang out on the front porch until in the wee hours of the night on weekends to have a good time before mother would open the door to invite Sandra and me inside and to tell Wayne she should find his way home before his mother start calling. I will definitely miss all those times but I will hold all of those times dear to my heart."

Soon, Greg had fallen off to sleep and it was silent, but in Sandra's room, she too was in her own world as she was thinking about Wayne being all alone there in his own place making preparations to getting use to his own surroundings. She was only thinking all about how the three of them grew up together and how they shared so many good all-around good things as sister and brothers. Sandra never thought about being in love with Wayne because she did not see it that way, only as a brother's point of view. "Come in the morning, I will get up get dressed, have breakfast with my family for the last time and start loading my luggage in the car to prepare to say goodbye to this home that I grew up in and lived through all of my schools years. I do believe that I will be just fine there in New York, living with my first cousin besides, it will give the two of us a lot of time to really get to know each other as it has been years since we last set eyes on each other. Maybe all of this was for the good and it was meant for me to travel to a place I never knew before, New York to gain some possibilities to add to my resume. This trip won't be as if I want return back because I still will have my parents and brother there."

Sandra said to herself, "I am quite sure as time goes by while I stay there in New York and not being here where I grew up will give me a lot of learning experience that I had never know because growing up here and being closed away from the things that were being done outside of as I call it, my so-called-world, did not mean a thing to my brother and me as our parents as well as Wayne's parents did not speak about what had happened or what was taking place in the city because living out here in a safe rural community, we were kept safe because anyone in their right frame of mind would dare to find their way out in what they would call a desolate living condition to try to start something. Now, all of that has finally come to the light as tomorrow I will enter a city that is full of bad things, as all I will have to do is be very careful of all my walks and all the places of my interest because of everyone living there and they will know when there's a new face had penetrated their city because of the way they look at things and then they will try to get to know you."

"I am hoping that my first cousin Delores will give me a good briefing on what to look for and what not to involve myself in to be taken in by so many scapegoats all over the city. Although Wayne and Greg are very concerned about my leaving from here to gain employment there in New York, I wish they would think of me as a person who will know that I am going there for a reason only to work and not associate myself with those who come up to me to win my trust. They know that I am a smart cookie and it takes a lot to win me over if that was the case them, while I was at the university there in Louisiana, one of those college guys who had everything going for them would have taken me and who knows, I probably would have remained there in Louisiana to look for work and a possibility gotten married but I had other thoughts and desires in my mind, working for the goods of all people and I believe wholeheartedly, starting off right there in a classroom teaching young minds would be the start of something big and new that would open up a whole new world for everyone win the educated minds of young people."

"I know at times I think the ideas that flows in my mind will make those individuals who are so caught up in their own ways of living, will bring them to a new realization of life and those old ways will be erased from all minds and change policies and procedures of the state of Mississippi, government forever. Since at this particular time this state had refused me to share my ideas, and I have to travel and live in another state, this will not make me think otherwise because I know in a year or two, all these outdated ideas will come to light and just then it will be a possibility to return back from which I did grow and was educated to help rewrite the pathways to a brighter life for everyone living in a closed society here. When I first hear of some changes that are about to take place here in Mississippi, you can bet your bottom dollar I will be on a train headed back home to get started. For now, I will leave tomorrow to head off to New York to get a good job to save my money so I will be ready when the time comes."

"I know within my heart that the wait will be worthwhile and who knows, once I return just then I just might run into a wonderful young man and I will become his life partner to have a couple of children to make my parents great grandparents as my brother to be a good uncle. I am so looking forward to that time because I have been taught that if you want something bad enough and you continue to wait and be of good courage, things will come to view. I am throwing a little of my spiritual belief in what I say to myself. Well! I think I better get some sleep because before I realizes it, day light will be here and Greg will be knocking on my door to say, alright big sister, this is your final day here as queen bee, because the king, which is me, will be replacing you in this household. Before I doze off, I want to remind myself that although I won't be here anymore for a long period of time, I am feeling sorry for Wayne as well as Greg because in their lives, there will be a voyage, but when the two of them get together, they will be able to handle it. Being away from them will give me a chance to learn a lot because if I teach or find another educated job, I know I will add to my mind new and many ideas as I never knew before."

Soon, Sandra was fast asleep and she had good night dreams about Wayne being left behind, not love dreams just ordinary dreams because there was nothing else for her to dream about as far as a love relationship because she knew of any. As she slept and when she was awaken, it seem as if she had just fallen asleep and sudden it seem as if someone had knocked on her door calling out her name. She felt as if she was in a never land of purity, but it was real because that knock came from her brother Greg being so excited as he were not because she was soon be leaving, but to get to the breakfast table to share their last good family breakfast together before the sadness worked itself in to make tears fall down from all faces once arriving to the train station to prepare to send her off to a city of many uncertainties as her first cousin Delores would be there on the other end as the train pull in to receive her and to take her to her home safe and sound to call back home to let everyone know that she arrived safe and unharmed to clear up all of the sadness that has built up the time she left.

Once in the hands of Delores, the responsibilities would rest with her, Sandra could start to relaxes to ask many questions about the city. After breakfast, her mother Catherine was on the phone talking to Florence to let her and Samuel know they would be ready to leave in about twenty minutes in order to be there in a timely manner to make sure all of her baggage were checked in and they would be able to spend some final time in quiet moments with Sandra before it was time for her to board. After breakfast, Greg kept a watch on the time to make sure everything ran smooth to look out the kitchen window to see Mr. Samuel and his wife walking out of their house to enter their car to drive over to follow them to the train station to drop off his big sister, where she will be here anymore thus leaving him as a lonely brother to fight for himself not only with his school work, but to help him deal with Wayne's crazy ways at time. "I guess I should be happy because I know just about six months she will make it her business to return home to attend my high school graduation and boy, I know she will think that she has by then have learned all."

"Okay," Greg called out to everyone to alert them that the Hunts were outside waiting in their car to follow us. As Elijah and Catherine walked out of the front door and they greeted Florence and Samuel with a good morning soon behind them came Sandra and Greg laughing and carrying on as they two said good morning for this was the day for all to say goodbye to a little girl whom they knew and she grew up with, finally she is now leaving her nest to take up residence someplace else in a strange city. Sandra said to Mrs. Florence, "I really am not looking forward to this move, but since things here are the way they are, I guess it is best that I put on my big girl shoes and walk away. I am so very happy for you Sandra and then I am sad because Wayne will surely miss from being around you as the three of you were all what this state needs." As they too loaded up in the car to make that drive, Greg and Sandra sat quietly in the back seat speaking when it was necessary because the sadness had kicked in and soon the tears would be rolling down all faces as hugs and kisses will surely be given.

The drive to the train station into the city was about a thirty minutes' drive and her train departure time was scheduled to leave at eleven o'clock which would give them at least a thirty minutes time together. Once they arrived and parked their cars and got out, Elijah, and Samuel, along with Greg grabbed all of Sandra's baggage that way Catherine and Florence could walk with Sandra as they enter the station with the three men carrying her baggage behind to walk up to the check in location so all of her baggage would be checked and her tickets for them be given to her to keep until she arrive in

New York to obtain them. After all of her baggage were checked and she was told the exact time the train will depart, all of them decided to walk close to the door she would walk through to be loaded to take a seat and just enjoy the moments left for them to be together before her train to New York would be called. As they sat quietly looking at each other, Greg said to them, "This is not a funeral but a sending off time for a wonderful young lady so let's cry and get it all over with because whether we want to believe it or not, this is her day, and I for one wish my sister well."

Catherine got herself together and said, "Guys Greg is so right because we all are here to send not only Elijah and my daughter off, but Florence and Samuel your daughter as well because she has been a part of your family from the beginning as your son did grow up with my family as well so although we will shed tears but in shedding those tears let them remind us of all the goods that has happened in our lives. Florence did say to the Logans that both families brought joy to all the things we did together and now that our children have all grown up and Samuel and my son Wayne has moved out of our home and into his own place, it has made us so proud although we would rather if he was still home, but he has been lucky enough to get a job here that would keep him close by where we still can see him each weekend. Catherine, my little girl Sandra has not been afforded that opportunity because the way things are in this stiff state, but let us look at it this way, going off to New York, will definitely brighten her mind and when the time comes she will be able to deal with all given situations because she would have already been exposed."

As the three men- Samuel, Elijah, and Greg- stood away from the ladies as they talked as they listened to them for they knew once that conductor come over the loudspeaker to announce the train arrival, the tears will flow. Sure enough that was exactly what did happened as Samuel, had said. Sandra got up from where she was sitting and walked over to her father and placed her arms around him and said, "Daddy, I love you with all of my heart and I promised you that I will not let anyone there in New York take the advantage of me."

As Elijah kissed his daughter he said, "I am not worried too much about that because I know my daughter. All I want for you is to do good at whatever you do to make mother and me proud. Come here my little brother Greg and give your big sister a big hug, and I want you to be the man of the house you know to keep our mother and father straight now. You don't have to worry so much about that because I got it covered."

"Yeah right," she responded. She walked over to Mr. Samuel to express her love for him because besides her own father he too has been a father figure.

The train was on the right track to head to New York, as people were getting in line to board as she walked over to her mother Catherine to hug and kiss her to say, "Mother, I am really going to miss you because you have been all that I want to be and I am so grateful that you pushed me to be the best young lady that I could be and to hold my head high and go after what I think is right for me. For those teachings, I love you and will always follow your advice." She walked over to Florence, and the tears just could not be held back because just yesterday as they all moved her son Wayne into his apartment, the same thing happened which were surely follow at this time with Sandra. Sandra said to all of them standing there to watch her get on the train that she promised when she return back from New York, she will still be the same girl that left from this place only to be more update on things. The conductor call out the last call for all boarding so Sandra walked up to the ticket agent and she gave his her ticket to be clipped to look around and wave as she walked onto the train to take her seat as she watched them from her window. Soon the train started to pull off and all hands were on deck waving as the train speeded up and soon to be out of sight on its way to the big city of New York.

As everyone walked out of the train station back to their cars, they stood outside for a while before they load just being sad because Sandra has departed from their space as Wayne did and now only one more left to depart and that is Greg. At least there will be a few more months before he will start making his move out onto a new beginning. As they stood there talking, Catherine asked Florence, "Can you tell me where did time apparently go? You and I were not watching?"

"Catherine, I don't know but I can surely tell you this much, it came upon us without any notifications."

Elijah and Samuel, said to their wives, "Listen, it is not over with because this is just the beginning because we knew that one day this would come."

Elijah threw his arm around his son and said to him, "We will be alright wouldn't you say son?"

"Daddy, we will be just fine because Sandra will be just fine there in New York being with Delores."

After they had finished talking outside of the train station as Sandra was now on her way to New York, as soon as the train soon was out of sight, Elijah, said to his wife and son, "I think we have finished up here so let the three of us get started going back to our home where our lives will continue as we keep our daughter and sister in prayers that all things will work out for her." Also Samuel and Florence did the same thing but the only difference to them was this: their son Wayne will still be present as he will come home each weekend to visit and to have dinner with them as well as with us as well because of Greg as they still have that bond.

"I really don't think things will be as lonely as it might seem just now because there will still be the presence of our daughter Sandra here as we look to see how well Greg and Wayne will still be so active in each other always speaking about Sandra. While Elijah was driving back home and Catherine, and Greg kept the conversation going so there would not be a silence of sorrow there in the car sudden, Catherine said to the two of them," I think our daughter Elijah and your sister Greg won't have a single thing to worry about because I know that she will be in good hands there with Delores knowing the type of person she is. When we get home, I am going to plan a good afternoon dinner and invite Florence and Samuel over so we all will be fulfilled regardless of the absence of our two children."

"Mother," Greg said to her. "I think that is a wonderful idea."

Although Wayne was very excited with his new position, his mind still was much on the girl he love, Sandra who has left him for now at a standstill as if he had been cut off from the whole world and he was out there all alone to defend those on coming girls who will be in his mist and he move around from place to place to try to help solve any farmers problems. With all those girls that will find Wayne exciting will surely come up to him to persuade him to make a play for them, but with his strength and love for the one he so much love will not even make a dent into his life because he was on track and there was nothing else or any other girl it didn't matter if she was white because that how things were set into stone that white girls are supposed to marry white guys, but in this instance in the life a little white boy who had grown up in the environment of two back little children, a girl and a boy as they grew up together to name themselves sister and brothers will not change his way of thinking about being with the one he has come to love from the time they became old enough to understand just what love is, and how all things can be because love conquer all.

Well, so much for Wayne's mother more so than his father because she will not be the mother-in-law of a white girl, but to soon be the mother-in-law of a beautiful black girl as she has known all of her life, but never expected anything like this to happen. Wayne knows in his mind once he is the husband of Sandra that this will be a good union as his children will grow up to know no prejudice among people because that is the one thing he plan to teach them as he will tell all about his growing up days. I guess you might as well say Wayne has looked into the future and have seen all what is coming into his life as will definitely start changing the way of the world. If the state of Mississippi, is ever going to change, it was now the time as Wayne thought more on it each day that the time has come and it is at hand starring those old southern individuals right in their faces which they refuse to see that, life for the living ways of their children are moving fast in the right directions and when those changes appear boy, won't they be surprised to see?

The old south that has held people back for so many years and generations will now no longer be at hand, but anew beginning will be born where anyone whomever they wish to be with will surely come and when the whole world finally jump on board, it will still be some that will refuse to give up, but try and keep that old southern flag blowing in the wind as only they will see, but as far as the young generations, they will not look toward those old flags but tear them down. Once Wayne and Sandra finally come together as one, and as things start to change, there will be a mixed of beautiful children running around all over the world to show that the rainbow that was created by the almighty father, has come aboard and that old outdated kingdom of people will exist anymore because a new day has been approved. Wayne had decided to give Sandra just about two years living there in New York before he will break his hidden secrets to her and hoping that she will accept his him not as a brother, but to look upon him as a boyfriend plus husband. Once he had sat down with her to tell her all the things he had hidden then she just might understand his reasons why.

As Wayne continued to ponder over all that he feel for Sandra it was a time also for him to get heavily involved in the duties that he has been assigned too from the head of the agricultural department. To tell all agents that in order for all the farmer in and around the counties of Mississippi, they must take everything in strive to assure all of them if they would follow all the guidelines that the department has put into place then at the end of the growing seasons, their crops would produce more than what they expected too. The one good thing about the department is they furnished each one of the agent a country vehicle to make their rounds each day therefore, not having to use their own vehicles, which was a good thing. Wayne was given an assigned close by location which to start off with a very few crop growers to deal with because he was the new kid on the block and the top officials had to make sure that he would get the experience needed in order to be given more tasks.

The second day of Wayne's assignment, he was learning to get familiar with his peers as he vowed to understand and to learn all the details which came with his position to make him a good agent, one whom the farmers could depend on for good advice. Ass the day slowly passed because he wanted to get back to his apartment to unwind and to concentrate on Sandra about when the time come and the time was right, how he would break it down to her. As the day for work has come to an end and Wayne had to go back to the main office to report to the big boss on how he spent his first day on the job and what he had accomplished, he felt good because this was something that made him feel like he was his own man, having his own job, own place and soon, as he hope will have his wife to really enjoy working for the good of a good life. After he had reported to his boss and was given the red light of his good deeds for the day by his boss of how proud he was to see such a first time young college graduate to take lead in the assignment he was given and to be able to work on his own without little assistance at all from his coworker, let the big boss to know that just maybe in a couple of weeks, he could be assigned to a bigger area.

After the little pet talk from his boss, Wayne was released for the day so he could hardly wait until he reached his apartment to just relax and concentrate on whether or not his future love had arrived in New York. After preparing himself something to eat which didn't take much preparing because most of his foods were already made by his mother when they moved him into his place Sunday so all he really had to do was to was his hands and warm it up and sit down in front of his television set to eat and watch all the things he like as he felt like making a phone call to New York, but he didn't know where too because Sandra did not leave him a number where he could call her. All Wayne had to do was to wait and keep his mind on his work because in a few days, he knew she will write to him with her number. Each bite of food he took into his mouth, he wondered if she had arrived as he kept watching his clock. It got to the point that he would not take it any longer so he picked up his phone and made a call to his adopted brother, Greg. I know he will tell ne if they have heard from her.

Soon, Wayne dialed Greg home number and he answered to say, "Hello my brother Wayne how are things going there with you tonight or are you lonely and wanting me to come over to keep you company?"

"No my brother, I am alright and I am enjoying myself but I just was wondering if you guys have heard from Sandra yet?" By this time it was about seven thirty and surely her train should have arrived there by now, Wayne was thinking.

Greg being the way he kept playing around with the yes or no answer so Wayne said to him, "Brother, please tell me if she has arrived there or not and stop your mess?"

"Alright Wayne," he said. "She arrived and was met by our cousin Delores, so they are now in the home of Delores taking it easy from her trip. By the way Wayne she did tell me to make sure I told you that she was there and in a few days after she get all settled in she will write to you."

"That is good to hear Greg because now I can have a goodnight sleep know she is there safe and sound."

"Wayne," Greg asked. "You are still coming home this weekend aren't you?"

"I plan to because you and I only just have each other to sit around and talk about old times you know."

"Wayne, I hope those talks will be carried out at the dinner table at your parents' home or here in my own eating at my parents table right?"

"Greg is that all you ever think about is food?" he asked. "What will you do once you finish high school and go off to college?"

"Right now Wayne, I cannot began to tell you just hope that my mother as well as your mother will pack boxes of goodies to help a hungry guy out. What will you do Wayne once I leave because then you will have no one here to be around when you come home on weekend to spend time with except your parents and a short time with my parents before returning back to your place. I can see it now how lonely you will be. I guess you might find one of those white girl there in your area to spend your lonely time with therefore having less time to come visit your parents my man, right?"

"Greg, right now that is the furthest thing from my mind because I am not so sure if that is what I want to do to get involved with a white girl that does not the least bit interest me right now."

"Listen my white brother, sometimes your vibes throw me for a loop and it is hard for me to figure you out especially when you keep saying that none of those white girls in the area interest you. I am your bother as you know and you know that you can tell me anything you want me to know, knowing that your secrets are good with me."

"Greg," Wayne opened up to him to say. "That is exactly what I am afraid of, you keeping all of my secrets because I know that you will make the mistakes and spill the beans so I think I will continue to let you remain in the dark at least for a while longer."

"Wayne if you are not interested in any of these while southern belles then tell me this much, are you so interested in a girl of color?"

" My brother, why are you asking me this right now as you know I am trying to get my life established to be the best I can?"

"Brother, I thought if I could get a clue then I will know more about you."

"Just let it go for now my brother and when the time is right, you will know because the secrets will all be thrown out on the table. When you are off to college, just make sure you find the one who you think just might be the one for you one day," Wayne responded to him.

"I truly can tell you this Greg your time is of essence because in only a few more months we all will be sitting in the audience watching you walk across the stage to receive the diploma where you worked so hard to get and then watch you leave to enter college so you will finally take you stand in society. I am sure by the time you are ready to set your sights high, things will have taken some turn and will allow people of colors to obtain the positions they worked hard to get".

" Wayne you have good insights because I hope that will be true and just maybe my sister Sandra will be able to return back home to pick up where she left off."

"Now Greg that would be nice and we all will be so happy to finally see that someone there in the general assembly of the government legislative found in his or her heart that the way things are set in the policies of this state will not be for the benefits for one particular race of people, but the changes will be for all of those who were born and live here, but to all people of colors, in order for this state to grow and be on the same level as others states who have are about to implement all the changes once were established. Wayne if all of this happens before I graduate from college, won't that be wonderful?"

"Yes Greg, it certainly will," Wayne responded.

Once Wayne and Greg had finished with their conversation about Sandra as well as all the changes that will soon take place once voted on when the voting rights will be for all people to go to the polls to decide on whom they would like to represent them, this will be a state that will be well talked about among other states. Wayne just had to let Greg know how great it was just having this conversation between the two of them as if they had been away from one another in a long time and they brought it all home by talking things out, but Greg still did not get to learn from Wayne what he had always wanted to know- his secrets. After they had said their goodbyes until the weekend as Wayne will visit, his mind wandered back on Sandra to say, "I am so glad she made it to the city and to know that she is well. Now, all I have to do is to wait until she send me a letter with her address and phone number where I can call her from time to time but I want make it a point to call every night because if I did that then she herself will start to wonder."

When they arrived to where Delores lived and they got out of the cab, as the cab driver got Sandra's baggage out of the cab and after he was paid by Delores. Sandra did suggest that she take care of the bill but Delores insisted that she would take care of it as she was her guest so she wouldn't think of her using her money to pay the fare. The place where Delores was living was such an eye opening because it sat in a quiet quaint place very quiet as Sandra said to her, "Delores you have made quite an impression on me with your home," as they walked inside and she took a really good look as how it was laid out because of the good taste Delores has. Delores had two bedrooms and two bathrooms so neither one would get in the way of the other.

Delores said to Sandra, "Come on and let us place your baggage in the room where you will be sleeping and I think we should go out to have a nice dinner once you change and but first I am sure you would like to call home to let them know you have arrived. I am sure Uncle Elijah, Aunt Catherine, and that little spoiled brother of your, Greg would want to hear from you."

"I think that would be a good idea and that way I won't have to hear Greg's mouth".

" Why don't you do it now while I go in and start changing my clothes to be ready when you are finished talking with them?" Sandra walked over to the phone took a seat and dialed their number to be answered on the other end none other than her brother Greg.

She said to him, "Why hello my little brother, your big sister has arrived here in the big city of New York, as my long train ride here was a very exciting one as I noticed so many wonderful landscapes as we rolled right along. Greg you have to one day come to New York to see it because it's a city with so many people and I never thought Mississippi would look just like a spoon of sugar. Let me talk with my mother and daddy before Delores and I go out to dinner."

"No," Greg said. "Get out of here, why you just arrived. Aren't you tired?"

"Just a little bit but I am sure a good New York dinner will liven me up."

"Here is Mother," he said.

"Daughter, how was your trip there?" she asked.

"Mother, I had a lovely train ride and I don't think it could have been any better. Delores was there waiting for me at the train station when it pulled in as we just hugged one another when I got off." Her mother asked about Delores, as Sandra said to her that she was in her room changing her clothes because they are going out to dinner.

"I bet you are excited about that. Sandra my daughter, I am so glad you arrived safe and sound and you are happy as I know in the coming days you will be more happy once you get a job."

"Where is Daddy because I want to speak with him?"

"Wait a minute here he comes and you know if he didn't speak with you he would just die."

Her daddy came on and she said to him, "Daddy, I am already missing you and the others but I am sure as time move on it will get better. At least I am here in good hands as Delores is taking me out to a New York. Isn't that grand?" she asked him.

"Baby girl, I know my niece Delores and she will indeed take care of you. All is well here as we had an evening dinner with the Hunts as your mother prepared dinner and invited them over to keep the family going."

"Daddy," Sandra responded to him. "I think that was a wonderful idea for mother to do that with the Hunts to let them know that even though their son Wayne has moved out, there is still some presence there still. Please let them know that I did arrived here in New York all safe and sound as they will want to know."

"I will do just that baby girl and you tell that niece of mine Delores that she better keep you safe there in that city where there are so much going on. Now, you two go on out and fill your stomach in that good food there which I have heard so much about. I am sure in just a few days, you will feel as if you have been there for a long time and you want ever think that much of this place."

"No Daddy, I could never think that because there is where my start began with my own family members as well as the Hunt family members. Have you guys heard how Wayne has been doing in his new surroundings?"

"You know Greg and Wayne talk a lot and I know if you ask your brother, he can tell you everything."

"I think I will wait to ask him all about it the next time I call. You guys be good and I will call you later on in the week."

After Sandra had hung up the phone, Delores walked out of her room to say to Sandra, "I think you better go get changed because we want to get out there to get good seats so we will be able to watch all of those fine men that frequent there also to have dinner and who knows, maybe looking for a good mate as well."

Once Sandra made a quick change, the two of them were ready to hit the streets as if Sandra had been there all along. "Delores," Sandra asked her. "What is the name of this exclusive place we are to have dinner"?

" Listen my first cousin, you are new to this city and all things are on me so don't even think about pulling any money out of your pocket to help pay for this nice dinner we will be having because it is my treat as I had planned this for your arrival as a gift from me to you for coming to live with me because at times. Not having any of my relatives here gets lonely so it is a privilege to welcome you into my home. Sandra I know you and I are going to have a wonderful time here. There is so much for you to see and to learn. Now, I have gone far and between to make these lawyers think that you are the best they ever would have because of your knowledge in the English language field just coming out of college with a fresh mind."

"Delores, what on earth have you done because I don't know if I can do that or will be able to. What will those law students think of me once they know they will have to sit down each morning in a conference room to listen to my ways of telling them how they should format their closing arguments for their bosses to finalizes their cases?"

"Believe me Sandra once you let those lawyers know all of your capabilities, who knows, they just might get rid of their law students and have you to do it all for them. Cousin, think about the money you will be making that will surely make you forget all about that dull place in Mississippi."

"Delores, I could never forget home because I have a need to keep my mind staying on it. Besides, my parents and my brother are very much a part of my life there you know."

"I understand Sandra and I would not want you to think otherwise about there."

Soon, Delores and Sandra arrived at this fabulous restaurant and were escorted to a nice table, one where they would be able to watch everyone walk in as the floor usher knew Delores and welcomed her in as always. "By the way," Delores said to the usher. "This is my cousin who just came up from that old crazy state of Mississippi to live with me and to obtain employment here." The usher said to Sandra how glad he was to meet her and he know that she will be happy living in a great city.

"I so hope so," Sandra said as she returned her thanks.

Delores suggested to the usher that if Sandra happens to come in here all by herself, she expects her to be treated as she has been treated. The usher said to Delores, "Now you know that nothing other than the best will be shown her way. Okay ladies, what would you two like to order because I have time to stand right here to make sure you guys order the best and to take your time making up your minds."

Delores said to the usher (his name was Carl), "Since this is my treat, I think I should order nothing but the best for her and myself."

"I am here ready to take your order," Carl responded.

Delores, being the big spender she was, asked Sandra how does a nice steak sounds with all the trimmings along with it. "That sounds good to me because to tell you I am very hungry because on the train that food they serve isn't the best."

"Carl, I'm ready to give our orders as two of your finest steaks with all that comes with it and a nice salad with French dressing for me, what about you Sandra?"

"I would like the same."

"What will you two have to drink?" Carl asked.

"For me, a nice glass of red dinner wine and I am not sure about my cousin here."

"Delores, I am not into wine so a nice cold glass of lemon tea will suffice for me."

Once Carl had taken their orders and left, Delores said to Sandra, "I forgot that you did not drink wine."

"Don't worry about that because I guess it is because there was never any in the house where Daddy nor Mother ever partake."

"What about college?" Delores asked.

"I never got involved as most of the girls there were only into getting an education so there was little time to be caught up in such things. "

Soon, Carl returned with their two salads and drinks to say to them, "Your delicious and most outstanding steak dinner will soon be out."

"Why thank you Carl."

Once Carl left their table, Delores said to Sandra, "Now that is a nice guy, but he is so young and he has a girlfriend as he is working his way through college also."

"What are you trying to tell me Delores?" Sandra asked.

"Oh nothing, I was just mentioning how nice he is but I never would dream he is your kind."

"My cousin Delores, please know that right now I am here for one thing and one thing only."

"I know," Delores responded, "to work." As Carl returned with their dinner, in walked a status symbol of a man, "Now that is as hot as can be," Delores stated. "I see him here quite often, but there is never anyone with him."

"Delores, why haven't you introduced yourself to him?" Sandra asked her.

"I am not that desperate right now for any of these slick men here in the city because I have been here long enough to know everything that look like gold turn out to be silver with no value within. There is a reason why he is alone maybe he is one of those guys who think their looks will make women fall all over them."

Once the two of them had finally finished their much needed dinner, Delores decided to walk around to some of the highlights of the city to show Sandra. As they walked here and there, Delores noticed some nice guys walking by as she turned around to watch by saying to Sandra, "How do you like that one?"

Sandra, being a new green southern girl just arriving into a big city was a little uneasy as she said to Delores that she should stop highlighting her about these guys because if and when she is ready, she thinks that it would be on her own time to get involved. "Alright my cousin, I want stress you further about these guys. Come on let us go home because girl, you will have a very long day at the first interview tomorrow morning, as I feel good about what is going to happen to you. After you get interviewed and land that high paying job after impressing those two head attorneys, you will definitely have a lot to call home to let your parents and little brother Greg know how excited you are," Delores said to her. "How do you think Uncle Elijah, and Aunt Catherine, along with Greg will feel? Why I can hear Aunt Catherine calling Mrs. Hunt to tell her the good news and Greg will definitely elevated it to your little white adopted brother and all of you will be as happy as can be."

"Delores, why are you placing the cart before the horse because it has not happened yet?"

"Oh Sandra but it will and believe me, because I know exactly all how the games are played here among employers here in this city."

"I suppose you do as it was you who is making all of this possible for me and I want you to know just how appreciative I am." As the two of them walked inside Delores' home, they sat a while just talking about old times there in Mississippi when she was there before she moved on to bigger and better things before they decided to turn in as Sandra was really tired from the long train ride.

"Sandra my beloved cousin, get plenty of sleep because come tomorrow morning I want you to get up and dress for the kill so when you walk in the

Ashley and Ashley Law Firm, by the way, it is two brothers who run that firm, they will look upon you to say, 'Who is this beautiful young lady, Delores?' Knowing who I am, I will lift up my head to say, 'Why this is the young intelligent lady I had spoken to you guys about who is very vast in English as that was her major field in college. By the way guys, she graduated from one of the top black established universities in the state of Louisiana, and she graduated with honors, can you believe those apples?'"

"Delores, I see for all the years you have lived here in New York, you have established yourself not only in your work, but also in your connections with some important people."

"You are quite right my darling cousin. When you know that you are good then why not show it so everyone will see that you are the best?"

"Is this how the Ashley brothers see you Delores?" asked Sandra.

"They are holders at my bank as they look to me for the assistance they need. I must say, you have it going on and I know you have no plans to ever returning back to Mississippi to live."

"Why no my dear cousin, only to visit my relatives from time to time. Do you know Sandra once I finished college and came back home to find a good job, I was turned down because of who I was, like you. I decided right then and there that I had to get away from that sick place with so many hateful people live and find another part of the world who saw me as me. Sandra there is no way that I want to return back there to live even if they offered me a job because the pay there would not even come close to what I am making right here in New York. Besides, I have the power to make decisions and to bring all of my workers under me to sit around the conference room table to make decisions as we all come to the conclusions that what we have agreed on will benefit everyone. Now, if I was there in Mississippi, my decisions would not matter to a hill of beans because old man white in charged would never take my word for anything because I will just be a person of color working there because the state said you must fill so many positions as required by law so the civil rights department would not be breathing down their necks. Now Sandra do you understand why I feel this way? To be honest with you, you should have the same attitude."

"Delores, when I am sure I have landed that position tomorrow, I will keep an open mind to accept that in the near future things will be changed and to be changed, it will start right there in old Mississippi with my brother and his generation as everything will take a turn around and then I suppose my whole mind will change as yours have."

Once they arrived by cab to the Ashley and Ashley Law Firm, Delores paid the cab driver as the two of them got out and walked into the building to catch the elevator to go to the fifth floor where the offices were. Once reaching the fifth floor and getting off, Sandra said to Delores, "How do I look?"

"You look just fine and take my cue, walk in as if you own the whole city with a sophisticated air about you as to say, 'I am here and I am ready for your decision.' Come on and pull it together," Delores said to Sandra. "This is your day to take control over the layout of all these law students to show them how to write papers."

As the two of them walked into the lobby of the receptionist's office, one of the secretaries said to Delores that she would let her two bosses know that they are here.

Delores turned to take a look at Sandra to say, "You see what I mean."

Soon the secretary returned back to let them know that they are ready to receive the two now as Delores said to the secretary thanks and walked straight into the lawyers office on into the conference room where their meeting would be held. "Delores," one of the Ashley brothers said to her. "It is so good to see you again and to see what you have to present to us because you know my brother and I are in dying need of a smart person who can write and set our court arguing procedures in place. Please tell us about your qualifications. First let my brother and I ask you of your name."

"My name is Sandra Logan."

"We understand that you have attended and graduated from one of the top black universities in the country, the University of Louisiana You see Delores has already filled us in on your good deeds. Well Ms. Logan, we were looking over your resume this morning and my brother and I were just so set back with such qualifications and all the letters you received from all of your professors there to encourage any employer to take you own so you can show all of what you are capable of producing. There are no doubts in our minds that we are not going to hire you because you have the job right now if you so desire to take on all responsibilities in being charged over all the law students who are working here to enhance their education to write cases for the court

Is Love Worth the Wait?

in our defense. So many are not up on the way words are supposed to be in place that the judges will understand what we are trying to say to win our cases. It is very crucial that the wording is right. So we understand from our dear friend here Delores you have what it takes to do the job. What do you think about the job Sandra?"

"This is happening so fast until I have to breathe for a moment and now, I think I am now ready to show you what I have to give." By then one of the attorneys called in one of the secretary to have her to bring in a contract for Ms. Sandra Logan to sign giving her the responsibilities and the salary she would be making.

When Sandra was given the contract after the attorneys had her signature, she and Delores read all the contents in it as Delores looked at her to ask, "Are you completely happy with what is offered to you?"

In that instant, Sandra knew that her whole world was about to open up and she said to Delores, "I am very happy," and she signed the contract and copies were given to her as well as the secretary to be filed.

One of the lawyers said to Sandra, "Now that you are on board let me call in all four of these law students to brief them on what to expect from now on. I think they too will enjoy working with you because you see, they are not that versed in the why cases should be written because that is not a part of the classroom preference, only to be taught how they should go about winning cases." As all of the law students walked in, they were introduced to Ms. Logan, by one of the lawyers.

He said, "Guys this pretty young educated English graduate from one of the top black universities in the United State in Louisiana will be your boss from now on to teach you the exact way to write your court cases with the right English words to be used."

One of the law student said, "Boy, are we glad to have someone to help and teach us because we are only taught in class how to win cases so this will be great."

Once Sandra's interview meeting was over with and she had met and introduced herself to the law students whom she would be teaching how they should go about wring their court papers for the attorneys, she was told by the two brothers who would be her boss because she would be working with the two of them assigned law students, she was told by her two bosses that they will be expecting her to report to work the following morning ready to go to it as they smiled. After shaking hands with each boss, she and Delores got up to leave when one of the attorneys said to Delores to wait for a few minutes as Sandra made her way out of the door into the waiting room for Delores.

After Sandra had walked out, the two brothers said to Delores why did she just now bring this smart lady to their attention. Delores responded by saying, "She was still in college when I first spoke to you two about her."

"Well, after listening to her intelligence, there were no doubts in our minds that we would not hire her to help build up this firm."

Delores said to them, "Now that I have given you something to help make your firm grow where just about everyone in this city will surely want to seek your assistance, now I want you two brothers to throw more business toward my bank," she said as she laughed and walked out.

Right now, the future for Sandra is in her hands and time will tell what will take turn in the upcoming years. How long will Sandra remain there in New York is not know at this particular time because in spite of her ability to motivate those law students there by viewing their work. Still she would much rather be back there in the state where she grew up in and in her young days had set her mind on teaching English to all students whether black or white, it didn't matter because all she wanted from them to know how important it would be to them once they graduate and enter colleges of their choice. Nothing about marriage was even on her mind because she knew what she wanted out of her future and she knew she had to make a go of it regardless of what will come in front of her. So being there in New York with appreciation to her cousin Delores was the start of something motivational for her as she know one day she would be making her final trip back to where she started to work for one accord as by that time the policies and procedures there in the state would have been changed by the movements of so many organizations to overthrow that old Jim Crow tightly squeezed. Once all of the charges had been overturned by the federal government to let all states know that this country was created for all people not, just for one creed but all creeds and the laws must be governed by the people and for the people.

Of course, this will be good new to Sandra and she will let her cousin Delores to know that she had a calling to go home to continue where she had left off, as she will leave all the things she had learned by living there behind and take up the things that were in not completion. Delores of course would be sad and lonely because she had hoped that Sandra would make New York her life and to forget about ever returning back to a place where she had been held down. Delores right away knew that she would have to do something with her life because all the years she had lived there in New York, she had not even considered marrying anyone and now that her life has taken a turn for the best for her cousin Sandra she thought she had better get started to find her a smart soulmate to live happy with as she hoped the best for her cousin Sandra.

"Delores, can't it wait for a while until I get myself together?" Sandra asked.

"Oh no my bright cousin, you must do it now while things are really fresh in your mind if they decide to ask questions."

"Alright," she said as she dialed the number and when the phone rang, you know who was the first to pick it up, her little brother Greg because he always wanted to be the first to know. As Greg said hello, Sandra responded by saying, "Do you know who this is?"

"Sandra what is going on up there and what is happening with cousin Delores?"

"There is nothing happening to Delores, and for me, I have landed a job on my first day looking for work. I only had just this interview and I had to make a good impression on these two brothers who are attorneys and have their own law firm with law students working inside the court with them. Guess what, I will be over all the law students here teaching them how to write their court cases for their bosses so when they are in court and began to submit their closing arguments to the judge their cases that they are defending will be well written thus causing the judge to make little or no succession."

"Now that the good news of your job success has been elevated to your family, let you and I put our heads together and you tell me how you are going to work this tomorrow."

"First of all, I think that I will set up a drawing board to show them the correct way to start off writing their cases and then establish the guidelines as to what they are saying making sure their wording are in the right content which will surely catch the eye of the judge when the cases are given to him once the attorneys submit them to him for further study."

"Sandra don't tell me anymore because when you put these cases together, you might be in the courts with the attorneys yourself presenting their cases as the judge will be so very impressed with your knowledge. Do you really think so?" asked Sandra.

"Why yes cousin, because right now you have it going on and you should be glad that you did leave from that hateful Mississippi, location. Why, this is a new world for you that has just opened up for you and as time passes, you will be well sort after by who knows, just might be the president of the united sates. I don't think you should go as that far because it would really take a lot of effort my dear cousin, Delores."

"Sandra are you saying that you would turn down a onetime shot at the top paying job in the administration of the president if asked?" Delores responded.

"I don't want to think at all about that because I am now just getting started and who knows, maybe one day I would want to return back home to teach English in a mixed high school to students who will be going off to college and I would love for them to excel regardless of what color they are."

"So, after all of what has happened for you and what is out there to still come, you still have your mind set on teaching in the south in a place that didn't even look at you for your qualifications, but your complexion to refused to grant you a position in one of their while school because they felt you were not good enough or they felt threaten by your knowledge to out shine those white teachers who felt that they were more qualified than you. Come on Sandra you and I both know that those white folks there in the south are afraid of a black person's mind because they have already known from way back that whatever we as a people put out mind too, we will succeed."

"Delores I am all up on that because I saw it as I grew up when Greg, Wayne ,and I would be out in some place together, how they would stare. It is nothing new with me because I know what the south has always been like. That good old boy network and please remain on the side of your town. You don't bother us then we won't bother you. I have conquered so far all that I set out to do, but there is still more that I have to do as time passes. I can say by being invited to come to live here in New York with you my dear cousin was a blessing in disguise because the decisions were placed on your heart to extend to me what was given you as you had no idea, but there was already a higher authority that had looked into your warm heart to be transferred to me. You had no idea at all when you had hooked me up with your bank clients that they would take me in on your word, but you must know they felt something good that was about to make their firm more successful. I have to say to you about the whole ordeal. If you did not see it, they did because what you had told them about me and they were waiting to meet me, this smart young black English student, coming from the south where there were so much confusion to take a chance to see exactly what I had learned from the all impressive black university, I attended. They must have read or they must have heard a lot to the fact that that particular university turn out brilliant minds, and this was what they had been looking for."

"Sandra you know the more you and I speak about those two brothers' law firm, the more I am in agreement with you because I only throw your name around to let them know that I had a cousin, who had just graduated from the university and she was in the market of looking for a job to enhance her career. They asked me what was your major, and I said to them English. I do remember when I said that, the two of them took a looked at each other as though they said, let us give this one a try because the ones we had who attended the colleges right here in this city did not really have it together as far as putting things into perspective when it came to teaching these law students how to arrange their cases to say they did not know because they were law students who were assigned to various law firms in the city to help learn all about how to go about with their cases once they would become lawyers. One of the brothers asked her about the date she would be coming? Sandra it was such a shock to me at that time as I had no knowledge about getting you hired there, but their minds were made up. I guess in so many ways, your old nosy cousin Delores was in the right place at the time needed to get you a job."

"I can say this much to you Delores, I am so thrilled and happy to be your cousin because you and I both have a lot in common. Let it be known right now at this moment that your cousin Sandra is all about business and I can assure you I will show those two brothers just how fast their lagging law firm will be up and running as it should have been because look out now, as I pin red roses on my own shoulders, Sandra has arrived and get ready law students because you will be met head on to a whole new way of writing if, you are going to become lawyers."

"You go girl!" Delores cried out. "Because I know once you put those cases together, those two brothers will wish they had you all along because if they did, then their law firm would be the top in this city. Delores, I plan to give myself just three months working there and then they will see all the progress they have made in the court system once they present all of their cases to win. I am telling you Delores, there will be a lot of changes coming and I can feel them as I speak about them soon to hit. I know there will be a lot of unwelcoming individuals at the start, but as things move along and everyone get comfortable with each other! Am quite sure everything will play out and when it does, just then especially the young people will start to see just how stupid the whole thing had been all along because of their parents fright."

"Sandra tomorrow will be another day and right now you must get some sleep because come tomorrow, you are going to need all the rest because of a new journey now that you are on. I will be alright Delores, because I am a worker and if you are a worker, you won't have to concern yourself with a lot because you know you have the ability to move mountains. Before I drift off to sleep, there is one more thing I would like to say to you," Delores responded to Sandra.

"I see I won't have to even worry about you because you have a made up mind. When a mind is made up and you stand firmly behind all what you have included into your, data bank of memories then there is nothing that can change you as I see that is exactly what had happened to you so I am going to leave you alone and get my sleep because like you I have to refresh myself for a busy day tomorrow at my bank because I know once I walk in the president will say to me, I am so glad to see you returning because it has been hectic around here with everyone, especially me, because I needed your input to a lot of things as you very well know that I have come to depend on a lot of your expertise on so many transactions."

The next day Delores asked her boss Mr. Greenspan, "Did you miss me? If that is the case let you and I go into my office to see all what you have messed up waiting for my return to get it right," she said as she smiled at him.

"I don't think I was that bad, but since I am not fully in the understanding mode of various loans, I have come to depend on your knowledge because of your vast wit to understand things fully and how they should be worked."

As he and Delores began to look into all of the transactions that had been developed in her absence, she said just a few mistakes had been made and it was an easy fix so the higher powers to be in the main branch of the banking system will never notice the time and dates they were made. Mr. Greenspan said to Delores, "Do you see why I hate to see you disappear on me like this?"

Delores being the funny person as she is, she quickly turned to him and said, "Is this why you keep me around to keep the heat off from your back and mine?"

"Sort of because that is why we pay you the big bucks. Oh, so you are going there also Delores, did your cousin who came from Mississippi get the job you had lined up for her?"

"Of course she did because you know whatever I do, it doesn't fail as I am Delores, you know," she said as she laughed.

"I am happy that she did. Maybe one of these days I will get a chance to meet her because if she is anything like you then I know the law firm that hired her will be well pleased with her work."

"You know Mr. Greenspan that is the most honorable thing you have said to me in a long time and I really do appreciate it a lot. You will meet her soon."

Since all notifications were out there for everyone to see and to obtain good advice, the ones who come to them for representation would surely be glad they did because now they were up running and rearing to go thanks to a wonderful, educated young mind who had been teaching four law students the ropes on writing so all cases that will be presented would not fail as the judge or judges review the cases submitted to them for decision making. Each week as the two brothers walked into the court room, they were well relaxed as they carried their brief cases with their documentations in them to start arguing with those prosecutors who are set out to destroy a person's life by trying to convince the judge or jurors that the individual or individuals that are being charged should be held responsibly.

As Ben and his brother, being the defense team, listened to all details of the prosecutors outlining their motives to rebut them with what they had to present, this way if the jurors buy into what will be presented then it would determine whether or not their client or clients would be freed. The war was on as each team starting establishing all motives to the court whether or not charges should be guilty or not to be entered in a plea deal or not. Since the four law students were present with their two bosses in court to give them the cases which they had worked on so diligently by the instructions of their teacher Sandra, they were not worried as they kept giving their information to their bosses that supported their cases to the jurors and judge as the prosecutors at times tries to twist the truth information at hand. As each side looked into all jurors eyes to describe their cases to them, the four law students sat quietly at hand to know without any doubt that they would not win, because they had researched all of the information they had thoroughly with the help of their instructor, as they knew it was a sure win once the jurors retired to their room for their decisions making before they would return with a verdict of guilty or innocent.

It took about fifteen minutes before the jurors returned back to the court room as all the law students sat still with hopes of wining to give shout outs to Sandra knowing if it had not been for her, things would been rough. The two brothers looked toward the law students to say to them, "Guys, we want to thank you for all the hard work you four guys did know this case and we two are hoping for an innocent verdict as you guys are." Once when the jurors came back the judge instructed everyone to have a seat at such time he asked the lead juror if a verdict had been made and asked the head juror to please read the verdict out loud so the court can hear.

The lead juror read the verdict as, "We the jury find the accused individual of all crimes not guilty."

Ther four law students were all in smiles as they looked toward their bosses to say, "We did it this time, as we could not have or would not have won if it was not for Sandra."

Ben, one of the brothers, said to them, :We must take Sandra out to eat at her choice to show her just how so much she is loved by us, not only as a sweet, intelligent young person, but a person who is willing to work for the good of all people to ensure that they are given a fair chance and since we hired her here in our law firm, our legal cases have skyrocketed all because of her teaching you four law students how to go about in presenting your cases to be heard. I am quite sure once you guys have finished with your training here with us, you will return back to school with a more open and broad mind to let your law professors know just how much you have learned by being in this program. You guys have about two more months to go before your time with our firm is finished and my brother and I will have to send in to your professors your working evaluations from us. Please don't worry, as I see it now, there is nothing for the four of you to worry about whether or not we will be fair because we will. I think we will allow Sandra to write your evaluations because she is the one who knows all what you do."

One of the law students said, "Now I think that would be nice because Sandra has been so good in showing each of us just how to put words into prospective and we just have been so privileged to have her."

"I must agree with you because we owe it all to a special friend of our for getting her here to this city as she was not up to coming here in the beginning, but her cousin Delores who is my brother's and my friend made it possible for you guys to shine. Now that we are wining cases, we are so happy because now our law firm has been recognized as the top ten in the city. If it had not been for Sandra we don't think we would have succeeded to this point so we are dedicated to Sandra as we are to Delores, our best friend. At night my brother and I can go home to our families and be at peace not having to worry whether or not we will have any cases of anyone to present to the court to keep our business running. I guess if you believe hard enough and surround yourself with good people to develop a relationship, things can and will work out for the good of any business."

Now, the most prestigious law firm in New York City, has become back to life and it is doing quite well with the thanks of a poor little black girl from Mississippi, who was invited by her first cousin Delores, to come to live with her with possibilities of her getting a good paying job would not have happened. With all honors going to Sandra by the two law attorney brothers, she would not have reached the potential that she has already gained. This was truly a blessing in her hat being so smart to be recognizes by others who at first did not believe this would ever happen, but thanks to a person whom they had become good friends with changed all of that as she convinced them to just hear her out and let her show them just what she was capable of presenting to them by her talent.

It was a good thing that those two brothers decided to meet with Sandra to let her show them how she could help the firm to relive it status again by showing them just how she could teach those four law students on loan from the university how to go about writing cases the correct ways to win instead of losing as that had been the case before. To the two brothers, it was a miracle, but to the four law students, having her on board to work with them was surely what was needed all along because if they had been taught how to write cases with the correct words, instead of just learning how to become lawyers, all those cases they spent time putting together as they thought they were right then the law firm would not have been in such shape it has been. Ben, being the oldest of the other brother, had his reservations about even trying to hire a person whom he knew nothing about, but taking the advice from a good dear friend, he took a chance and now, he can stand up and feel good about himself knowing that he and his brother had made the right decision. There was one thing neither of them knew just yet that in about another year Sandra being home sick would make her plan to leave New York to return back home to Mississippi to obtain the position she had always wanted as she studied for it to be the English teacher she had always vision herself as she would stand in front of her classroom teaching English to students.

While Sandra and Delores sat quietly, Sandra asked Delores, what she was thinking as she all of a sudden stopped talking. "Oh really nothing as I was just thinking about a lot of things about you, Greg, Wayne, and the whole family."

"Exactly what type of things Delores?" she asked.

"Believe me Sandra everything that I was thinking about were so very good until I don't think I would change a thing."

"I know you Delores," Sandra said to her about when she is thinking about something she had a plan. "No not this time my dear cousin because it all on you and when the time comes, you will know. For all that it is worth, I dare not say or tell. Let the two of us just leave it where it stand for now because as times move and you are ready to accept, then you will know. Once you get to that point, you will realizes as you look back over all the times you and I had conversations will know those conversations were geared around what will take place. I don't think I want to know anymore Delores, because to me it seem as if you are trying to hook me up with someone here in this city, as you have already explained to me how slick these guys are here meeting nice young professional girls and use them for their own means and then they drop them like a hot potato."

"No Sandra, because you know that I would not ever want anything of the sort of happen to my little cousin from Mississippi. I am your protector while you are here, and that is just what my uncle and aunt expect of me to look over you and to guide you in the right way as possible since I have the skills of mapping out these guys here. Come tomorrow night since it will be

Friday, why don't you and I hit a few night clubs that way you can see for yourself. Besides, we don't have to work come Saturday so you and I can just dance the night away as so many guys will fill this wonderful club I know."

"Okay," said Sandra. "But I am not promising you anything."

"Neither am I promising you anything, the two of us are going to have a good time as neither one of us ais looking for a relationship at this time you know."

Soon, she and Delores, decided to call it a night to return home to sit up in the rest of the night to talk about all what the two of them experienced being out to this well talked about club. As the two of them arrived home, they started to laugh about their evening to say as they got inside about what dull guys that frequent that club only to see how many young professional ladies they would be able to smooth talk to their liking to get them into their games. Once inside from laughing about those fine guys they had met, they took a seat and said to each other.

"Delores, what about that handsome guy who came over to our table and asked me if I wanted to dance with him to the nice tune being played?"

"Sandra don't you know I did because I knew what he was about or up to because I have seen him here many of times before when I use to come here long before you came and then I peek his whole card of using girls. I knew right away when he came over to ask you if you wanted to dance that he thought he had found a little soft girl who was looking to be blessed through the night. Well, I wasn't worried because although he had never asked me to dance because I think he did know right away that I knew his game so he remained far away from me."

"I am thinking that he didn't realized that you and I were together or I was just someone who you decided to sit with at my table. Well as it stands, he soon found out because in all of his dazzling tries, he was surely let down as you came off the dance floor and he walked back over to his table alone to try another lonely girl."

Sandra said to Delores that she wasn't thinking about getting to know him because she had always been told that when you go out to a club, be ready to meet Mr. Smooth talker because that's what most clubs have to give.

"I know for myself that if you are looking for a relationship to fulfill your every need, you surely will not find it in a night club," Sandra continued on telling Delores.

"While you were in college there in Louisiana Sandra, I am sure you and some of your classmates frequented a few clubs to run into the same situations," her cousin Delores said. H

"ow so true you are in that because not only were their those guys from campus there, also just your regulars guys who constantly hung out in that type of environment to capture young girls heart."

"I can see it now, you being married and Greg being married as well and the two of you will be giving your parents some grandchildren as Uncle Elijah, and Aunt Catherine just enjoying their lives having their grandchildren by their sides now that will be about the best thing they could ever ask for."

"I wonder about you sometimes Delores, if you will ever find that one person who will sweep you off your feet that will surely make your parents happy."

"Who knows Sandra maybe one of these days, I just might stop playing hard to get and untie myself with my job and let my hair down and get buck wild, not the way that you might think off, just enough of my wildness to get a good man's attention."

"You really deserve a good man Delores," Sandra said to her, "because you are a good person and you have so much to give through all of your good qualities."

"Sandra what good qualities are you speaking about? I didn't know that I had any," she said as she laughed to make it sound like a joke.

"Sometimes, we as individuals cannot see our own good qualities as it takes someone else to tell us about them and now, my dear cousin, Delores, I have seen all of your qualities and I am the first one to tell you because I am inside telling you not, standing outside looking in."

When she talked to Wayne he told her, "As my brother Greg tells me as he and I talk just how fast things there have changed and how much I would not recognize how Mississippi has been built up as people of all races are living in the same locations and working together which should have been that way all along, but with the laws of the southern governors with their hate, it would have never been changed if the federal government had not stepped in. Now my sister, it will be possible for you to get that English teaching position in an all-white school because all schools are now as one and you have the choice of which one you want to teach in."

Is Love Worth the Wait?

After having a long conversation with Sandra to hear that things there in New York were going well with her as she continued with her work, he promised himself after he go to visit his parents this weekend, he would just come right on out to tell them that the reason why he had not dated any white girls as they would expect him to was because he had been in love with a black girl all these years and he was hoping to marry her one day soon. He knew from telling them about this, they would surely ask who she was as he felt it was not the time now to let them knew that it had been Sandra all along so he said to them, when the time is right that is if she accept then I will let you know who she is. He was so sure that more so his mother would be shocked rather than his father, because his father had always said to him, "Son, if you decide to go out to find you a nice girl, it wouldn't matter to me who she might be just as long as you and she find comfort in one another and to produce a few grandchildren for your mother and me to spoil." Wayne really didn't think it would matter the least to him, if he finds out that it is Sandra because at least he had known her since she was a child and what a good relationship we had.

Wayne thought, "Mother, on the other hand would probably flip out because to her the Logan family has been all family to the three of us especially when we all shared some wonderful dinners on holidays and other times. I ask myself, would this really be what my mother would expect from me? Then I would come to the realization that it would be what I wanted and my mother would just have to accept my decisions or live the remaining of her life without it. This would definitely not be what I wanted to happen since the two families has so much in common and I hope this decision of mine would not tarnish the built up relationship that Sandra's mother Mrs. Catherine and my own mother had developed for many years. I know if I open up this can of worms, I will have to let each one out one by one slowly so all of them will not come out the same time. This will be a working condition I will have to make sure I fix right so everyone that will be involved will be as happy and joyful as possible. "

"Besides worrying about me, I think my parents as well as Greg's parents will not be so upset once they find out that Greg will bring home the love of his life to meet everyone as he will tell them that he met his future wife while in college and now the two are going to get married. I think once my mother see that this lovely girl that will be marrying Greg is an Indian Cherokee, she will accept all changes. My mother will say to my father that something like this should have happened long ago and we would not have worried so much. I know Greg's parents will not be upset because as I have heard them speak many of times that their past history consists of Native Americans in it as well as some white. I know they will welcome their new daughter-in-law into the family as I am sure they will welcome me as well. I don't think anything difference will change between each of our mothers but I think the friendship between the two of them, will grow stronger. After all, they taught me from the time I was a small boy running around the house playing with Sandra and Greg that we were as one in the sight of god, because he, had made it that way that no color of a person's skin really matter to him."

After Wayne had finished going over things in his mind, it was time for him to get out to his duties because come tomorrow being Saturday, he would drive off to visit his parents for the weekend as well as walk over to the Logans to check on them that is if the two mothers had not planned having a meal together to past the time since neither child would be present. Wayne thought, "When I get there, it will not be the same because my little adopted brother Greg won't be there because he is finishing up his last year of his field of studies at the University of Louisiana, in New Orleans. I can see many changes are coming at a fast pace. Sandra will soon be moving back home because she said that she will submit her resumes to the Board of Education here in Mississippi to be offered a job teaching English in one of the school that has been integrated, preferably one of these high school as far as I know now, Greg too will be coming back to teach chemistry also in one of these white school where all mixture of students will be attending."

"To be fair to say, I have never thought that all the problems that existed here long ago even before the federal government stepped in to make changes were not the students at all, but the problems came amid the adults of the families, thus teaching all their children that it was wrong for other race of students to be in the midst to prevent them from learning what they were supposed to. Now that things have changed and as I see buses filled with all race of students, I feel vindicated as I wished all of this had happened while Sandra Greg and I went off to college that way, we all could gone to the university right here in Mississippi. Since those changes had not been implemented at time, three of us had to do what was best for each of us. Now, when Sandra and I have our children, we will not have to worry about doors being shut into their faces but rather, they will have a choice to go to any college they choose . I use to hear my parents say to me, wait and be of good courage because surely changes would come. At that particular time being a small little boy, I really didn't understand to much of what they were say and surely I never would ask questions about it because I just did not see things that way or I just didn't understand since I was too busy playing."

After Sandra had hung up from taking with Wayne to see how he had been handling so many things there since she and Greg had left, she could not help but feel a sense of the release that had been bothering her from the time she departed there concerning Wayne as to why he was so lonely. Sandra said to Delores how her mind is now at peace after speaking to Wayne to hear that he is doing alright and he had accepted the fact that Greg is not there to help him through his trials. "I was really worried there for a long time because I just didn't know how much he would be able to stand and for how long because he did not have any friends there whom he could relate to."

Delores opened up to say to her, "Girl, why are you so worried about that skinny white boy, because if he wanted too, he could find someone to be his friend. Besides, you and Greg have your own lives to worry about, not his."

"You see Delores," Sandra responded to say. "I knew you would react that way that's why I was a little hesitant to say anything to you about him."

For the time remaining for Sandra to live in New York, Delores was sure not to mention anything else about Wayne becoming Sandra's husband just to wait until it take place as it was sure to happen. Delores, has been having these weird dreams and when she awake, all she could see in her visions the two of them standing before a minister reciting their vows for life. Delores kept saying it over and over in her mind that there will definitely be a white skinny boy as her Uncle Elijah and Auntie Catherine's son-in-law. "I have seen it and I know it is going to happen maybe not as soon as Sandra return, but in the near future as she get settled, it will come true. Once this does happen and Sandra decides to tell me about their her wedding then I will open up to let my cat out of his bag to say, I knew you would marry him because it was in my mind and it would not let me be. When it take place then Wayne would not be that skinny white boy to me any longer. I think he is a good guy because he has not dated anyone since Sandra has been gone.

As I continue to support my cousin, I will definitely keep her interest of my best in my heart as she will soon walk out of my life and leaving me here all alone in New York to carry on with my life as I was doing before she came. If anyone one of those brother attorneys ask me anything about why I didn't encourage Sandra to remain here, all I will say to them is that I tried to but her mind was so set on returning back home to obtain what she had always wanted to do and that was to become one of the best there ever had been there in the English department of teaching students."

The two brothers then assured Delores that there would not be any doubts in their minds that she will not be one of the greatest because just look what accomplishments she had made with them while she been working. "We will have to say, we could not have done it nor would our law firm would have gained the attention as it has if it had not been for her being able to do what she did with the four assigned law students in working with them in helping them to write cases correctly. Even the judges would often ask the two of us who did we have preparing these cases for us? With all of this given to us, we are so grateful to her after watching her take complete control over the four law students on loan from the university to write and prepare all of our cases to go to court with, being lost many of times. The reasons why are because the contents of the cases were not written properly until Sandra decided to teach the four of them right ways in heading up their cases. After watching her and seeing all the correct phrases to be used caused our cases to be won in court as the judges found that whoever did the research on those cases should be congratulated because since they had been maintaining the court bench, there has only been a few cases they came across had been written in the right contents. One of the judges had indicated to us so many times about the ways our cases presented themselves appeared to have been the work of a very smart individual who have been taught by some wonderful professors or someone with great understandings. Of course my brother and I dare not let on to tell them who had come all the way from the state of Mississippi, who had learned all he could from one of the best black university there in Louisiana just as the top one in the state of New Orleans."

"I guess things back there in Mississippi were so bad until all the smart ones make way to other states where they can be utilized from what they had learned. It is too bad and it is really sad that such states down there in the south has that feeling about a race of people who are a different complexion who have so much to give that could make all of the growth there so much better. All we can say is this much, it is our gain and it was their loss because although they did not honor her back there in her state, she came to us in our state to honor us with her smarts. Ben and I just hope that she will forever remain here and maybe one day she will decide to become a lawyer to join our firm, the firm that she help to succeed." Since the two brothers were saying so many nice things about Sandra Delores dare not tell them that she had planned to depart from being in New York come next year to return back home to the state of Mississippi, because she felt a need too because that is where she wanted to be as she has always knew that she would be such a good mentor to so many students in teaching them English.

As things continued to swell back there in the grand old Mississippi, Wayne with his determination to one day marry Sandra had arranged a calendar to be placed on his refrigerator to mark off each day that would be getting closer to the return of Sandra coming home from as he viewed as a very long vacation she was so well to have after graduation from college to now come home with great enthusiasm to tell everyone about all the things she entrusted herself too while in the great city of New York. Wayne was quite sure she would have a lot to speak about as she will be sitting in the company of his parents as well as hers. One good thing about coming home was she would be here to celebrate her brother's graduation from college where he would be just in time to reap all the benefits that has been afforded to not only him, but to all races of young minded individuals by the federal government new drawn up laws to support every person.

Each new morning as Wayne awakened he would rush to his calendar to mark off a day that would bring him closer to his hoped would be his future wife return home to be with him forever. He knows that this would definitely be a well thought about big decision he will have to sell to her and hope her acceptance would be a positive answer. Each new day as he prepared for his work with the agriculture department in working with farmers, his mind was stayed mostly on Sandra than on his work although he did complete his tasks each day that were pleasing to his boss, but thinking of her probably did make him work more diligently more. Each night as Wayne would sit in his living room watching television, he would come up with many ideas on ways he could and would make Sandra happy by first finding a house for them that would definitely suit her every need to raise their children. With the two of their incomes, it would easily avail them to meet all of their expenses right off the start as she would be holding down a teaching position and he, as an agent for the department of agriculture. He thought about buying a nice home outside from where their parents live to be free of a lot of company from both parents only to come over maybe some weekends.

Of course this he would leave up to Sandra to decide, since he would have all of the others things to handle such as maintaining the lawn, and all other things that would definitely make their home a pleasure to see and to enjoy. Wayne wanted everything so fitting to Sandra's needs and he would go out of his way to make sure those things he wanted for her would be at her beck and call. "By the time me and Sandra would have married and started off with their lives, her little brother, as my big brother would too have gotten married and landed a good paying science teaching position as his wife too will obtain so they too, would do the same thing as Sandra and I, but the only thing I would see about it is this: I know Sandra would not want her brother and his wife living to close to she and I because they would always be presence in our atmosphere and the two of us would not have any spare time to ourselves to live according to the vows we made when we said yes we do. It would not be that Sandra nor I would want them to be close by, it will just be as we would see it that seeing too much of them would put a dent in both relationships."

Each day as Wayne would come home, he would walk up to his calendar to say, another day has gone by and the time for my beloved future wife will be soon coming home to be with me to be happy. "Maybe as we were growing up and things were not available then as they are now was somehow a blessings from the skies because it is a possibility this feeling I developed from playing with Sandra and her brother, Greg would never had happen. The time as I see it now and understand that a lot of changes had to be made by someone that is higher than anything here on this earth. We just had to wait and remain good to our needs because those things would soon be coming down the pipe and now look, changes has turned all dark things around to be opened up to all walks of life where all people could have the fruits of life and be able to live to marry to whomever they wanted too. Now, once Sandra and I and even Greg and his future Indian wife decide to get married then we will be able to walk hand in hand down the streets in the city to be as one not to be looked upon by all those old closed minded white people.

"I know in time as my parents as well as her parents get use to the ideal of our marriage, everything will work out just well and we will be a bundle of joys to the family members as well as others all around. I expect just a few years there will be mixed marriages in every section of the state of Mississippi, enjoying the life of perfect setting and none will have to worry about whether eyes are looking or not. As Wayne continued to wonder about all the things that will soon be taking place right there in his neighborhood, he also was wondering what Sandra was doing there in New York. Whatever she is up too, I know she is happy, but not as happy as she will soon be here with me."

"Hurry up time and move faster to Sandra time of returning back home here so she will hear what I have to tell her that will change her mind for good in a positive manner. I must repair myself about what just might come, but knowing her the way that I do and the years I have known her, I think her answer will be good at least for the first spoken words after she finally come to understand all of these years, she was the one and the whole time she being there in New York, not wanting to get involved with anyone for a serious relationship, it was I who she had blocked out of her mind to make herself get heavy involved with her work to take her mind off having an affair. I am quite sure that her first cousin Delores had spoken to her many of times about me as I know that I was not one of Delores' favorite people because she thought that I was trying to get next to Sandra. Of course I have always known that Delores, did not accept me because the three of us grew up together and she just could not understand why she and Greg even wasted their time playing around with me when we were young living in the midst of each other and Delores just could not understand why her Uncle Elijah and Auntie Catherine would always invite me and my parents over to their home for dinner at so many times."

"In so many ways, I can understand how Delores, did feel because she being much older than Sandra had to go off to New York to seek work after she had finished her college career because here in Mississippi she was refused any type position because the city hate planners felt as if she did not have the knowledge to work in any establishment there because her color was not suitable for the white public if they walked into an office to see her seating there.

I guess her treatments then has grown cold inside of her and she somehow took it out on me. I think if Delores, would just sit down to talk with me and understand just how I too feel about how she was mistreated then she would grow to like me and she would understand that her uncle and aunt had built a bond with my parents, by living across the street from each other attending to their lands and their two children and I developed a closeness by playing together as children.

I am truly convinced once Delores finally realizes that I am in love with her cousin Sandra she would have many changes about things to see that there are some good understanding white people in this world. Only those hateful few who refuse to let go to let things progress the way they should go that will help to make things much easy for everyone one. Who knows, maybe Delores will want to be a part of our wedding as the time get near and she will be able to give Sandra a few encouraging words to live by since she will be the wife of that skinny white boy, as she always related to me as. I can see it now, just what a big happy family all of us will be and when we start to have our children, life will surely light up the world because as people look upon Sandra and my children, they will not see those old days gone by. By Delores being up there in New York, she herself just might fall in love with an Italian, a Jewish, a white, or even a Spanish guy, other than a black guy to marry."

"You old devil you," Greg said to him. "Because I knew you had a secret girlfriend there in your location that you had meet just waiting to surprise all of us. What is her name? Come on Wayne you owe your brother that much now."

"If I told you then you will know and it will no longer be a secret would it now? No my dear little brother, I think I will continue to be in secret until I think you will be able to handle it." With all of Wayne talking about his secret love Greg still did not figure it out that he was speaking about his dear sister Sandra.

Wayne said to himself, "If Greg finds out this just might send him into a shock knowing we grew up together." Wayne hurried up to get off the subject about his love affair to ask Greg, "When have you decided to get married?"

"Well, I truly can say it will not be until a year after she and I have graduated and have gotten into a working status so we will be able to afford a nice little home."

"I know your parents will be so proud of you to have a daughter-in-law."

Greg said to Wayne, "Not only will my parents be happy to have a daughter-in-law, but your parents will as well."

"Now my big brother, the only thing that will be left for you and I to do is to make sure our sister Sandra find herself a good guy to marry; also that way ther three of us who grew up together and played together reap the benefits of life by becoming three married people. You know," Greg said to Wayne. "Maybe the three of us could buys homes in the same location and live close by one another. Wouldn't that be grand ?"

"I must agree my little brother, it would be grand but I don't know if Sandra would like that, knowing how she is. I don't think she will have any problems with your wife or even my wife just as long as we are in the presence of each other. I am looking so forward to my graduation so we can get our lives started."

After Wayne had finished speaking with Greg and hung up the phone, he said to himself, "Something has got to give or else my whole life will be blown out of proportion. I think just before Sandra gets ready to make her move back here from New York, I should tell her so she will not be caught blindsided by news she was not expecting to hear. I hope in my heart that once I tell her she will walk away to be alone by herself to take everything in."

Greg, Sandra's little brother, on the other hand after sharing things with Wayne has decided to not make a big fuss over the girl he had gotten involved with while in college by letting everyone right up front to know who she is and why he wanted to marry her. Greg had already spoken to his parents about the possibility that once he had graduated, he and his beloved first time ever girlfriend Sadie, plan to become husband and wife in about a year after the two of them have graduated and are gainful employed within the new establishment, he wanting to obtain a science teaching job and Sadie, hoping to endure a position as a mathematics teacher to save enough money so when they decide on a date, they will have enough saved without asking either of their parents for help. Greg had said over and over time after time that he think that he would be married long before his sister Sandra because she is somewhat particular about guys she meet as they just might not be up to par for her after she had spent a lot of quality time in New York, and she had learned all the ins and outs about guys with a little help from our cousin Delores.

Being already engaged was something new for Greg because he had hoped that it would be a long time before he would even think about getting involved, but being in the midst of so many beautiful young inspiring bright minded women there at the university there in Louisiana, his wondering eyes fell on Sadie to learn that she was from Mississippi, as well as he and when the two got together to talk, they both found out that they had a lot of the same interests. This as Greg tells it started the ball rolling and soon it would lead to something else that would be most worthwhile to their growing relationship. Greg was not sure at first since this was he and Sadie's last year there at the university, if he should wait before he would ask her if she wouldn't mind one day becoming as one by being his wife. Since neither one of them had ever talked about getting married as he was so sure that Sadie, had planned to return back home to make a lot of changes there within her own family now, she would be the family first time college graduate.

Once Greg had decided to build up enough nerve to walk up to her to say, "Sadie, I am wondering if you and I cannot become engaged right now before we leave from here so when we return back home, we can let everyone know that although we came to do what we set out to do now, you and I have grown to become think we are ready to take the next step in becoming as one."

He hopes when this does happen, Sadie will say to him, "Greg I thought you would never ask me because as you and I were in college, you just don't know how my heart yarned for you to ask me to be your wife one day because I think you are one of the finest young men that I have ever met. You and I have found out as we talked that there are so much we have in common."

Of course, this would put a damper in Greg's throat but he soon will get over it and come to accept how things can and will change. By Wayne becoming the husband of his sister, there would be nothing changing because it will bring a closer relationship for both sides, his family as well as my family. Greg knows getting use to calling Wayne his brother in law and not his big brother, will take sometimes getting used to it, but after a while, things will mellow out. Wayne getting marrying just might be the blessings from the stars in the skies because I will become an uncle to their children one day as his wife will become an aunt to Sadie, and my children as well and the two families will have plenty to keep them busy. After a few years this once old hateful place will not be the same with all new growth and new changes to become something that never existed before because of hate.

As Greg walked around on campus alone to flush out a lot of things going through his mind about his marriage he was wondering how all of this new would set with his parents once he tell them. "I also am wondering how Wayne's marriage would also fair with his parents. You know I finally figured out what Wayne has been telling me through all of our conversations on the reasons why he never found any of those white girls interesting to him because he had always been in love with my sister and now, I know he is waiting for her to come home. This secret will just be mine not to say anything about it because I don't want to rock his boat of surprises. I know my sister doesn't know anything about his plans and I am sure not going to expose him, but let him be the one to decide on how to handle his plans. As bad as I want to call out to Sandra to warn her, it would not be the right thing for me to do before Wayne decides to make his move. Of course, I won't to tell Mother and Daddy all about what I know as I dare not spoil anything that my adopted white brother had hidden all of these years."

"Sandra my dear sister, you are in for a waking because if you have never been surprised before, you are about to be soon once you return back home to gain the position you have worked so hard in college to obtain one day. That little skinny white boy as our first cousin Delores has always related to will be asking for your hand in marriage and I don't know how you might feel but for me, I will sort of be glad because at least you and I know him and we know just how much things has really changed here in this once hated state. Besides, my dear sister, I think he will be a good husband for you as he has really planned for the two of your future. I don't have a problem by him being the complexion he is because he didn't have a thing to do with that part. All you need to know about him as you already do know that he, does not look upon the color of a person's complexion, but he look into the heart of goodness. Although Wayne is a white guy, my soon to be wife is Indian, with a fair complexion too. My heart wants to reach out to tell Sandra all about it, but my mind says do not let the cat out of the bag."

"When Wayne and I speak over the phone as we often do, I will make sure I will not let on to him that I have already figured him out as he left his front door wide opened and I just walked right on in to see through him. If I didn't know any better, I would say that he did it this way hoping that I would figure it out knowing that he was in love with her and he wanted to marry he. I think he is testing me to see if I knew how he felt about Sandra. If he doesn't know, I will never speak of this to Sandra his parents or even my parents, because I think if I did, it just might put him in a scary position to be around afraid that his parents as well as mine would say to him now Wayne you know what you are doing is just not right because you grew up with one another and you did a lot together so we see you as a son, as his parents would say to Sandra you know how much Samuel and I adore you as our daughter and why would you and Wayne want to violate all what we have built up? Of course Sandra would tell them that all of this was a shocker to her once she returned back from New York to be confronted by Wayne with this news. How do you think I felt when he sat down with me to tell me?"

Many times once Sandra had returned back home to learn of it, she would be on the phone calling to her cousin Delores to ask her all of her opinions on what she should do. Of course Delores, being that strong headed black woman who had not let go of all that he came up in as she was forced to move away to New York to gain her popularity, she would say, "Girlfriend, let your own mind be your guide and if you think that he is the one then go for it besides, you cares about the color of an individual is this day and time because things are changing fast and he just might be a good husband for you."

Sandra would say to Delores, "Do you think so my dear cousin?"

"For you, yes I think so for me, no way Jose. Sandra you have made lots of strives in your short time of life and you have done those things with so much pride. Now that you have been confronted with your childhood sweetheart, I will not stand in your way for getting what is good for you."

Once Sandra come up against this, she just might accept his proposal and give it a try. These are all things that will surely be discussed by Sandra, her brother, and both of their parents. Greg thought, "There is still time to rectify the whole situation by Wayne if he would change his mind, as I know being his little brother, he will not do that because he want what he want and that is my sister. I have realized that if a person see something that has taken over his mind and he or she knows just how much their lives can be there is nothing anyone can do to change the way they feel. There is one thing I have learned as I have fallen in love with Sadie, the girl of my dream, you can't change any thoughts that had been transformed into your mind you know will see you through all conflicts and trials to walk through with the one you love. If Wayne is going to make my sister happy and give her all she needs, then I say, 'You go boy,' because she is yours."

Since everything that had been in the mind of Sandra's brother Greg will soon become a thing of the past once Wayne has come to his right frame of mind to let the cat out off the bag as he had been holding tightly together not allowing anyone to give it a second thought of what all he had been feeling about this beautiful black intelligent girl, who he grew up with alongside her brother Greg to finally let his parents as well as Sandra parents and brother to know just how much he had always loved her, and now much he wants to marry her to have a complete life where he and she could become parents to their children where each side would be please having grandchildren to look upon, not because of their mixed colors, but the grandchildren they had always wanted to share time with as grandparents. In the meantime, Wayne had prepared himself for the return of Sandra back home to Mississippi, as she had told him as they had long talks over the phone that she should be leaving New York in the next year, just before the new school year start up so she would be able to gain a teaching position. Of course this had excited Wayne so much until he just did not know what to do. At his work, he was just so over joyful until his coworkers would ask him what had come over him because since he had been working there in the agency with them, no one had ever seen him so full of spirits.

While Wayne was dealing with his promises of a good life for his soon to be wife, he hoped Sandra she was busy back there in New York, preparing to clear up all of her tasks there she had created to be given a great going away surprised party by the law firm that she help to save and to build up to become one of New York, outstanding law firm to be named the top one in the state of New York. All of this was because of a single smart black girl who graduated from the university of Louisiana, maintaining all A's in all of her subjects while there to be discovered in a city where she had never even once visited if it was not for her cousin Dolores, who had been affiliated with a big banking branch there for many years once she left from Mississippi to find her dream there as, she did and once Sandra had graduated from college, Delores invited her to come to New York to live with her for a while to obtain a good paying job to see if she would like it enough to remain there for years to come. It all sounded good to Sandra, but her mind was on being the English teacher she had gone off to college to become right there in Mississippi to teach the students English in one of those high school there as it did not matter whether it was a white school or a black school, but to give her the upper mobilities she knew she was worthy of, she rather teach in an all-white school to get the students to see that it doesn't matter if the teacher was black or white just as long as they were being taught.

The next year there in New York City was a very hard year for Sandra because as it got closer as her time to depart to return home, her two bosses continued to offer her more money to remain with them to continue to help their law firm to grow even bigger with a sure possibility that other branches could be opened up in other states under their name to employ other fresh lawyers coming out of law school to get a start in life. Sandra did know if she did accept their offer then she would be on the road most of her time to look over all the daily activities to teach them how they better could enhance their daily activities. This would be too much for her to handle and if she did accept then it would take her mind off what she had always wanted to be an English teacher.

Sandra said to Delores, "Please don't take it the wrong way about all of this that is happening to me so fast but I just wanted to get your opinion."

"Sandra since you have been here with me and I do mean, it has been wonderful to have my dear cousin here in my presence where we have grown together, I knew all along that you had not been that happy because your mind was back there in Mississippi to be close to your parents and brother Greg. Sandra you must know that once you return back to Mississippi, things are not going to be the way you left them because Greg will be soon graduating from college and who knows, he just might marry some nice little girl he met while in college and he will not be living with my uncle Elijah, and aunt Catherine. You will find yourself all alone there with them until you decide to meet a nice young guy to fall in love with to move out on your own as his wife as you dive head heel over in love with your teaching."

"I do know one thing that's for sure that little skinny white boy Wayne will be around peeping at you if you don't know it Sandra."

"Delores, why do you keep saying that about Wayne as I have said to you many of times that he is Greg and my adopted brother."

"Oh yeah, keep telling that to me because deep down in my heart and soul, I can feel something otherwise. You know all the time that you have been living here in New York, I heard it from Greg that he has not even dated a single girl the whole time that you have moved. Now you tell me this my dear cousin Sandra what does that tell you? I know for a fact that he is in love with you and has always been. Couldn't you see anything that was not as it should have been each time you were in his presence?"

"Delores," Sandra said to her. "What has given you this indication that Wayne who has been a brother to Greg and I for all these years have now come to the point in his life that he is involved with me?"

"Why Sandra it does not take a cow to eat all the grass in the field to know his stomach has been filled and this is what has happened to Wayne in my opinion that his stomach has been overrun with the love he has for you since your absence in his presence. I know for a fact that he is madly in love with this little girl who has grown up to become a wonderful lady as he has taken a look in the directions that she is the one he wants to marry as you have stolen his heart from day one although, you never looked at this situation that way. Sandra the truth of the matter is, this skinny white boy has fallen in love with you and there is nothing that anyone can do about it because when love hits you whether he is black or white, there is nothing that anyone can do to change love feelings. Cousin Sandra I bet you once you return home from New York, he will be there to do all the things that will be right with him to open up his arms to welcome you back as his face will be filled with a shining light of joy, once you see his actions of the joy on his face, you might understand all what I have been telling you about that skinny white boy about being in love with you."

"Delores, I wish you would stop calling him that name skinny white boy because whether you know it or not, my brother Greg and I have never looked at him in that context because we three grew up together and color was never a part of our up bringing."

"Of course Sandra you won't have that problem because you had been lucky because of your parents and Wayne's parents were the best of friends and he was taught nothing about racism, as the three of you guys grew up to see the big picture of color was not an important thing to succeed in life, but to live together in harmony where you and I both know that it has not yet gotten to that point. Just think, whenever I decide to visit home there in Mississippi, I will always find it worthwhile to visit you and your beloved white husband Wayne to see just how the two of you are accepting life as a bowl of milk and dark cream," she said as she smiled.

"Now Delores, I never expected to hear that sort of thing coming out of your mouth but then too, I should not be surprised because I have known how you have felt about Wayne since the first time meeting him. I would have hoped that since we are cousins and we have a lot in common, you would have grown to accept him as one of the family member. Oh no my cousin, I don't think I could ever do that and surely, I couldn't ever bring myself to find love for him in my heart. Maybe I would try too if the two of you are married and I have to let bygones be bygones if I wanted to continue to have a family relationship with you. I know in my heart that it would be a hard thing for me to do because whether or not things has begun to make a change there in Mississippi, I still just cannot get over the wrongness people of colors were treated for so many years and now, since the federal government has decided to step in to do something about the ways people have been treated there because of the pressure being placed on the justice department by the organization of the civil rights division, they are now beginning to act as if they have been truthful to everyone soul through all these years to try to right all the wrongs that were carried out. I understand that I cannot blame the young whites for the things being carried out because they were just like you and me, children and they had no authorities to change because their parents keep them thinking they were the better of all races but now, those little children finally awakened to come to the realization to realize that all those things being done were wrong to human kind."

"Sandra it is good to see and to know that they are trying to make this a better world for everyone to live in if this means, they have overthrown their parents teaching to make them believe that they were better than anyone on this earth and they had a creed to keep by maintaining their white race to make sure no other race would penetrate to mix it up, but that will not be happening because their white lilies daughters and their white perfect sons have decided that they must try the grass on the other side of the tracks to see, as they have started too. Sandra I see you and Wayne will produce some wonderfully skin toned children because it has been spoken many of times that a mixed soup with so many ingredients is better anytime than just plain soup with no spices. I am making myself happy for you Sandra because I know this is going to take place and when it does, please know that in spite of how I feel about that skinny white boy, oh let me change that saying, how I feel toward Wayne, I will be happy for you and I will try to embrace him only because of you my dear cousin."

"Well Delores, what can I say, because you have put it all into your own perspectives of how you feel and for that, I can appreciate you much more than ever. I guess now, it is left up to me if this does happen once I return home to take my stand but I don't think so because if all what you have said is true then why haven't my little brother Greg has not informed me?"

"Well Sandra you know how Greg and Wayne are as so called brothers in keeping secrets from us females to let us know exactly what they want us to know and with this turn of events, there is no way that Greg is going to tell you anything where he himself is not sure off. Delores, have you and Greg been in secret communications together behind my back discussing something that should have been told to me by my brother?"

"No Sandra I can assure you that Greg and I have not been secretly calling one another. I suppose Greg feels just as I do, thinking there is something going on with Wayne but he has not put it all together yet. By the way, you do know my little cousin, your brother Greg has met and fallen in love with this girl he says will be his wife one day once he graduate from college next year."

"Now that, Delores, I did not know because when I speak to Greg he doesn't tell me a thing about his personal life there on campus, but only to let me know that he is doing great in all of his subjects and soon hopes to graduate to start his off his career in the school system. Never once he mentioned anything about a girlfriend until now."

"What is her name since the two of you hold secrets?"

"Her name my dear cousin Sandra is Sadie, and she is right there from the same area at a distant location. Just like Wayne your husband to be and she is a mixture of the color of Indian and Asian descent. I bet she is a pretty thing because my brother Greg only likes beautiful girls with a lot on the ball as far as smarts Sandra related to Delores."

"My, my, it looks as if I am going to have some wonderful mixed little second cousins running around everywhere," Delores said. "I will soon be able to say that that old south has taken a turn for the best and all that old kept secrets in the closets has finally broke out and is now filling the whole world as it was intended to be with great minds of mixed generations."

"Delores, where do you see yourself in the next few years because you do know that you are not getting any younger and you have broken all barriers by holding a key position in a major city with one of the world's largest bank? You know, you have talked against all white people, but take a look at who you are involved with each day and look to see how you have made things possible for them to borrow funds under your control as most of them are white business men, as you followed all policies and procedures to let their loans be approved to further their business. You even became good friend to two of the now prominent lawyers because you thought by introducing me to them would expand their law practice, which it did. They were your two best white friends and you didn't make any exceptions to the rule."

"Sandra I had a job to do and it didn't matter to me what color they were just as long as I carried out what I was supposed to be doing for my corporate headquarters. I am not in love with them, just on a friendly business relationship. If you think that I am going to roll over and marry one of these white guys here in New York, you are sadly mistaken my cousin."

"Do you think that you will ever meet that one person who will make you happy to maybe one day want to marry?"

"It is a possibility as I have told you about the history of my past relationships with these guys. I am a successful black female woman who migrated here from the state of that racial state of Mississippi to make a name for myself which I have shown and now, if I don't marry, I can say I will be alright. It is not about whether or not I will marry, but the light is on you because there is someone who is back there in good ole Mississippi that really love you and awaits patiently for your return to drop his bomb upon your mind, heart, and soul."

The year has passed by so fast until all she could think about was her little brother Greg was about to graduate from college and she did know from him that he had met a nice girl while on campus, attending school there and fell in love with her to hope one day she will marry him, because she was not only a mixed person, but she had a good heart and she held from the same location as he, just a few miles living apart. Of course, their cousin Delores knew all about that situation and she did not have a lot to speak on to the race of this young girl because she was close to being in the minority and she was quite sure she too had come up against the same closed doors and she had while living there in Mississippi, before relocating to the big city of New York for a better life and more respect for being looked upon on her ability to perform a job and not on the color of her skin. While Delores was busy pondering over whether or not her cousin Sandra would one day wind up in the arms of the skinny white boy, she has always made notice too Wayne as she felt she did not trust him or any white person because of all the past history, Sandra was busy rearranging her priorities to prepare herself to soon depart from New York to return back home to Mississippi.

For the time being Sandra was not even thinking about whether or not Wayne had a thing for her because her only desire at the time was to get her application out there so the board of teachers hiring would take a look at her accomplishments to see that she is well qualified to gain a teaching position there in one of the high school English class room that awaits for qualified English major, Sandra was feeling good because she had the feeling that she would be called upon by the Board of Education to offer her a job to teach English as she had always wanted. Sandra said to herself as she was about to send forth her resumes back to the state of Mississippi that she would soon hear to be offered a position there to put her on top of the world as this will surely make her parents happy to have her coming home to be in their presence as well. Of course Sandra would be living with her parents until she decided that it was time for her to move out on her own to allow her baby brother Greg to take up residence there until he is fully and gainfully employed.

Not only would they miss from seeing Sandra, but Delores, one of their best friends who was responsible for introducing Sandra to them, would be missed because they would not be seeing her as much because of the growth of their law firms as they had opened up others firms in their name to employ new out of school lawyers to handle other matters. The two brothers can truly give all of their financial status to Delores and to Sandra because it started with Delores being a good friend in the banking funding business to help them to survive as they were about to go under before she mentioned to them that she had someone who just might be able to keep them a float, if they cared to meet her. One of the brothers said to her, "How wrong can it be to hopefully have a person with smarts to come aboard to help us to rearrange what we have been doing in all the wrong ways that has not helped this firm to grow." The two brothers gave Delores, their go ahead to see if she would be able to help them out to turn their law firm around as it was established by their father and it needed to remain as a family business.

Once Sandra returns back home that will be a happy time in her life because she will be feeling nothing but joy in her life to know that just maybe it was all in the plan not to allow her any employment there once she had graduated in order to allow her to go off to some other place to gain experience to return in back in full force to show the state that she loved so much to be recognized by someone that was not affiliated at all with the laws of Mississippi to take in one of their citizen who had good qualities to come on board with them to show what the well talked about citizens from the south had to offer a big city who had all the possibilities to fit into their society, as the city power to be took a look into the intelligence of this little southern girl to see just how smart a southern university had turned out, they had no choice but to let her exercise her rights to her own authorities so the ones here in the city had always thought they were above southern students got a shock of their lives.

After the great showing that Sandra had produced, there would be no doubts in the minds of these city students that they could surpass what the southern students were being taught. Not only will Delores be sad to see her cousin leave, but so will all others here in the city of New York will also be missing her as well. Sandra kept saying over and over in her mind that she had only just a few more months left for her to enjoy New York and then it would be time for her to catch that train for the long ride back to dear old Mississippi to which she came to regain her voided space there in her family home where her mother, Catherine, let her bedroom remain the same as she would always talk with Wayne's mother Florence about how good it would feel to have her only daughter back home living again. As Sandra would call to talk with her parents, she would always say to them, "Hey guys you know my time is getting short here in New York, and I will soon be coming home. Once I hear from the Board of Education there about giving me a teaching position, I will be packing up to prepare to make that move back to my stomping grounds. Of course this made her parents happy to hear as they were hoping for the Board of Education to hurry up to make a quick decision.

Is Love Worth the Wait?

Greg being the overprotective brother as he had been over his only sister, once he got wind of a possibility that Sandra would be coming back home to live for good, he said he better call Wayne their adopted brother to let him know of Sandra's intentions. As he waited until Wayne had gotten home from work so he would be sitting down relaxing to accept the good news. Greg thought since the three of them have been brother and sister through all the years, there was nothing he thought about otherwise to think anything that could have been in the mind of Wayne about his sister as he had before he left to attend college. The idea he once had with a possibility of Wayne could be in love with his sister just flew away from his mind and now, since he had grown up and about to be on his own as well as Wayne having moved away from his parents' home and is now on his own, Greg had no idea that Wayne will get up his nerve to ask his sister Sandra to marry him, but as Greg was telling Wayne all about Sandra moving back home soon, Wayne was trying to figure how just how he would break his new to his parents as well to Sandra's parents as well in person. He was sure there would be a lot of misunderstanding, but he hoped that regardless of how they might say, they just don't know how this could have happened because they had no way of seeing this coming because the friendship between to two families had been nothing but families.

As Greg and Wayne continued to talk, thoughts were moving fast in the mind of Wayne asking him just how was he going to handle this situation that he had kept hidden from everyone through all these years in darkness which at times his own parents asked him many of times why he wasn't dating any girls. The only answer he would give them to ease their minds would be, "In time when I think I have found the right one," but he know he didn't need to look because she had been there in his sight all along, as he grew up together with she and her brother. Wayne had finally made up in his mind to let them know when Sandra return back home from New York that way, they can stop asking him about his dating crisis.

Since Wayne has been tormented by his parents as well as his best friend, brother Greg he had made up in his mind that come the weekend, when he is due to visit his parents to have dinner with them he, had decided that it was about time that he stop hiding himself in darkness about his dating decisions and open up and let his long stayed cat out of his bag once and for all to see just how they would handle it. Wayne said to himself that he was tired of hiding the truth from everyone and he hope after telling them the way he has felt about Sandra all these years would put an end to things and everyone will be able to move forward. He knew that his parents just might accept it and come to grip with it, but after he let Sandra's parents and brother know, will they accept it, after all these years they have treated him as one of their own. Wayne had a lot on his plate to deal with come this weekend as he has gotten himself brave enough to finally let his dating situation be known.

Wayne should ask Sandra, "Now that you know and you know that your cousin Delores was right, how do you feel about what I have told you?"

Sandra would say as he was so sure of it to say, "I just don't know because not only am I coming home to accept a job offered to me by the education board to teach English in one of these high school that has now been mixed to hear this news has just blown my mind. It is something I will have to think hard and long on because I make any decisions." Of course, in the midst of Wayne's night of sleep were these ideas running through his mind not yet been told to Sandra nor the others just that he was thinking about how this thing would pan out. Sandra was still in New York making her decision as to when she will leave New York, and there were a lot of things she would have to clear up there before she would hand her keys over to the two law brothers, who would definitely miss her once she greet them with her final goodbyes. Sandra would definitely miss her cousin Delores because she had been such inspiration in her life and she had taught her so much, as she learned so much.

Wayne's decision to open up was a big hurdle in his life to deal with as he was hoping to come out on top of it all as Sandra would not turn him down, but agree to allow him to become a part of her life once she had accepted his proposal to marry him one day. He knows that the first thing Sandra would have to do is speak about all of this surprise between her parents, as well as Wayne's parents to get their catch on all of this. Wayne news of having been in love with his adopted black sister would surely travel far and near in and around the neighborhood among relatives and just friends. There was one thing for sure that he was not too sure of and that was would his co-workers, once they found out, continue to accept him as one of them as they didn't believe in mixed marriage or would they just shun him to the point that he would probably quit his job he held there in the agriculture department, as he had impressed his boss?

Is Love Worth the Wait?

Talking about a piece of candy that would be hard to get rid of, this would be it to see just how much all those individuals he had been working with, take his decision to get married to a black girl in strive and congratulate him. All of these thoughts were in Wayne's mind and they were running everywhere hoping the best would come out of them. Wayne had made up in his mind to make a call to Sandra in New York to check on her to see just how she was doing without giving her any indication as to why he called other that speaking with his adopted sister. Of course, he would ask her if and when she had planned to say goodbye to that big city to come home, without alerting her of any other thing he wanted to tell her. Wayne was trying to be very careful not to rock the boat not just yet as he was a little hesitant in calling Greg to tell him because with this sort of thing, he knew that Greg would waste no time in calling Sandra to ask her if she knew anything about Wayne wanting to marry? Wayne said to himself that he could not afford not at this time to let Greg know because he wanted to break the news to Sandra once she arrive home from New York. There would be one thing for sure once he call Sandra to find out exactly when will the time frame be for her to come on in so he could meet her at the train station.

Wayne thinking all through the night as he slept about all of the things he would be telling Sandra if and when he would meet her at the train station if she so make it a desire of hers for him to do so had not given all other things an even thought to just how ell all of this excitement would blow over with Sandra and even with her brother Greg as her parents and his parents as well, before any of this would become concrete to their needs. Mayne this certain shock would be something that cannot be handle by everyone, but with Wayne's way of thinking he was sure it would soon pass over and at any given moment, it all would seem as if it never existed, but to await from a deep dream he was having. It was a hard night for Wayne to fall off into a deep sleep from thinking so much about Sandra so he got up out of his bed as it was being late, but he just could not wait to call her the next night so he decided it was time for him to make his move now so he dialed her up to hear her voice as she said, "Hello."

Wayne said to her, "Sandra I know it is late there in New York, because of the time zone but I just had to hear your voice to see how you were doing."

"Wayne what has gotten into you calling me at this time of the night?" Sandra asked.

"Well, you did tell me that I could call you up at any time you know when you left from here."

"I know I did Wayne but I am sure you realized that I didn't mean for you to call me in the late part of the night to disturb me from my sleep."

"I am so sorry to have awakened you but I just had you on my mind and I thought since I was not able to sleep, I would give you a quick shout out."

"Now that you have called and gotten my attention Wayne how are things going there with you at work and with your parents?" Sandra asked him.

"As far as I know about my work, everything seems to be going well as I just received a raise giving me more money to prepare myself for what is to come my way I hope soon."

"What is it that you are trying to prepare yourself for one day Wayne?" she asked.

"I don't want to spill all of my beans just yet because I really want to give myself more time to take everything in. Tell me about yourself Sandra," he asked.

"What is it that you would like for me to tell you?" she responded.

"Well, for a starter are you seeing any of those professional smart guys there in the city who have swept you off your feet or are trying?"

"No, I am not even involved because since I have been living here, I must confess I have met a lot of them, but thanks to my cousin Delores to school me about just who they are and what they are looking for in a young country girl because they think all girls from the deep south are not so hip to their way of living."

"If they know you the way that I do, they didn't know that there was such a person with smarts as you so they decided to look in other directions," he said as he laughed.

"Wayne may I ask you a question and I want nothing but a true answer now because you know this is your sister asking as you know, you cannot fool me?"

"What is it Sandra?" he responded.

"It has been almost four years that I have been away from Mississippi, and yet you have not met one of those nice young white girls in the surrounding area to date and with a possibility to marrying, why is that?"

"Well! I don't want to get into it over the phone and you and I need to be in the presence of each other before I give you an answer. Have you mentioned to Greg at all about what I asked of you?"

"Greg is busy getting ready to graduate and as you may already know that he has met and fallen in love with the love of his life there on the campus and I know for sure that the two of them plan to get married in a couple of years once they have gained employment and saved up their money to start off."

"Are you telling me this is exactly what you are trying to do yourself, Wayne? I think I can truly say that is true. Well, Mr. Wayne when I return back there, I think that will be a top priority on my list to do to get you involved to get married Sandra said to him. How do you like that my brother?" she asked him.

"Sandra you just don't know how good that makes me feel to hear you say such nice thing." Little did Sandra know that he was speaking all the time about marrying her once she returns home. Wayne did say to her that he was saving himself for that special someone and he knows she is doing the same thing for her mate. "You know Sandra if I am going to be able to get up to be ready to take on my work day, I better get some sleep."

"Wayne, I am glad you placed that call to me even though it is late, but after you and I have spoken about things, I can fall asleep to prepare myself for a good day of work as well. Now I have something to think about that will just might benefit the two of us. "After the two of them had said their goodbyes, Wayne had a very positive outcome to what he knew would work out for the two of them. "I can sleep tonight because I just had a good talking relationship with my future wife."

In the meantime after Sandra had hung up the receiver, Delores walked out of her bedroom because she heard Sandra talking to someone and she wanted to know if there was something wrong back home with her parents. Delores would soon find out that it was Wayne that had called to see how things were going with Sandra. "Girl, haven't I said to you many times that that boy Wayne as you want me to call him not that skinny white boy is in love with you? Oh no, you keep telling me that you guys are just brothers and sister. Sandra it doesn't take a red bird to see what is happening to him especially when he call you at this time of the night to check on you. Tell me, what a so called brother as you and Greg put it, will wake you up this time of the night to just talk?"

"If you have not figured this whole thing out as of yet, let me tell you that there is a rotten apple in Denmark, and no cheese remaining in Wisconsin, because Wayne has bought all of it and just waiting for you to join him in eating it up. Wake up Sandra to smell that eight o'clock coffee brewing."

After Delores had spoken her mind, Sandra looked straight into her eyes to ask, "What if that is true as you have said many of times then what can I do about it or what is there to do?"

"You know you are leaving here in a few more months to return home, and I suggest that you give this some consideration about what you will tell him if he ask you when you return about becoming his wife. Sandra you being my first cousin that is all the advice I can give you because it will be your decisions to make whether you think you can move passed this brother and sister relationship to become Wayne's wife. I am not trying to put false hopes into your life because if it was me there would not be any hesitation on me to say what I feel."

"Delores, you don't have to go any further about Wayne because I already know just how you feel about him, and you don't even really know him. In spite of all the things you find that is not suitable to you just because he is a white boy, there are so many good qualities about him that you don't even know about. I am not saying to you as you and I talk that I wouldn't marry him, I am letting you know just what a devoted sweet guy he is and the color of a person's skin doesn't matter to him because he was brought up in the midst of color in Greg and my presence. There's a lot that you missed while you were growing up back home about people because the brother of my father who is your father, had so many difference opinions about people thus not allowing you to see a person for whom they are so you have built your whole life judging just on the color of a person and not what is in his heart."

"Sandra I was not expecting that to come out of your mouth but then too, I guess I really do deserve hearing it because you have made a valid point through all that you said. I tell you what if this thing happen between you and Wayne, I will make it my point to grow to like him and accept him into the family, that is, if you decide to jump over the other side of the fence. Now, there you go again Delores, speaking those hated words about jumping over the fence. I really do think Wayne will be a perfect husband and will do all the right things because he does not look upon the outer surface of a person, but the inner surface and just maybe he has looked inside my inner space to know that he will find what he know he deserve out of life. Maybe you are right about this whole affairs as some people would say the grass is greener of the other side so they cross over to feel that green grass but for me, I think I will continue to enjoy the green grass for which I am standing on now, until I think that something better can will come to my rescue and pull me over. I am wondering to myself exactly what Aunt Catherine and my dear Uncle Elijah along with Greg will have to say about this whole thing?"

"Delores, there is nothing for them to be torn apart for because what you have alluded to has not happened and it just may never take place so be at peace within yourself. I think Delores, after I have left and all of these good things that has happened to me, I will soon forget because I will be back home embarked on the one true thing that I had always had my mind geared too and that was, being the best English teacher in the state of Mississippi, as I could be. Of course, I will think about all the good times I had there in New York, and will probably miss some of the night life but I don't think I will miss it to the point that I would want to return there to live out my life. My dear cousin, Delores, I will be happy to leave this to you because this city is a part of you and I don't think that you could be happy living in the south again because let you and I face it, you have out grown the slow southern life as it has nothing to offer you anymore since you grew up to get away from there. I am quite sure I will regain my momentum back once I am back living my life in the south because as you know, I never did wanted to leave from there in the first place."

"It was you Delores that encouraged me to get away to obtain a good job which you knew being there with you in New York, it was sure to happen because of your great connections there and you had the right people in your surrounding that you could call upon and sell my knowledge to them that would want them to hire me for what they were looking for. For that, I will always be so indebted to you. While I am on this discussion, I want to let you know that once I am settled back home and have the right professional people around me, I too will be able to offer you the same chance to you as given to me."

"Sandra," Delores stopped her right then and there to say. "All of that my cousin sounds tempting, but please don't count on it because as I see it now, it will not be happening because there is no way that I plan to give up on all that I have worked so hard right here in New York and obtained to give up and move back there in Mississippi."

"Delores, please don't be too hard on your home state because there, is where you got a start from that forced you to leave there to relocate."

"That is one thing that is true Sandra but returning back will not happen because as far as I see it, there is nothing back there to make me to return is to visit relatives for a spell and to get away from there as fast as the train will move down the tracks. You see my dear cousin Sandra that is where you belong, because you have so much to gain by being back there, because to get right down to it, you never left mind wise only body wise. Who knows, only time will tell whether or not you and Wayne will tie the knot and become husband and wife to produce a few kids where both parents will have the opportunities to fuss over who will keep them to enjoy being grandparents."

"I think Delores you have put the horse before the cart as far as my marrying Wayne to settle down to have a few kids which is something that is not even on my mind so just put a spin on that for a while because I have my own mind set to what I want to do. Please excuse me if I got into a territory that I was not supposed to Delores, rebuttal. I have to admit, since it will be you, it would be nice to have a couple of beautiful mixed second cousins to look after if I must say so myself."

Time was drawing near as Sandra had promised her bother Greg that she would be back home in time for his graduation from college to see him walk across the stage to receive his degree, just as he was presence to her graduation also to see her march across the stage also to receive her degree. Of course Wayne being a close knit adopted brother would be there as well because he would not miss this for the world. It was a pity that the Sandra and Greg could not have been to see him march across the stage when he graduation, but during that time, privilege afforded to them had not yet been implemented to them by the federal government at that time. Things for changes to the south were still being worked out by the human rights department in Washington, D.C. Wayne very much wanted the two of them to be there to see his accomplishments, but it was not possible. Changes began to take shape two years after Sandra had left from there to go to New York to live with her cousin Delores.

Once Sandra had heard about what had taken place there in Mississippi, and all other southern states, she wished that she had remained there to be a part of it all that way, it would have been possible for her to get what she wanted as far as job wise. Since it was not possible, she thought just maybe her leaving did her a favor at least she found appreciation in her work as she threw her knowledge around and everyone who met her, wanted to have her in their presence to give them good ideas of how things should be written in language. Although Sandra regret coming to New York to seek a good job, she soon became use to the idea of being away from the south at least she knew when she return back home, she would definitely have a lot to tell everyone in and around about her stay in a big city, where most of the people there had never even had the opportunity to visit or thought they would not go there in their life time. Time was moving so fast until Sandra sometimes lost track of her scheduled departure date to say goodbye not only to the good people there she had met during her stay there, but to her dear cousin Delores, who will definitely escort her to the New York port authority train station to wait until she had board and pull away headed down the tracks.

As Sandra with her head out the window of the train waving goodbye to Sandra until she could no longer see her then she will know that she had left behind the best thing that happened to her for the duration stay of her time there, her cousin Delores. She could never forget the two lawyer brothers that went out on their limb to accept her on the words of their good friend, Delores. After seeing all what Sandra had done for their law firm, they realized their decisions to hire her were the best ones that the two of them had ever made and all thanks were given to Delores, for giving them a new business start. Of course Delores, didn't need a lot of thanks because each day as she entered her office, thanks had filled her desk by all business counterparts there within the city because she was the reasons their businesses exist by the funding that was made available for their existence. Delores, applied the funding through the bank that operated solely by lending monies to businesses for operational purposes in the return for higher yield on their dollars.

Sandra had already received her job offer from the state of Mississippi board of higher learning offering to hire her and it was the desire of Sandra to return back home to pick up the pieces where she tried to put together before she left. This was a great time for her because she did not feel any remorse about leaving because she never did have any desires to be there in the first place only, from by the urgency of Delores, offering her a better life. In just one more week, Sandra will call it quits there in that big vast city to pack and head out. Back there as she arrive there surely will be someone there who will be welcoming her home as he plan to meet her at the train station instead of parents, as he will work that out. Wayne was so sure that once he ask her about being at the train station to greet her, she will not disappoint him that way, she could make a surprised entrance in the home she long left behind to shock her parents. As of now, her parents as well as her brother Greg has no indication of when she will be leaving from New York, because a definitely time have not been given to them.

One night while Sandra and Delores, sat together at her home on the couch, Delores said to Sandra didn't she think it was about time that the truth be told so when this thing finally hit the fan, it will not be any surprised to anyone?

Sandra looked Delores in the face and asked her, "What type of surprises you are speaking about?"

"All the things that I have been telling you all along about Wayne. I can't say what is right or what is wrong because I am in the dark just as you are as you pretends to be in the light of things. I wish that I knew all of the specifics as you Delores, and just maybe I will be fully abreast of it all. Sure Wayne calls me and he and I talk quite a bit over the phone, but nothing pretending to any relationship he wants with me."

"Wake up Sandra do you think that he is going to right away blur it out to you before making sure that you want deceive him? I know you have never been in a serious relationship, but you are about to be in one now and believe me as soon as you get back home, it is going to happen because that white boy wants you so bad that he even can taste you."

"Has it not made you think and wonder why he has never dated any white girl, all this time of you being away, as he calls you his sister? Wouldn't you think that he would at least have said something to you about, he has met a nice girl and he is thinking about dating her? Sandra if you have not thought about it, think about it now. He is in love with you and only you and it doesn't matter if you are a black girl or you and Greg had adopted him as a brother. That is just how a relationship get started, once a person get close to you to find out all of your ways of likes and dislikes. That was just what Wayne did pretending to be your brother and all the time that brother mess was a joke, because he was loving you. Sandra if you have not thought about it, I think it is time right now for you to start looking into it, as I see it one day you will become Mrs. Sandra Hunt, the wife of Wayne Hunt." Just as Delores finished talking about it with her, Sandra became very quiet as if she was trying to put two and two together that all what Delores had said to her just might be something true.

It was now Friday evening and Wayne had gotten off from work and was home packing a few clothing to take with him to visit his parents, as he had made up in his mind that come what may, it was time for him to let his cat out of the bag that had been locked up for so long to tell them, all about his plans. How they would accept it would definitely bother him a lot if they say they do not approve of it, but that he hoped would not be the answer he will want to hear. If they agree with him on his decision making to marry this lovely black girl whom they had known all of her life then he would have to elevate it to her parents in hopes that they too will agree although he had been like the second son they never had. If they too agree after long discussions then in secrets he would have to let Greg know the one brother he has held in high esteem for all the years as someone to whom he could count on to help him solve any problems he had.

Wayne thinking hard on his decision while he was still at his place packing, he was just a little nervous about the whole ordeal because this he,\ has never done before because he has never dated before. He was so sure that his parents just might ask him why he decided that Sandra would make him a better wife other than a white girl. If they ask him that then he would day to them, "Because white girls never did interest me as I never had a feel for them not because of who they were, it is because I could not find love to share with them in my heart. With Sandra my heart had always been with her even as we were small children running around playing together hide and seek, my heart was her for the taking. Maybe I should have told her all about this long before but I just could not find the right time to do it because when I wanted to, the words just would not come out that way. Once my parents drill me a lot, I have to be patient with them as I am sure the same things will happen with Sandra's parents as well."

"Once I tell them this weekend, I would like for all of them to be secret about it for a while until Greg has graduated from college and I have spoken to Sandra about it. I much rather to tell her myself other than them. I will ask her parents to please act as if they did not know anything of it because it would not be the same if I didn't break it to her myself. After I call to tell Sandra about letting me to meet her at the train station when she arrive, once we are on the way to her home, I will tell her my way. Knowing her cousin Delores, as I think I do, she probably already have told Sandra a little something concerning how she think I feel about her. I have tried many of times to win over Delores, but it was a losing battle because she just don't have any use for white people and you know if Sandra and I get married, there will be no way on this earth that she would agree to it unless a rock fall out of the skies onto her head. I hope Sandra had spoken to her many of times about what a nice person I am and I am not one of those white people that look at a person difference because he or she may be black but I see them as a person from the way I was taught. I think once she figure it all out, Sandra and I will be parents of some beautiful mixed spice of life children."

After Wayne has built up a mountain of thoughts up in his mind as he has imagined what his and Sandra lives will be once they are matrimony together, it was about time for him to head on out traveling in the directions of his parents' home for the weekend to spend quality time with them as he was for sure break out to them what he had been holding inside of him all these years. "If they are ever going to know, I feel it is the time now to shine so once the three of are sitting at the dinner table having a good dinner cooked by my mother, is when I will break it to them gently to get their reactions." Wayne walked out of his apartment and got into his car to head out to release his information as he turned on his radio listening to some of his favorite songs he loved so much before reaching his parents' home. In the meantime, his mother Florence had made a call to Catherine, early that day to let her know that Wayne had said that he would be visiting her and Elijah too while he was here. Catherine said to Florence that it will be a happy occasion to see him since it has been a while he had been in their presence.

"You know Florence, Catherine said to her. Since our children has left and going in difference directions, things here are not the same. At least you see Wayne more so that Elijah and I see Greg with him being away in college and Sandra far away in New York."

"Seeing Wayne will be a happy occasion for all of us I think. Florence is there anything you would like for me to do to help you out while Wayne is here?"

"Thank you Catherine, but no thanks because I have everything I need to make his stay good."

"You know how I will be glad to cook something for him to take back home with him to have for the week to eat, you know?"

"That would be nice Catherine," Florence said. "But with all the foods I plan to prepare, he will have more than enough to carry back with him. Oh Catherine, this is going to be a good visit for Samuel and me just knowing that our son is here with us if only for a short visit. I know how you feel because in a few weeks, Elijah and I will be going on down to Louisiana to attend Greg's graduation from college. Will Sandra be able to make it there?" Florence asked Catherine?

"When I spoke with her last evening, she said that she plans to catch a flight for her first time to fly in there to attend the graduation ceremony and to see some of her old professors that taught her all she know and after that she will catch a flight right back out because she had to clear up a few things there in New York, before she return home to be ready for the opening of the school session this fall to start her job as an English teacher that she had been offered. I know she would love to see you and Samuel, as well as Wayne too, but her time just will not allow her to. We will have plenty of time to see her once she has returned home and then the three of us can sit down at the kitchen table to have a delicious conversation over a cup of hot tea or coffee, listening to all what she has to tell us about New York."

"Florence, I am quite sure she will have a lot to tell you and I about the city where we never had the opportunity to visit."

"Catherine, I am so proud of her and I know you and Elijah, are too. Please, don't even mention anything about Greg because that sister of his is the joy of his whole life and he could never find any faults in her."

When Wayne finally came home, he told them, "Mother and Daddy, you have to realize that the day was coming that I would be out there on my own as I grew up into a man."

"You are so right my son, but your mother and I just didn't want to hurry things, just wanted you to grow slow. I guess we could not understand while you were growing, we could not hold you as a small boy until we were ready to let go."

"Look at you my son," his mother said. "You are a man and now you are out there free to date some of those pretty white girls to decide on the one you just might marry one day and give your father and me some grandchildren." Of course Wayne did not reply because he wanted to wait until they were having dinner before he would open up and let them know once and for all. His mother said to him, "I am cooking all of your favorites and in a few hours, dinner will be ready where the three of us can sit down to enjoy a good dinner as a family, as you tell your father and me all about your work and dating experience."

His father Samuel said to him "Son, why don't you and I go outside and have a seat on that bench where I built for you under that old oak tree when you were a small boy. There are many memories still hang under that tree where you and I shared together."

"I think that would be nice daddy, so we won't get in Mother's way here in the kitchen."

"You two go on out and I will keep the back door open so I can hear what the two of you are talking about."

Once Wayne and his father sat down to begin to talk, his dad asked him several times if he had found that special someone in his life living there in the location where is working to be serious about. :Daddy, I did not come home to let you and mother know that I am dating or found a white girl to date. I came home to enjoy being here with you two for the weekend and to tell you something that is going on in my life that I think you need to know, as a matter of fact you and mother need to know."

"What is it Son?" he asked.

As his mother was listening at the door, she also asked him, "Wayne please tell us because just like your daddy, I too want to hear this especially if you have found happiness."

"I am sorry guys, but it will have to be over dinner as the three of us eat filling our stomachs."

"Samuel, "Florence said to him. "I think I better hurry up and finish this cooking so we can prepare ourselves for the news that our son is bringing us to give you and I hopes in becoming grandparents one day." A Wayne and his daddy continued to talk sharing old times, Wayne asked him how were things with Mr. And Mrs. Logan, since Sandra was in New York city and Greg was away in college.

"To be honest with you Wayne, Elijah and I talk each day about not only you, but we talk about his two kids as well and I know how much they miss them as your mother and I miss you. When you left us Wayne Florence and I thought that we would not be able to go on, but we took a little at the same thing that had happened to Catherine and Elijah to see how they were feeling and then the four of us just bonded more and more to surround Greg with our love because we still had him to give us hope that all was not lost. Each day, we became stronger and soon, we were alright because we had two good friends where we knew we could go to for release. Whatever it is that you are going to tell us my son, I know we will welcome it whatever you have to tell us. I am not promising you that at first, it just might be a little hard for us to accept but I think we will embrace you with open arms. You know how much your mother and I want you to be happy and if whatever you planning on telling us that we should know then I have to go along with your decision even if it will be hard at first for your mother to digest. You know my son, things here in the state of Mississippi, has made major changes since the federal government has stepped in to let these states in the south know that if you continue to practice your hate policies then the funding will be cut off because every child and every race of people should be able to have the rights of life to work, and hold positions just as the white has done for years, holding back what could have been the harvest for every individual regardless of the color to reap in every southern state. We are so glad that we taught you to see Sandra and Greg as someone you could look upon as a sister and a brother to become as one. Since that did happen, look what life has provided for you as you grew up, a concrete relationship. It's a good thing that you decided to come home this weekend to visit with your mother and I because I know whatever you have to tell the two of us will be something we will cherish."

"Do you really think so daddy Wayne responded to him? Yes son, in my heart I do believe things soon will open up for you and you will have a joyful life. Take a look at how you and Greg have stayed in contact with each other as well as Sandra. You call her often in New York City to check on her I have heard from Catherine on how often you make calls to her because you are concerned about her being there in a crazy city. You and Greg are always talking about crazy things because that is just what brothers do at times. This shows the love you two have developed among each other. You know in a few weeks, Greg will be graduating from college and I know he will be returning home to work in the school system as he has been offered a job teaching mathematics to high school students. I know on weekends you two will be hanging together and I can see how happy you will be."

"That just might be true too daddy, but what I will tell you and mother tonight over dinner just might change the course of things."

"Wayne, I don't think whatever it is you are planning on letting your mother and I know will make a big difference maybe just a little shocked. The way I see it, the three of you guys will soon be together again as before, but in a different capacity." Soon, it was about time to walk inside to wash up and take a seat at the dinner table where the surprise anticipation was ready to be thrown out on the table in hopes that his parents would not fall out of their chair over the news that he was about to shock them with. As the three took their seats and Wayne said to his mother just how good everything looked as he was sure that it would taste as her foods always did, building up his nerve before he told them. First, his father said to the two of them to hold hands in prayer as he recited a good one thanking for their son's presence and whatever it was their son had to share with them would be received. As the foods bowls were being passed around, Florence said to her son Wayne, I know I am ready to hear the news, as I know your father is as well.

After Wayne has filled his plate with some of his mother's nice baked chicken, along with green peas, scalloped potatoes, macaroni and cheese, and hot buttery dinner rolls he said, "Now that I am about ready to eat a good cooked meal, I want you and Daddy to brace yourselves what I am about to open my mouth to tell you."

"Please Son," his mother said because she was eager to hear as she was all smiles.

"I have no better way to tell you other than I am in love."

Just then his mother yelled out, "Hallelujah my son has finally met a nice white girl and fell in love with her. I am so happy because I thought for a while that you might never find someone." Wayne's daddy was overjoyed as he asked him how did he meet her and where is she now.

Wayne said to them, "Please don't take this the wrong way when I tell you who she is."

"Wayne, I think your mother and I will not take it as being a bad thing once you let us know who she is."

"I have thought about telling you guys for a very long time but I just had to get up enough nerve to come forth so now, I am letting the cat out of the bag without hesitation."

"I am in love with Sandra."

"Oh I see she is name as same as your adopted sister Sandra. I think that name says a lot she said to him."

"Mother, you don't understand; it is Sandra my adopted sister."

"What did you just say son?" his daddy asked.

"I just cannot hold it any longer inside of me because all these years, I have always been in love with her and that is why I never dated anyone else as you wanted me to. You were hoping that it would soon be a white girl but I have never had any interest in white girls. Since the three of us were young children playing around the yard together, I saw her as the person I knew who could one day make me feel like a whole person. I supposed your hallelujah cheers have just dropped Mother now that you and daddy know all about my secret. Please don't be mad with me because I am in love with Sandra because she is a black girl, but that is just the way it is and there is nothing you two or anyone else can do about the way I feel. Daddy, how do you really feel about what I told you guys here at the table? I would like to know to get your opinions because the way you two taught me to never judge a person by the color of their complexion."

"Son, I and your mother are a little shocked but I am sure we will get over it and move forward after we mention this whole thing to Sandra's parents."

"No please don't do that because I want to let them know tomorrow when I stop by to visit them on my way back to my place. For now, you are the only ones that I have told, not even Greg or Sandra and I will appreciate it you didn't say anything to them about it. I want to be the one to let Greg know as I find a way not to break his heart."

Wayne's his mother said to him that with this surprised news, he had a big pill to swallow. "Mother and Daddy, I want to know how do you two feel about it and maybe one day she and I will become husband and wife?"

"Right now son, your daddy and I are thrown for words, but if this is to be then we couldn't be happier for you at least we know Sandra as she too has been like my daughter but now, I guess that has to disappear and eventually become our daughter-in-law."

Wayne's father spoke out to say to him and his mother, "Why not let this good news, although shocking news, become something that has been distant to come our way and lifts you up high as a wonderful son who found his life partner. When are you going to ask Sandra's dad for his daughter hand in marriage son?:

"First of all, since I have gotten all of what I had tied up inside of me for so many years, I am going to enjoy this wonderful dinner mother prepared and then I will think on all what I will say to them tomorrow as I visit. Mother, please if you can find it in your heart to keep it a secret and not tell Mrs. Catherine, anything about this tonight if you and she talk over the phone. I want son, although it will be hard for me to do but I respect your wishes as you will tell them tomorrow and then she and I can have our say about our surprised from her adopted son to soon be a thing of the past and you will be her son-in-law."

"Samuel?" Florence asked him. "How do you think Elijah will accept it when the two of you are out and about"?

" Florence, you know Elijah and I are the best of friends just like we are true blooded brothers as I don't see whether there will be a problem because he will feel toward Wayne just as I feel toward Sandra as two people that should be given every opportunity to a filled life as we have had."

"I know he will not look back over all the years his children and our son played with one another to have grown up still remaining together as they moved in difference places and into different fields would change anything. I think once Wayne sit down with the two of them tomorrow and explain the way he feels, I think they will come on board as you and I Florence. Heaven knows, you and Catherine will burn the telephone up talking about it tomorrow night once Wayne has left. Son, we want you to know that we as parents could not be any pleased with your choice and who knows, once the two of you are married, we just might be having a couple of mixed grandchildren running around the house just as their mother and father did as they grew up. Won't that be nice to see, Florence?"

"I am so excited until I can hardly wait until you tell Sandra, Son. When do you plan to tell her Wayne?" his father asked.

"Well, in a few weeks she will be moving back home because he has been offered a teaching job here in one of the high school, as she will be teaching

English, her passion all along before she moved away for lack there off by the Board of Education because it was detailed with only all white school with only white teachers until the federal government stepped in and changed things."

"I am glad that she has been given the opportunity to teach what she went to college for because she is a very smart young lady, or should we say, our very smart daughter in-law. Do you think she will accept your proposal right away after you tell her or do you think she would want to have some time to think on it Wayne?" asked his daddy.

"I know at first it will be shocking, but knowing Sandra the way I do, she would have to share it with her mother and father, as well as Greg before she gives me an answer. I already know and understand that this will be something that she never expected to hear from me because she was my sister and me, her brother. I guess you and daddy know that I have been saving all my money to put down on a nice little house not far from here where Sandra and I can live so she will be close to her job. Well son, if you will need help in getting started, your father and I will be willing to help because little do you know, we have saved quite a bit of money for you to use one of these days."

"I didn't know you and daddy had saved money for me mother."

"When you were a small boy, he and I decided to open up an account in your name to put money into it each month as it grew over the years to be well over fifty thousand dollars. So you see, if you need help, the money is there waiting for you and since you will soon have a wife. It will give you and Sandra a lead way to save for the future of your children so they too, will be afforded the same opportunity once they grow up. Wayne son, you will be just fine because we have all that you need to help you get started off as a first time husband."

"Daddy you talk like I will get married more than once. I just said that because I know the way you feel toward Sandra you will only marry once in life. I want to make her as happy as I can and to show her exactly how much I love and adore her because the way things has changed, we want have to worry about people watching the two of us as we walk into a store or walk down the street, as the old south has changed into a whole new life and everyone, color or creed are mending together for a new life of the world."

As the evening began to fade and Wayne and his parents had finished with their dinner, Samuel decided to take his son out back to sit down as one on one as man to man to have that long talk while Florence was inside the kitchen clearing the table and putting away left overs so she would not hear what the two of them were about to get into with their conversation. It was hard for Florence, not to be in their presence as she would like to share her opinions about her son's desires to marry the girl he grew up with and called her his adopted sister. Samuel thought if he being the father would be more attended to the situation than his wife because men somehow seem to feel the way sons feel when it comes to marrying someone because they themselves had to face up to the music themselves and now it was easier for them to relate in giving out their talks. As the two of them sat talking, Florence kept going back and forth to the back door to see if she could hear from was being said to finally pushed open the screen door to say, wait for me because I am almost finished with the kitchen duties so I can join in with you two.

Wayne said to his mother to just remain inside because this conversation was between he and his daddy as he was receiving advice that would guide him in his decision making. Finally, his mother said to him, "Oh well, I guess I will keep my comments to myself and not get involved because I see you two men rather be alone in this time."

"Mother, I have said all that I needed to say to you about what I wanted and you agreed with me just how supportive you are so now, let Daddy and I have this time together as one on one. I know when you get with Sandra's mother, the two of you will talk for days."

"Florence, Wayne is right, why not leave this time for father and son bonding together to prepare for a daughter-in-law? Son, his father said to him. "You know how much I have valued all of your decisions and how much I have grown to love Sandra as well as her little brother Greg as if they were my own because the three of you have grown up to love each other as a family and now, since you said that you have always loved Sandra I have no other reasons to not accept your decisions. I am happy for you my son. I can see from watching the expression of relief on your face that you are happy and you are glad to know that your parents accept what you want. So my son, if you are that much in love with that beautiful little black girl that you grew up with and loved her all these years unknown to any of us then I encourage you to go get her and I want you to the happiest young white man around with your mixed wife. When all of this love affair takes place and you two set the date for marriage, please handle it with pride and don't look back as to what those narrow minded individuals might be saying about it. Just go forth and be happy because you are the one that will make yourself happy, not any of those people that make a lot of noise talking. I don't have to tell you right at this time about whether or not Sandra's parents will accept what you will tell them when you meet with them tomorrow, because I know they will be as your mother and I are, happy for you. I am sure Elijah wouldn't mind having you as a son-in-law because he know exactly how you are and what you want out of life."

"At first, when you tell them he and Catherine might be stunned and shocked, but after they have listen to you, I know they will be favorable. So whatever your mother said to you tonight about your decision, let it be known that she is just so thrilled that you are finally going to bring her joy. You see son, I know your mother because I have been married to her a long time. It is all good and now, let us go inside for the night to have a glass of wine to celebrate the good news."

"Please Daddy, don't let this whole thing slip when you are out talking to people not just yet."

"Don't you worry your head off Wayne for now your secret is tight with me and with your mother as well. The two people we probably will be discussing it with will be Sandra's parents. What about your brother Greg? When will you let him know?"

"I had thought about telling him once he had graduated and Sandra had returned back to New York City to clear up her business and then I will tell him once he is back home from college before she get here. I am hoping he will be happy for me to know that he and I will always be close around still seeing each other as true brothers. I understand that our status will changed from being adopted brothers to become brothers-in-law."

"Wayne the sound of that has a certain ring to it and boy, I know there will be a lot of joy in and around this neighborhood once the light has been turned on. Let me ask you this Wayne when you and Sandra finally agree to everything, do you two think that you will plan a big wedding or you will visit the justice of peach to tie your knot?" his father asked.

"I will leave that to Sandra her mother and my mother to make all of those arrangements." You know, there is a large benefit hall that will hold a lot of invitees as I am sure you and Sandra will receive a lot of gifts because this marriage right here in this neighborhood will be something of new, not expected."

"Hold on just a minute Pop," Wayne said to him. "I think you are moving too fast as if you would like to see it happen tomorrow."

"No, because I know you have to let Sandra know but is it wrong for me to be thinking ahead of myself I know once Elijah hears it, he too will be acting and thinking the same as I am. I am ready for some excitement around here Wayne because to be honest with you, we had almost given up on you ever getting married to produce some grandchildren, as I and your mother have so desperately wanted. You know we were not blessed to have a daughter, almost did not have you because there were a lot of complications, but you came on in. That is the reason why your mother clings to Sandra so tight because she was the daughter we never had. Take this class of wine to be saluted."

"Wait for me," Wayne's mother said, "because I am a part of this whole thing and I want to be drinking this nice fine glass of wine in the congratulations to our son."

Samuel said to Florence, "I think one glass will be enough for you because you know that you cannot hold your wine and when you start drinking, you start acting out."

"Hey, once our son and our daughter-in-law get married, I can drink all the wine I want to because I will be so overjoyed and I just might be dancing in the streets. Wayne if you would like for your father along with Sandra's parents to take a look at some nice home for you while you work, we can do that because we have the time on our hands."

"That all sounds really good but I think when Sandra and I come together to start this thing off, I think she and I can do it but I am not saying that you guys can't look, but let it be her to decide on whether she like the ones you come across. I know you Mother and Daddy, how you will try to surprise us on our wedding day with keys to our new home. You just said that we should allow Sandra to make her own decisions about the ones we find, didn't you?"

"I did, but Daddy, you, and Mr. Logan have ways of doing things as I am sure you two men along with Mrs. Catherine and you mother will join in with them."

"Wayne your mother and I promise not to make a move until we have discussed it with the Logans. Son, his mother said I guess you are aware about all of these ladies here in the neighborhood who belong to the ladies' club will definitely get involved because you know how they too feel toward you and Sandra as they have watched all of you grow up together through the years along with their children and will want to make this upcoming not yet scheduled wedding plans a big thing."

"I think all of this is not up for my discussing because I will have other things to think about such as if I will continue to hold my position there with the Agricultural Field Office once everyone there finds out about my marrying a mixed girl."

Wayne's daddy said to him, "Who cares if they like it or not, it won't be their choice to live with her and it surely won't be their decision to let you go because of all the changes that have taken place will keep your job stable because of your work performance. Of course you will not want to continue to keep living there in the location that you are now living in as you have said that the people living there in those complexes there are not that good and you don't think they will ever change. That is why I think you should allow Elijah and me to look around for a nice little home close by this neighborhood where you know you will be happy because you and Sandra will be among good neighbors. There are more Agricultural Field Offices in and around so maybe you can put in a relocation request to move back in this area."

"Daddy, I never thought about that possibility but I will check into it."

"Wayne, I am sure it will make you feel better if you could be transferred to a closer location to feel much happier than where you are now."

"Daddy, don't get me wrong because where I am working now, I enjoy my work and all of my bosses are great to be working with. It is just that I am not really happy living where I am because I know just how those racist people are and if and when I marry Sandra they will surely get out of control. Besides, it will be too far away for Sandra to travel to her school and job and I would like for her to be close by so she won't have to drive so far."

"Wayne you do what you have too and you let Elijah and me attend to what we have to. Believe me my son, everything is going to be alright and everything will work out in the favor of you and Sandra. One good thing about it all, you know you will have two guys to give you all the support you will need."

"Wayne do you have a feeling that the three of us has beat that horse to death and it is ready to rest?" his daddy asked. Florence had gone into the bedroom to make up the bed that Wayne slept in when he was living there to make sure he would get a good night sleep in order to get up early to have a good morning breakfast before he make it his business to visit the Logans to discuss his wanting to marry their daughter to make her his wife for life. Although he wanted to call Sandra, he decided to wait for another time because he did not want to move too fast. Besides, he knew that she was probably making plans to fly to Louisiana to attend Greg's graduation to meet up with her mother and father there to spend some time with them before she fly back to New York to finish up her business, as Wayne will come back home with them as they pack up his things to bring back to be housed until he is ready to move into his own place and soon get married to the girl he met. Being there at his graduation will give Sandra a good time to spend time with Sadie, Greg's girlfriend to get to learn about her.

He said, "Of course, I will not attend because I think it would be best if they all could have their moments together. Besides, I have a hectic schedule come next week and if I wanted to get off, I don't think my bosses would allow it to be."

"With so much is going on with the agricultural department, this is a crucial time of the year because year end is about to come to a close and all reports have to be to the federal government before a certain time in order for them to put out in the index to the world just how much yields have been produced for the world because farmers has to be responsible for feeding the whole world as products are shipped to and from the countries. Since I have been assigned to so many farmers to make sure they have followed all growing guidelines, it is a big responsibility that has been laid upon me to supply to my bosses each week just what progress has been made that has turned out for the good of the department. I love my job and I am glad to have studied in this field because I know goods come out of it and I can walk away feeling good about all I have done."

"Come Monday morning Daddy, I will take your advice and see if I can be transferred to a closer office here in this area to accommodate Sandra as well as myself to be able to worry less about her safety. Coming home to spend the weekend with you and Mother was a good decision I made because now that I have told you guys everything, I feel so good about myself and I am not all bottled up inside thinking that you guys would not accept what I had to tell you."

"You should never think that way son," his daddy said. "Because regardless who you have made it your business to get involved with, we as your parents are here to do nothing but to support your decision whether it is a good one or whether it is a bad one. We are here to help you work out all of your soul salvations because that is what parents are supposed to do for their children to guide and model to them the right direction."

"The more I talk with you Daddy, the more I understand all about life and this is exactly how I want to be with my son one day, giving him strength just as you and mother have done for me."

"You will Wayne because you will have a good, loving wife to support you."

"Not only is Sandra smart, but she is also good person and I am sure our children will have a good upbringing just as you and mother have provided for me, as well as her parents have done for her and Greg."

"I think that I will say goodnight to you daddy as I am tired because I had a long hard day and driving here made me even more tired. I am not going to shake your hand as most fathers expect from their sons because it is a man's thing. I am going to give you a big, tight hug to let you know that I really do love you and Mother for believing in me and wishing the best for me. You have done so much in giving me a good life which I will not forget to know that I can always count of you guys if need be."

By the time Wayne had finished hugging his father, his mother walked out of his room and he said, "You too come here mother so I can hug you to because you guys deserve it."

"I just turned your bed down and there are fresh towels in the bathroom son for you to take a shower. You go and have yourself a long warm shower to call it a night."

"By the way Mother, thanks for such a wonderful dinner because it was well worth waiting for," he said laughing.

"Why, you are very welcome because I am quite sure when you and Sandra get married Catherine and I will be doing a lot of cooking because I know you two will be spending many weekends here with us she said. Hold on mother, you know that Sandra likes to cook as well and I am sure she will invite the two families over some weekends to our home for a well cooked dinner. I don't think Sandra would want you and her mother to spoil us to the point that she will forget how to cook."

Wayne's daddy said to him, "Son, I think you better step back out of that conversation because you know just how much Catherine and your mother, tries to out due each other with their cooking."

"I know how they are Daddy, and the two of them can win door prizes you know laughing as he left them to go into his room to take a shower and fall to sleep because come tomorrow he will have to build up his nerve to face the Logans to let them know his reasons for coming home this weekend." As Wayne allowed the warm water to run down his body, he kept thinking about whether or not the Logans would accept what he will tell them or would they give him a no for an answer? If they do then he just want know what to do other than maybe he would convince Sandra to elope with him and get married. He know if he did that, he will not be welcomed into the family anymore. He must be positive.

Come tomorrow just before Wayne made up his mind to leave first and foremost, he had to make a stop over to the home of the Logans to see them because it has been a while since he has laid eyes on them, especially now that Greg has gone off to college therefore, kept him from running home every weekend. Of course this visit will not only be a friendly visit, but it will be a visit to let them know just how he has carried a secret around locked up inside of him for many years, know the time was not yet right to reveal his secrets to anyone, not even to him mother and father. Since he has now gotten up enough nerve to tell his parents about his hidden secret he held within himself all these years, he felt as if it was worthwhile telling them as he did by making time to visit them. Of course, his mother thought that he just wanted to see the two of them since it had been a few weeks, not expecting to hear anything what he brought out to them, over a nice dinner at the kitchen table. It did happen and they were glad to know.

"Now, will that same atmosphere be when I open up to tell Sandra's mother and father tomorrow as with his own mother and father?" he asked himself. This is something he will have to sleep hard on to hope for the best. If his mother had her way, Mrs. Logan will already know about it once he visit them, but he pleaded with his mother not to call and tell her because just as he surprised the two of them, he wanted to do the same thing for Sandra's parents to get their take on what he has to say. At first, Wayne had a hard time falling asleep but soon as he relaxed his mind, the sleep came upon him and soon he was out until morning. As he lay awake listening to the sounds of the noise his mother was making in the kitchen as she was preparing breakfast, he decided to get up to dress and join his father as the two of sat and talk over a cup of hot coffee until breakfast was ready.

His father said to him, "Well son, this is your big day to tell the Logan all the things you opened up to your mother and I about. I know you just might be a little uneasy, but listen to me son, it is not like you don't know them. You have a life time with them as seeing you as a son too. "What time have you planned to stop by?"

"I plan to leave from here around mid-day because I want to get back before dark to my place so I will stop by to see them right after I leave from here."

"If Catherine calls before you leave, I promise not to say a word about anything to her. You know after you have talked with them about it, she will definitely call me to ask if Samuel and I knew anything about what Wayne had said to them. Will it be alright if I open up and began to talk about it son?"

"I can't see what hurts it will cause because the two of you will know. 1 just want you to assure her that it would be in the best interest not to let Greg nor Sandra know anything about this whole thing because Wayne said that he will find a way to break it to them. They had a good breakfast, one like Wayne had been use to when he lived at home with all of what he liked in the morning, scrambled cheese eggs, bacon, hot biscuits, stewed apples, juice and coffee. Now, this is a breakfast that I miss from having each morning before I go to work."

After getting up early to spend at least half the day with his own parents, before visiting the Logans. Wayne pushed himself from the kitchen table after having a good hearted good breakfast, and decided to go back into his bedroom to make sure he will not leave anything behind as his mother got busy making sure what was left from their big meal the night before, would be packed in containers for him to take back with him to have for the following week so he would not have to try and cook, saying to him, "Wayne, I have packed up everything for you to carry you through the week."

"Thank your mother," he said as he was somewhat a little weary about saying anything to the Logans but he know, it was now or never because if he did not then his own mother would definitely tell it because what he had shared with she and Samuel was definitely burning up her heart so whether he wanted to or not, he didn't have a choice.

"Well Mother and Daddy, it is about time for me to say goodbye to you two and move on over to the Logans to tell them."

"Son," his father said to him. "Don't beat yourself up before you hear what Catherine and Elijah have to say about it. After you have said what you had to say, then you just wait until you hear what they will have to respond back with. I am quite sure the two of them will be favorable. They know you son, and they know exactly how supportive you have been to their daughter during her time away in New York, keeping in contact with her to see if everything was going there for her. After you ran it by your mother and me, we now feel good about the whole episode because we are welcoming this marriage for our son. So what if she is a black girl and you, being a white boy, love runs deep you know and there isn't one thing anyone can do about it when love take place. You have our blessings and you go get the blessings of the girl you plan on marrying."

After those comments from his daddy, Wayne said to him, "I really do feel good about this whole thing, and I am so sure they will give me the long awaited answer I have always wanted. I am out of here folks and on to the Logans so wish me well. I will call you guys tonight to let you know how things came out."

As Wayne's parents stood outside greeting him goodbye with a hug and kiss, he backed out of the driveway, headed down the street to stop in from of the Logan's home. As he pulled up, Catherine came to the front door and stood on the front porch yelling over to Florence that the two of them must get together to have coffee cake and tea to talk about old times. Florence yelled back to say, "You know we will girl," as she looked to Samuel, as the two of them turned around and walked back into the house, because they did not want Catherine to think that they knew it all along.

As Wayne stopped his car and got out, he said to her, "Good afternoon Mrs. Catherine."

"Wayne, Elijah and I saw that you had come home and we were hoping that you would stop by to say hello to us before you headed out. Come on inside she said to him because you know that Elijah is waiting to see you because that is all him talk about, his two sons not being here for him to hear your arguments about things. As Wayne walked inside, Mr. Logan stood up from his recliner to greet Wayne saying to him son, I think it was about time you showed up to see Catherine and me. Have a seat so we can talk how you like your job and where you are living. Wayne can I get you something cold to drink?" asked Catherine.

"No I am fine as you know mother filled me up with a lot as well as packing all of the leftover from dinner last night to carry back with me to have next week."

"I asked her if I could prepare something for you but she said that she was fine and you know I would have loved to have made you one of my banana pudding to last you all week. That would have been nice to have but I have quite a bit already out there in my car in cooler. As Wayne sat still in his seat not saying but allowing Sandra's father do most of the talking, finally he said to him, I have a slight feeling there is something on your mind that you want to talk with Catherine and I about. Is that true Mr. Logan asked. Wayne knew right at that moment he know that felt something coming from him that they might be shocked to hear. As Catherine sat next to Wayne on the couch she said to him, whatever it is that has been bothering you or is now bothering you, we are here to hear because we are family."

Before Wayne would open up to tell them, in the back of his mind he was thinking, "I don't know because after I tell you two, we just might not be family, but enemies." As he sat there trying to get his thoughts together to come out with what he was about to let them know, he kept thinking about what his daddy said to him at the breakfast table to let what is was feeling out because if he continue walking around with all of it bundle up inside of him it would just destroy him and he would not be any good to anyone

"Okay Wayne, "Mr. Logan said to him. "I respect your wishes, but before you leave from this house this afternoon, Catherine and I will know."

"Do you really want me to tell you all that I have to say to you?"

"You know Wayne," Mr. Logan said. "If you told the truth and you were willing to stand on your words then it will set you free and you will have a different feeling about yourself knowing you have come clean. so I don't think what you are holding inside of you can be that bad because we have known you since the day you were born and we watched you grow up with Sandra and Greg as brothers and a sister."

Wayne decided to ask them first before he opened up to them if they would hate him if they knew. Catherine said to him, "Why Wayne how in the world could we hate you about whatever you are going to tell us because we love you just as much as we love our own two children? Elijah and I might be a little shocked, but have known we can never hate you so come on out with it because I am sure you would like to get on the road before dark catches you." There were moments of quiet as Catherine and Elijah waited patiently for Wayne to start.

"Mr. and Mrs. Logan, I want to tell you as I have been wanting to tell you long ago that I am in love with Sandra and have always been since we were small children playing in and around the house. I want to marry Sandra to make her a good husband as you me and know how I am. If you have not realized it or not that is the reason why I never did date any white girl while in college or even now that I am working among so many in my work location because they have never appeared to me. Sandra has always been the love of my life and I really don't care who knows it."

As Wayne continue to pour his heart out to the Logans about his feelings, Mr. Logan asked him, "Is that is why Greg would ask you sometimes to tell him the secret?"

"I couldn't tell him because I knew if I did as he at the time didn't understand because I was much older, it would drive a wedge between the two of us and our friendship would be nothing and I didn't want that so I continued to hide my feelings about Sandra all these years."

Do our daughter and son know about this?" Mr. Logan asked.

"No, they don't know and I would appreciate it if you two did not mention anything to them about it. I want to be the one to tell them and especially to tell Sandra."

After Wayne had spilled his guts to the Logans, they just sat still for a few minutes as they did not respond but were gathering their thoughts as to what they would come back to tell him, as he sat still as could be didn't know if they were going to say to him, "Listen boy, you get up and get out of this house to think we are going to allow you to marry our daughter to drag her through the mud."

Instead, Catherine placed her arms around him and said, "Wayne you know if there was anyone else who told us this, Elijah and I would have had a problem but now that things has changed and life for the two will be in a brighter stake, and we have no choice but to welcome you in as our soon to be son-in-law."

"Can I have the two of your word that nothing of our conversation will mentioned to Greg or Sandra? Wayne, Elijah's and my mouth are shut tight until you tell us to open them, Wayne, I supposed you are now free of your heavy burdens you carried around with you locked up inside all these years."

"I guess you can now run free and want look back but rather, keep a happy smile on your face knowing that one day soon you and our daughter Sandra will get married once she is back from New York."

As Wayne was about to leave, Catherine said to him, "You know the sooner she knows, the better she will be able to accept our proposal."

"I know that because that is why I want to ask her to let me pick her up from the train station when she arrives, so I could tell her without being around." Mr. Logan asked him about Greg as he would be coming home after he graduates from college.

Wayne said to him, "I think Greg and I will be alright with it besides, you know he himself will soon be getting married as well."

"Has he mentioned anything to the both of you about his girlfriend?"

"Her name is Sadie, and she is a mixed Indian and Asian girl. I think it is time for me to be leaving because I would like to get home to put all of that food mother packed for me in the refrigerator."

As the three of them were walking out to the front porch to wave Wayne off for a safe trip, Catherine noticed that Florence was walking around in her yard as though she was checking on her flowers buds but really, she was checking out to see what a sendoff we were giving Wayne. Florence saw that Wayne gave me a big hug and Elijah, and then pulled off. Catherine made it a point not to look toward Florence direction so she would not have questions to ask as Wayne had warned us not to say anything about what he had said until he spoke with Sandra and Greg. As Wayne has gotten out of sight and Catherine and Elijah, returned back inside to continue enjoying what was left of the day, they said to each other, "What a surprise we received today, just like a big unwrapped Christmas gift. We just have to get used to calling Wayne our son-in-law instead of our son when they marry you know. All these years, Wayne has been in love with our daughter as he called her his sister. Catherine, you know once Florence and you get this together, you guys will have a lot of planning to do as mothers-in-law as well as daughter-in-law."

Elijah said to her, "You do know our neighborhood women's auxiliary will play a major role in helping to plan this big event for all to see."

Now that Wayne had gotten all of what has being lingering upon his chest all of those years, has finally been released so now, he can rest in the hopes that once he open up to Sandra to tell her, he hope that everything that he had been longing to see fulfilled will put an end to his aggravations not being able to have a peaceful night sleep because of the burdens he was carrying. Wayne was happy on his way home knowing that he had just two more individuals to open up too and this would be the sure thing if his little brother Greg will accept it and agree that it would be the best thing for his sister Sandra to be the wife of the guy he had always looked up too for any advice. As the music on the car radio was bumping, Wayne began to sing alone with the songs being played because at least he had a good visit and he was able to release himself from such the strain he was carrying inside of him, being so afraid that his own parents as well as Sandra's parents would reject him, but none of what he had expected did not turn out that way.

Also home to his apartment, Wayne had decided to go right inside to make a call to New York City to speak with Sandra to let her know that he had visited not only his parents, but he stopped by to visit hers as well not to tell her anything about what they talked about concerning what he wanted to do. He realized that once he began to speak with her, it would be hard for him not to speak anything about his plans so he knew he would have to be very careful because he knew that Sandra could read into lines of communications. For sure, he definitely would like to know when she would be flying out to attend Greg's graduation in Louisiana, and when she planned to depart from the city for good. Of course through their to be conversation he would surely ask her if he could be the one to meet her when she arrive home. Knowing Sandra the way he does, she just might ask him why he wanted to meet her when her parents could do the same thing. He would say, "Well, I think it would be a surprise to them if they look to see you in my car driving up into their driveway." Wayne had it all planned and worked out as he hope it would work out as he would shock her with his surprise.

As Wayne walked into his apartment and place his night bag down on the floor, he walked into his kitchen to place all the foods that his mother had packed in his ice chest to be placed in the refrigerator. After that, he was sure to pick up his phone to make that call with joy in his heart and soul, knowing that he had gone home for the weekend and he, had gotten the approval from his parents as well as Sandra's parents as well to become her husband as she his wife with his high hopes and all the negatives attitudes of people who just might object to his affairs to this black girl would not be a matter of interest to him because he, with all of his determinations had reached the top of that mountain which he had been climbing to let the whole world know that if you continue to fight for what you think is right then changes will happen. Wayne just could not take it any longer so he picked up his phone and dialed Sandra's number to not only hear her voice, but to hope that through their conversation, she would feel his happiness to ask him, what had happened to him that had him all jolly?

Of course, he would not be able to share with her all of his joys instead, he would skip around the curve to throw the light back on her asking about her remaining time there. "Sandra how are you holding up knowing you will soon be leaving from there for there with no plans to return to live there?"

"You know Wayne, I will be flying out from here when Delores and I come next weekend to Louisiana for Greg's graduation from college as well as spending some time with everyone there who will be in attendance. I know you had said that you rather remain home instead of trying to go there to accept Greg and surprise him when he comes home with Mother and Daddy, right after everything has been packed up to bring away from school because his reign there for four years will have ended."

"So tell me, how is Delores these days?" Wayne asked.

"You know my cousin Delores, with her opinionated self about things other than that, she is fine."

"Sandra once you and Delores, has flown back to New York City, and you finalize your job missions there, please let me meet you at the train station, because I have something to discuss with you."

"Wayne would it be impolite if I now ask you what is it that you would like to tell me?"

"No, it would not be but I just want you to hear it alone away from everyone. Please don't let your parents or brother Greg know the time you plan to depart and with all respects, tell Delores do not make a call to them to warm them of your coming because if she does, it will spoil my own plan."

"If that is very important to you Wayne then I will make sure Delores doesn't call them ahead of my departure time. Wayne whatever you have to tell me, it better be good." After the two of them had their long talk, Wayne decided to say goodnight to her until she let him know the date and time she would be leaving. You take care Sandra he said until I hear from you. After they had a good conversation and he decided to take a long warm shower to prepare for his day of work that would soon be forth, he felt good because he knew things would be the way he had been hoping for.

In the meantime, after Sandra had hung up the phone, Delores was listening to some of their phone conversation said to her, " I hear wedding bells ringing because that white boy is telling you too much and you my dear cousin refuse to accept that you will be his wife once you have returned back home."

"Delores, I don't know what you are talking about because I am going home to work in the school system because I was offered a teaching job there teaching English, the love of my life. I am quite sure that is farfetched from Wayne's mind about wanting to marry me. Sandra you can say what you too may but I am not ruling that out. Delores, just think about what you are saying, you know Wayne, Greg, and I basically grew up together as brother and sister so I think anything else that you says are wrong."

"Okay my dear cousin, Sandra. I plan to stick to my words and when all come to the light then I will look toward you to say, I was right."

"Delores, if what you are saying is true, what do you think my parents as well as his parents would say?"

"I don't know maybe they will agree to it or they will disregard it. We will just have to wait and see, won't we?" Delores said.

"By the way Delores, there is one thing I would like for you to promise me."

"What is it Sandra?"

"Please don't call to let my parents know of my departure."

"Why is that Sandra?" she asked.

"Because Wayne said that he wanted to meet me at the train station once I arrive there. So please don't slip and say anything about this while you and I are in Louisiana attending Greg's graduation next weekend. Can I trust you on this my cousin?" Sandra asked.

"You have my word on that although you know how bad I would want to tell them, but to respect your wishes, I will do as you said, keep my big mouth shut. You know I will definitely miss from having you around here in my presence once you leave as well as those two brother lawyers and the whole staff from relying on you for your expertise on things. Girlfriend, I have to say this much about you, you came to this city as a complete stranger and turned it upside down by bringing some of that southern smarts with you to show these northern so called smart know it all people, just how things are done if you have the capabilities. You know Sandra you can write your own ticket to anything that come about within this big city, because your name has been put out there for everyone to know just who you are."

"No Delores, I just want to leave from here to return back to my roots where I would have made a difference there long before the changes that has happened there if, the Board of Education had looked upon my learning skills and not my color. I could have still been there, but since that happen, I am happy I had the opportunity to come up here to be recognized."

"Being recognized, yes you have been elevated all the way to the mayor's office as he will surely be attending your going away party to congratulate you for all of your great accomplishments you have done for the city. Now that day, I can hardly wait to get here because that night, I plan to put on my finest outfit and walk in that hall with you with my head held high knowing it was all because of me your cousin, who introduced you to the two brothers whom we will be seated with them at their table. The only one thing ! Regret is the fact that your family won't be here to see you be honored. Sandra it seem as if your whole world has turned around for you not only will you be teaching what you have always wanted to do, but your life has been opened up to a new life."

"One day you will look back over all of what you went through and what good things came your way, you will smile and a possibility if you have a few children, you will make it a point to enlighten them on what all you had to endure to reach the height you are now."

"Yes Delores, I know you are right about all what you said and take a look at you yourself, because you had to endure a lot because you reach the status where you are because of rejections there in Mississippi that caused you to move away to show the south that with one's intention nothing that they threw out could not hold you back because of your determination to excel to higher heights. You came to New York, and you worked your way up to your position you hold right now and you gained the loyal and respect of many businesses because you had firsthand knowledge of the financial world which was your college major. The bank headquarters, took a chance with you to let you show exactly what you could do for the system and girlfriend, you proved yourself. "

"If only you were given that chance back there in Mississippi, when you graduated from college, you probably would have help make the situations of things there much better because you would have been a people person to assist everyone not just one group of people. I guess you can say Delores that you as well as I have both been blessed to be able to utilizes our college education and now, since things has changed back home for the betterment for all people, my brother Greg will not have to do as I did, leave from home to exercise my education with a strange city of folks who took me serious and did not look upon me by the color of my skin. He will be welcomed into the school system as it was once favored to all whites that gave the black schools nothing so we knew we had to learn or be left behind so we decided to learn as much as possible because those black teachers that taught the black students, instilled into our minds to not let the odds that the system set up for us become our power brokers. They often said to all the black students, the world will be looking to see if we would make it or fail."

Unfortunately, with all of the changes that has been implemented, those policies and procedures established long ago for keeping people of color down have turned around for the good of the whole country as everyone has begun to marry in all races to show that is exactly what was intended to be all along. Once Sandra returned back from the city to see all of what has taken place right in her own country home setting, she will then understand finally what Wayne had said to her, but until then she will just have to face it on her own to understand. Time was drawing near for Sandra and Delores to prepare for their trip to Louisiana to be there for her brother's graduation and then after their return back to New York, they will be faced with another exciting time, the honoring of Sandra for all the work she had done for making the city's law firms the way they are in handling cases to free up the courts. As Delores and Sandra began to pack for their trip, Delores said to her that it was no use take a lot because they were only going to be there for just two days and then they would be flying back.

Is Love Worth the Wait?

Sandra said to Delores that this trip there will be a very important trip because her brother Greg had finally followed in her footsteps as she knew he would as the two of them discussed where they wanted to go and be while they were all growing up to include Wayne as their adopted brother during that time. Sandra said to Delores how she so grateful how everything turned out the way she had hoped they would, with Wayne making his career in the field he majored in, as well as Sandra finally getting into what she had always wanted to do, an English teacher. Delores said to her just how proud she was to see what her family members had turned out to be with Greg entering into the field of mathematics and you know, he will be good at it because growing up he had a mind for solving problems as other of us could not solve.

"Once you and I have flown to Louisiana and returned, Sandra, just watching you to pack up everything to go home, this place will be so sad until I realizes that your presence is no longer here."

"Delores, you will be just fine as before, because you are a strong woman Sandra replied to her. Delores, I want you to think about what I am about to say to you. As you regain your daily routines once I am no longer here, you must believe that all hopes won't be lost because you are still a young attracted woman and with your high position there in the bank, I am sure there will be a guy come knocking on your office door one day to be your knight in shining armor."

"Sandra if that is true then I wish he would hurry up and come on by so I can become someone's wife before I am too old. Just think about it Sandra you are lucky to have someone that has been in love with you all these years unknowing to you, still have high hopes. I am still not sure if you know what you are talking about because I think you are seeing things that are not there, but you are going on the assumptions of how you view Wayne as you think you might see something there which are not. If something come out of this whole thing that is true, I really want you to keep silence and do not make a hint to my parents, not even to my brother until I myself figure this whole thing out."

"Sandra I promised you that I will not say a work to my uncle and aunt, not even to my little cousin Greg. I am sure when this atomic bomb drops, there will be enough surprises to go around without my meddling into your affairs. Sandra it is surely going to take place and that, you better be prepared to accept it," Delores said to her. "As I see it now, you and Greg both will be jumping the fence, you involved with a white boy and Greg involved with a mixed girl. Now I can go along with Greg's choice because at least she is close to our race, not like Wayne completely all white."

"Delores, if there is one thing I wish you could overlook or have a different perspective off and that is, the color of one's skin tone. I think if you could come to accept what is then you will be able to move forward to look at things clearer. Take a look at your situation Delores, you have been exposed to all kinds of people because you have been fortunately enough to be given a position that will allow you to serve all Sandra replied to her. You know, once I get back home, I promise you that I will not allow myself to look at the color of a person's skin because you know I will be teaching English to all races and that will be good."

"Come now," Sandra said to Delores. "Let's you and I discontinue this conversation for this night and make sure you and I have all what we will need to take on our trip to make my brother, your cousin Greg, happy to see us. What about taking him a gift Delores?" asked Sandra.

"I really don't think at this time it would be feasible because the more he receives from everyone, the more he will have to pack up and knowing Greg as I do, he will put all of that responsibility on Daddy, as he stands around entertaining Sadie, his future wife to be."

"You know Uncle Elijah will not mind packing up his son's belongings because he and Aunt Catherine will not want him to lift a finger as he is their baby boy Delores," reminded Sandra.

"Once you and I have gone there to see him march and return back here then you and I will have time to go shopping together to buy him something really nice so you can take back with you once you leave that sounds good at least I will have time to decide just what to get him. I just cannot believe it, there will soon be two wedding close at hand within my family that I will have to attend ," said Dolores.

"Wait just a minute cousin, please do not count your chicks before they hatch from the nest because there is no sure thing that this will be happening to me you know, as I will be so busy preparing English charts for my class of students to bring them up to their standards where they are supposed to be. "Delores just had to mention one important thing to Sandra about teaching English to those supposed to have been the cream of the crop white students, taught by all of those announced white professional teachers who they placed way above the back teachers in the all black schools to see just how much they know.

"Girlfriend, this is your time to shine to let the school board education administration know just how dumb those white students are and to show the scale of the black students margin and then they will know how wrong they had misjudged the black teachers below the white teachers. Now won't that be a slap in their faces?"

"I don't think all of that will be necessary now since all the things that did occur back then has changed and now everyone will know," replied Sandra.

All of that would be nice though to finally show those so called established perfect southern belles, they did not have the intellect as the blacks teachers who learned all they were taught and keep their learning close in their minds to be mentors to all the back students they taught to let them know that what they learn no one could take it away from them because they had good guidance. "Sandra after I say this much then I am going to close the subject. I really think what has happened within the federal equal opportunity bureau, is the best thing that could have taken place because now, it will be known that this should have not happen. I guess better late than never."

"Delores, you made our flight reservations to and from Louisiana, didn't you?"

"I did and our flight to Louisiana will be leaving from JFK Air Terminal Saturday morning at exactly six thirty with expected arrival time there at ten thirty. I understand that the ceremony will get on the way at two thirty and by four thirty, everything should be over with and the graduate students will be able to clear out of their dorm rooms to turn in their keys to the dorm residence overseers."

"Just think about it, my little brother will be walking across the stage to receive his long awaited degree, as he studied so long and hard for. I know Mother and daddy are as happy as they were for me when I too graduated. It was the joy of their lives and when Wayne graduated too, his parents were just so overboard for he and me."

"That's good Sandra the reason why you are going to be their daughter-in-law soon. Oh, did I say that? You know I didn't mean to let that out Sandra."

"Yes you did because you just cannot help yourself smiling. There's one thing for sure, we all will finally get the chance to spend some time with Greg's girlfriend to know her better and Mother and Daddy I am sure will be so delighted with her because right now as I have spoken to her about Sadie, mother would say, 'she is such a lovely girl and I am sure Greg will be so happy having her as his wife. You know your father and I are looking for you and Greg to one day give us some grandchildren so we will be able to spoil them as we did you two.'"

"I have to go along with what Aunt Catherine said about grandchildren from you and Greg because that is the one most important thing all parents look forward too from their children, giving them something that will make them happy in their finally years on earth, so the family name can be carried on. I am not worrying so much about Greg producing your parents some grandchildren. I have a little concern whether that while boy will be capable of the same thing Sandra. He looks so fragile to be a father."

"Delores, what is wrong with you about whether or not Wayne can produce children? That is a subject you should not be discussing with me because I have said to you many of times that I don't know anything about what you are talking about. Delores, you know one thing that bothers me, it is you. With all that bad talk you have been throwing around I am so afraid one day it will come back to hit you in your face and by no shock to me you just might wind up marrying a different race yourself and then what would you like for me to say? Would you like for me to say to you the exact words you said to me?"

"I think if you did change and moved on over to the other side, you would be a better person and then you will know how Wayne felt when all you did was talk about him. Delores, just maybe if I did marry Wayne, I am sure I would have a good life because I know him better than any of those guys I have met here. At least I will know that he was not trying to run a scam on me as these New Yorkers are."

"On that point Sandra I will have to agree with you as far as Wayne is concerned. He is just an old country boy raised with good values and grew up in the midst of you and Greg. Now that you have mentioned all of that to me, he just might be able to shine Sandra Delores said to her. Being here in New York, I really didn't have to worry too much about you because you had the insight to look right through these players here to make your decisions about them. There's one thing that you have that is positive in your pocket and that is, you did not let yourself be taken in by the so called professional guys giving a different side of them to pull you in to be used and thrown away, as they would go on to the next victim. Cousin, not only do you have smarts, but you also have style and know how to use it too."

Finally the day and time has arrived where Delores, and her cousin Sandra were busy getting into a cab to take them to the air terminal to make their flight at the time to depart to fly off to Louisiana to attend her brother's Greg graduation, as well as to meet up with other members of the family to spend the short time she and Delores would have there before they would have to catch a flight back to New York to get ready for Sandra's going away party to be held by the law firm she had made so out- standing as she will be awarded the key to the city of New York to take back to her home town Mississippi to show everyone there what you can obtain if you are given the chance too. She mostly will show it to the Board of Education once she has been interviewed in person by the head figure. While she and Delores, were in flight, she made a comment to her just how much she was looking forward in meeting Greg's new girlfriend who will one day become his wife.

"That is all well and good Sandra," Delores replied. "But will your brother be glad to hear the news about how Wayne feel about you once he is told?"

"Listen Delores, I don't want you to say a word to him about what you think is true because this is not the time to get him upset because this is his day and he has worked so hard for you to come up with that silly stuff you keep talking about. Cousin, you can call it what you want too but I know the different because I have always smelt this rat," she said as she laughed.

"Don't worry my dear cousin Sandra I will not say a word that will cause Greg to ask questions. Like you said, this is his day and I do want hm to be happy because he really deserve it. After all my dear cousin Sandra he has followed in your footsteps to become the best that he can. At least he was not afraid to let my uncle and aunt know of his intentions once he did graduate from college and get a job to plan for his marriage with the girl he met while on campus. Greg didn't try to hide things to make believe they were not true as you have Sandra."

"I sure can say this to you Delores, whatever comes of it, it will still be a surprised to me because I don't think I have given Wayne any indication that I am interested in him other than what we have in common now. Listen Delores, please stop speaking about it."

"Delores, start preparing yourself for landing as the stewardess is telling everyone to keep their seat belts fasten until the plane come to a complete stop once we land. You know my parents have already reserved our room right next to theirs so we all can be together to have a goodtime in lifting up Greg, in his finest moments."

Once the two were off the plane and held a cab to take them to the stadium to meet up with the other family members, Sandra said to Delores, "So much has changed since I was last here as I look around to see all the changes that has taken place. Louisiana, is truly a new look to me."

"Well," Sandra replied. "Delores that's what happens when you have been away from the south for so many years until when you return, you will not recognizes a lot of it. Don't worry, once you are back for good here in the south, things will once again come to you and you will remember the sights as you did before you left." Soon the cab pulled on campus to the stadium and as the two of them waited for the cab to stop, they took a look and saw her mother and daddy, along with Delores' relatives who had come to see Greg march. They got out of the cab and Sandra paid the fare as the two of them took hold of their one overnight bag and walked over to where everyone were waiting to be seated as they gave hugs and kisses to one another so glad to see their presence there. Delores said to her Uncle Elijah how great he looks as well as her aunt Catherine.

Delores own father who is the brother of her Uncle Elijah, gave her a hug and said to her, "How are things there in New York?"

"Daddy, Sandra and I have been having the time of our lives, enjoying all the highlights there to be enjoyed in that city."

Her mother Lora said to her, "You know your little sister is thinking about enrolling into this same school as all of you have done. I guess it will be a family tradition."

"But Mother, Sarah has a full three more years to think about what she wants to do."

Sandra said to her, "Do you know how fast time flies? Before you realize it, she will be marching across the stage receiving her diploma. I guess that means, I am getting old because my little sister, Sarah is growing up real fast. Sandra parents said to all of them, it is time for us to take our seats because the graduates are about to come down to take their seats."

Just as everyone were taking their seats to greet all graduates, Sandra said to Delores, "There is Greg in his finest taking his seat looking over toward his family members all in smiles knowing this will be the last day here in this city before he depart and he has no plans to return because he came here to get what he set out to do and not only did he, get an education, but he met his future wife as well as she too was marching to receive her degree as well and she too, will return back home to gain employment there in the field she majored in. As the president of the university was standing in front of the his podium making his speech to not only the graduates, but he was letting all of the parents who had sent their children to the university to be further educated, gave all of them his many thanks because their children were the reasons why this university is the most outstanding black university within the state of Louisiana, as well as the far most outstanding one amid other states as well."

As the president continue to speak, Sandra looked toward Delores to say, "Isn't this a good turnout as so many people are here for this event?"

"I have to say Sandra you, me, as well as Greg made the best decision in our lives to attend here because now, since things have changed, the opportunities are vast but I still would not come back here to live," she said. "You see Sandra I have out grown the south and now, I am a city girl who have learned all the city ways and if I came back here to the south, I would not know what to do because I would be lost. But for you Sandra you have not lost all what you have been use too here so that is why it will be easier for you to come back to live."

Soon, the president ended his speech as he started to recognizes the most outstanding students to come up to take their rightful place here on stage as he will present to them, their degree and along with it, a certificate of outstanding merits. Greg was one of those outstanding graduate because just as his sister Sandra did while she attended there, he too held for the whole four academic years, a grade point average of all A's. When his family heard what the president had said about him, Delores said to Sandra, "It must be something in the water to give this family smarts."

Of course Sandra was not really happy with what Delores just said because she knew just as she and Greg showed their smarts, there were more students there showing the same. Beside from Greg being recognized, the president also presented all the ones he had called up on the stage to be presented with the same appreciation. Little did they know, the girl that Greg would be marrying one day was presented with the same as the others which made Sandra as well as his parents happy for her. Soon, after all had been presented with their degrees and a shout out to every graduate by the audience, the crowd began to break up as the parents were following their graduate children back to their dorm to clear thing out because in a few weeks, summer school would start and rooms would be needed for the upcoming applicants. After Greg ran down to give his mother, father, sister and cousin Delores a big hug as he laughed with all joys as they all walked back to his dormitory to pack up his things, he saw Sadie, walking with her parents as he said to his family to wait a minute because he wanted to go over to meet Sadie's parents.

"Greg," Sandra said to him. "Instead of walking over to meet them, why don't you bring them over here to meet all of us because you know we would love to get to know her since you have been telling everyone that you plan to marry her soon."

Greg did exactly what his sister had said to him and they all came over and the reunion began to unite. Greg introduced everyone as Catherine said to Sadie's mother and father that she was so glad to finally meet her because she was all what Greg talked about, Sadie, this, Sadie that, as they laughed. Sandra and Delores, said to Sadie, "We are so glad to meet you and if and when you two guys decide to tie that knot, please know that we will be in the midst of your wedding planning."

Sadie's parent said to her to come on so they could help her pack her things so they could get back on the road to travel home before it get to dark. Catherine said to Sadie's mother, "I think we better do the same because this son of our probably have a truck load of stuff to take home. I am sure we all will be getting together pretty soon." Greg walked with Sadie for a few steps kissed her and said soon.

"Greg," Sandra asked him. "I thought they were going to remain over night at an hotel and leave in the morning?"

"No, because Sadie's father said he had to get back to work. I am sorry to hear that because I was looking forward in getting to know them more but oh well, there will be plenty of time as she will become Mrs. Greg Logan, one day. As they enter into Greg's room they could not believe all the stuff he had gather over four years. Sandra said to him, when I was here attending school,

I never had this much stuff but then too, men are different from females. His father and mother said to them let's get busy and start taking all of this stuff down to the car. It's a good thing I have my truck to put all of these things in the back of it."

Delores said to her cousin Greg, "I just cannot believe you have this much stuff."

Greg said to her hand Sandra, "By the way, where are my graduation gifts from the two of you?"

"Little brother, let me explain something to you," Sandra said to him. "Delores and I had made plans to go shopping for you, but we decided to do it once we return back to New York that way we could take out time to decide what you really needed."

"Greg my dear little grown up baby boy," his mother said. "Please don't push it because they will take get you something just as your father and I will. First things first, and now the thing we all need to do is to get all of your things together, so you will not be charged by not turning in your key. We have all been checked into the hotel of our choice as a gift to you to surprise you with what we have planned for your night."

Delores asked her Aunt Catherine, "Will there be any strippers on the scene?"

"Now Delores," her cousin said to her. "You know that is not who my parents are because you know we have more class than that," she said as she laughed. After everything had been cleaned out of the room and Greg walked down to the office and turned in his key to the dorm staff, the lady who took it wished him well in his career and it was a privilege to have him stay there for the full four years without a single incident.

She said to his parents who were standing there with him, "I know you are so proud of your son, as I am as I watched him over the four years, a well manner young man and I know he will go far."

Greg's parents said to the lady that they thank her so much for saying those nice kind words about their son because that is what they had always taught their children to show respect to others. As Greg turned around to walk out for the last time and as he got to the door, he turned around to say to the lady that had made such a nice comment about him, "Well, I don't think I will be seeing you again but I would like to say to you and the other staffers that it has been my pleasure to be in your company for these four years because I have learned a lot because you help me to grown. Goodbye and I do hope that you will have another young man to come to you as I did with good family values." Greg walked out the door with his parents and they got into his father truck as Sandra and Delores had already gone over to the hotel to check in to their room to rest before it would be time for the event for Greg get started. As the three of them droved over to the hotel, Greg asked them, "Exactly what is that you guys have planned for me?"

"Son," his father said. It isn't a big deal just something your mother and I thought would be beneficial to you for all the hard work you have done over the past four long years making such remarkable strive that you have. We decided to let you enjoy yourself as long as you wanted too before we all have to get up early in the morning to drive home."

"Tell me about my brother Wayne why didn't he come?"

His mother said to him, "Well son, Wayne did want to come, but you see his job right now has him stressed out making sure all reports are correct before they are elevated up to the agricultural federal government office for the year relating to farmers." Elijah and Catherine had made an agreement with Wayne that all that he had said to them about marrying Sandra will not be told to him. so they had to walk a tight rope getting him through this.

As they drove on to the hotel, his mother turned around to look in his face to say to him, "You are happy aren't you son?"

"Why yes mother because I don't think I could be anymore happier seeing everyone her for my graduation and introducing Sadie to all of my family members. This is a good day."

"When we get back home, knowing that I have been away for four long years, I don't know how I will be for the first few weeks because everything and everyone would have changed so much. I imagine I probably will not recognize to many of the kids of my age that is, if I can find them. Well, I do have to let you know most of those guys you grow up with either have joined the military or even gotten married. What about Wayne's parents, how are they?"

"Well son, you know how Florence is as she calls me all the time and even bring her favorite coffee cake over for the two of us to have a slice and a cup of hot tea. She is fine as Wayne come home not every weekend but some to have dinner with the two of them. I think I would enjoy a piece of her coffee cake as it make my mouth water. I know she will be glad to see me and to let Wayne know that I am home so he will be coming home every weekend to hang out with me."

"Did I tell you and daddy I have been offered a job in one of the high school teaching mathematics to high school students come this fall?"

"I just cannot believe it with you already gainful employed and Sandra receiving notification that she too will get what she always wanted to teach English. Of course she and I will not be working in the same school because the school I will be working is about five miles from home."

"It doesn't matter Son," his father said. "At least you two will be home for a while as we already know your stay with us will be short once you save your money to buy your home for you and Sadie." Greg doesn't know it but just as Wayne's mother and father had done about his future, Catherine and Elijah had done the same thing with their two children to set money aside to help them get started. Neither parents will let them know the exact amount they had placed aside for them, but it sure will be enough to almost pay for their home in full. They decided to wait until Greg work some so he can save his money to be responsible. If they told him then he would rush right out to try and persuade Sadie to marry him now without waiting. Catherine and Elijah, though to let him work for a period of time until they think he is ready to hear the good news.

The night that had been planned for Greg entertainment went along as planned as when all of them came into the dining room to have a well thought of dinner, set up by his mother unknown to him as she made all arrangements with the hotel at the time she made their reservations. As dinner was served, all of a sudden as Greg looked around to see all of the party ladies coming up to him to dance for him as well as he was pulled out on the floor to dance, as he said to his parents, "I know you did this for me and now, I am going to show off with my dance moves," as Sandra and Delores sat still with their mouths opened not believing what they saw in Greg.

Delores said to Sandra, "Now that is the type of moves you should have been putting on those guys back there in New York, because if you had then you would not be moving back home to be involved with Wayne." She whispered in her ear so that her Uncle Elijah and her Aunt Catherine would not hear. Little did Delores did not know that they already knew all of Wayne's plans as he had briefed them.

Greg was having the time of his life because after this night, this type of fun with him just might not happen again until he will make his outstanding dance on the floor once he get married to Sadie. As the excitement continued on the floor, Sandra and Delores, enjoyed the fabulous dinner that had been chosen by her mother. As Greg would not let up on the floor from dancing with all the four ladies that were entertaining him, his mother asked his father, "Do you think he will come off that floor to eat?"

"Catherine, you know you asked for this because you wanted him to be happy and you wanted to give him something that he would remember for a lifetime so even if he doesn't eat, we can always take it upstairs in a carryout bag that way when he decide to eat, it will be there for him. I really don't think he has any appetite now because that young man of our are having the time of his life after graduating from college. We did good Catherine, didn't we?" Elijah asked her.

As things continued to show around Greg Sandra and Delores said to them, "Guys you know that we will have to fly out tomorrow morning early as you three head back home to await my arrival you know.

Catherine and Elijah wanted so much to tell Sandra what she would be walking into once she return home, but since they had made a pack with Wayne not to tell her, they said to her, "We know and you know going home without you, will be a lonely trip, but after this night I am sure it will be a quiet trip because I know Greg will be so tired from all of his dancing that he will fall asleep."

"Daddy, why didn't Mr. and Mrs. Hunt, come because I know Greg would have been more than glad to have them here as well?" Sandra asked.

"Well, I think they probably have something planned for your brother once he is home that way, Wayne will be there to enjoy that gathering since he himself could not come to be with us. Sandra have you started packing yet because you know it is only a couple of weeks before you will be rolling in?" her father asked her.

Before Sandra could answer him, Delores with her outspoken self said to him, "Uncle Elijah, you just don't know how hard I have tried to convince Sandra to remain in New York, because I think her future would be better, but she is so set on moving back to teach English to a bunch of students."

"Well my niece that is her calling and you know Sandra as well as she and her father know that, once she had set her mind on something and she know that is her calling then nothing different would change her mind."

"I know one thing, I will miss her and I know the law firm she is working for and built up with be besides themselves come next week when they present her the key of the city by the mayor."

"You see Daddy and Mother, Delores has grown to hate the south because when she graduated from college she was denied opportunities there so she will never return regardless of how things has changed."

"You are right girlfriend, I have become a city girl and all of that country stuff has been left way behind me to no avail. It is with sadness that my dear cousin will be leaving but I want you and aunt Catherine to know that I am so glad that I encouraged her to make that move for the years she had stayed with me at least she has grown in all aspects of the country. Now, if and when she get tired of teaching school, she know she has the capabilities to set her sights on other things to her endeavors."

As Delores kept talking, Sandra was afraid that she would slip up to say something she wouldn't want her parents to hear as they too have been like real parents to Wayne and they all were raised together as one family. However, Delores with her sly self did ask them about that white skinny boy Wayne.

"How is he doing?"

"Delores," her uncle said to her. "I am a little shocked that you would say something like that about Wayne because he is just like my son and Catherine and I cannot find anything better to say about him, but he is a wonderful person. Now tell me, where did you get that attitude about him from?"

"I don't know Uncle Elijah, but I just find something that is not right with him," and just then Sandra made up in her mind to cut her off from talking about him to turn the conversation around toward Greg.

"Look Delores, at all those dance steps he is making out there on the floor, do you think you can do all of them?"

The party lasted about two hours in that time Greg was almost worn out so he thanked the ladies that entertained his graduation accomplishments as they walked him back over to the table so he could have dinner, but since he was so tired, he could not eat a thing and all he wanted to do was to go to his room to rest. His father said to him, "Son, we set this all up for you and now you are telling us that you are tired?"

"I know Daddy but I have not danced so much in a very long time and you know if Sadie was here, I could have held out." His mother had already said to the server to put his dinner into a carryout container because her son will be having his dinner in their room.

Delores said to all of them, "Is this party over with already when I am just getting started to walk out there on that dance floor to show these southerners how to really show them the way the New Yorkers entertain."

"You come on Delores because you know we have an early flight to catch in the morning so knowing how slow you are, we don't want to miss our flight." As the five of them stood there along with Delores, Mother, and Father celebrating Greg, they all decided to make way to their rooms for a good night sleep.

You know They all will have to meet up in the dining room for a light breakfast before they hug, kiss, and to greet everyone a safe return home until they would all meet up again for other events which will soon come. Once Sandra's parents and brother Greg made their way to their room as her mother held Greg's dinner because he would be staying in their room so they could just talk and enjoy him for all of the accomplishments he had made over the four years being there at the university. Instead of eating his dinner, Greg just fell across the bed to sleep, but his father said to him, "Son, not so fast because you have to eat something since you have drained yourself out on the floor of your energy so sit up and start eating. After you have finished, you go into the bathroom, take a long shower, and get into bed. There were two queen size beds for him to take one as being their baby boy. After Greg had eaten and his mother handed him a pair of sleeping shorts, he went into the bathroom to take a shower.

Afterward he came out and said to them, "I love you guys because you are the greatest," and then he was in another world.

Catherine and Elijah sat up reading over his certificates and being amazed to all of the wonderful things he had allowed himself to get involved with for the total period of time being away from home. "I think Catherine," Elijah said to her. "We made the most and best things by our children as we possibly could. Look how the two of them turned out to be. Sandra soon to be coming home to take a teaching position and Greg already has been given a mathematics teaching position. Who would have ever thought all of these good things would have happened to you and me as we were busy being good parents to our children?"

"You know Elijah, as I said to you many times that things will not ever remain the same just because you and I didn't have those privileges, it didn't mean that our children would not be applied with changes. You know, I am sort of sorry to hear all the negative things Delores has felt about the south, as things were not put into motions before she left but I think over a period of time, she will change."

"Please don't hold your breath to that," Elijah said to her. "Because I know her and how she can be. I wish she would make negative comments about Wayne because she not being here around him, she doesn't know just what he is like." Speaking low and soft so that Greg would not hear their conversation, they said that what Wayne has opened their eyes too.

Elijah said to Catherine, "I think he will be good for her. How do you think our son who is sleeping over there will feel once he finds out? You and I have already been told by Wayne to let him be the one to break it to him the reason being he thinks that since to two of them have a closeness as true brothers, he would be able to make him have a better understanding of just how he feels about Sandra other than a sister. As much as I know how Florence wants to call to discuss this with me, she too is holding onto what Wayne had mentioned to her and Samuel to be silent until he let Greg know as well as Sandra when he picks her up when she comes home from New York arriving on the train."

Back in the room where Delores and Sandra were, Sandra said to Delores, "Why did you want to go there with my parents about Wayne when you and I had talked about not saying anything about him?"

"I am sorry Sandra but as I took a look and saw how so much fun Greg was having out on the dance floor, something jumped inside of me because I could see you out there having fun with a good black guy and not that white boy if that is ever going to be such entertainment."

"Still Delores that was not the time to go off on your wind bend.

"I know but now it's all over with and come tomorrow, you and I will fly back to New York to prepare for your leaving me for good to go home. Greg seem so happy didn't he Sandra?"

"My little baby brother was having the time of his life and I am quite sure if Sadie was present, we would have to take him off the floor because he would have spent all night out there. I think he and Sadie are going to be two good people together once they are married, if I do say so myself, cousin Sandra."

"This is one marriage I know I have to attend because I just might bring with me one of those New Yorkers to cut a step or two with me," Delores said laughing.

"That would be nice," Sandra said to her. "Then maybe you would mind your own business."

After Sandra saying what she said to Delores, they turned in and before they had a clue, morning was upon them as they rushed to dress to go downstairs to meet up with the others who had already made their way downstairs into the dining room for a quick breakfast because it was now a time constraint for all to prepare to be on their way back to their destination. As Sandra and Delores arrived to meet the others, they had always taken their seats at the table and unknowing to Sandra and Delores, their taste of breakfast had been ordered by the one who had put all of this together in honor of their son and brother Greg. Sandra and her father said to the two of them, "Come on and join in this fine breakfast with the others because you know you two have to make sure you get to the air terminal on time to catch your flight back to New York, and we, like you two, must hit the road to take our son home."

Delores said to her parents that she promised them that it will be a very soon visit not because of a graduation, but for a period of time to spend quality time with the family a she will be presence for Greg's upcoming marriage. Her mother said to her, "Delores that won't be for another two years and you are telling your father and I you won't be coming home until then?"

"Not really mother, because it just might be sooner than you think," as she took a look toward Sandra as she wanted to tell them about a possibility that Sandra will be marrying that white boy who is just wild about her. Sandra took a look at her to say in her mind, "Please shut up your mouth because you are just all over everyone's road trying to find directions to park your car in." Greg was so busy eating until he was only thinking about getting home to catch up with his future wife Sadie to be spending quality time with making their plans.

Delores asked Greg, "By the way little cousin Greg was Sadie lucky enough to be offered a job position as you?"

"Delores, my future wife was offered a position long before I received mine as she will be giving an administrative position in the Board of Education to become the director over the hiring of teachers."

"Wow," Delores said. "Now that is an accomplishment."

"Just think Sandra if that type of position was available when I graduated from college who knows, I just might have never settled in New York, but these good changes had not taken place so, therefore, forced me to leave."

Sandra's mother said to all, "We better end these conversations and start saying our goodbyes because time waits for no one you know."

As they stood up to begin hugging and kissing, Sandra's father Elijah said to Greg and his mother, as well as to Delores parents, "Come on and let us prepare to leave," as they hugged Sandra and Delores to say, "You guys get busy to get into your awaited cab to take off to the air terminal."

"We hope to see you guys real soon," Delores' parents said to them.

Delores' mother said to her daughter, "Please try to concentrate on your life and stay out of Sandra's."

"It is hard to do Mother but I will try to do as you say." Sandra hugged Delores' mother to say thanks but it is just who she is and there's no changing it.

Soon, everyone was on their way back to their homes as Sandra and Delores were now in the air terminal waiting to be boarded on their flight back to New York. Delores said to Sandra as they waited until their flight number was being called, "Attending this good graduation of Greg was a good thing and it was so good to see everyone there for I had not seen them for such a long time."

"Yes Delores," Sandra responded to add a little more to her response by saying, "You are something else Delores but I still love you as you are my cousin, sometimes you just get carried away and don't know how to get in your place wanting to tell everything."

"Are you speaking about Wayne, Sandra?"

"Yes, you know I am because you had no right to open up your mouth to say what you did as you are not sure of all the things Wayne just might be thinking. I guess now you are a mind reader."

As their flight number was being called and everyone were busy lining up to give the ticket agent their boarding pass, Delores whispered in Sandra's right ear to say, "I am not a mind reader but I know what I feel and right now,

I feel that I am right about what is going to take place with you my dear cousin once when you return back home to start off with your teaching career."

As the two of them gave their boarding passes to the agent and walked through the hall to get on their plane and after taking their assigned seats, Sandra said to Delores that she hoped that this conversation would not continue all the way to JFK Terminal. Delores said to Sandra, "I want to say one more thing and then I am finished with it for a while. I know what I feel and at night while I am asleep, I see it coming in my dreams as I know you will become Mrs. Wayne Hunt, something you keep fighting off because you don't want to accept what is to come." After that, Sandra turned her head and began to look out the window of the plane as it taxis down the roadway off into the skies.

Delores tries to keep a conversation going by saying to Sandra, "Come next week you will be overshadowed with excitement from all of your working peers wishing you nothing but the best."

"Sandra?" Delores asked her. "Will you be glad to be going back home?"

"Think about it Delores," she said. "I never wanted to leave there anyway, because of the situations there then and when you encouraged me to leave, I thought it would be to my advantage to make that move and I can't say that I have not enjoyed it, because I have learned a lot and have made many strides as well as opening up a lot of new and foremost avenues in the big city of New York. Cousin Delores, I owe it all to you although you worked my last nerve at times, but you and I were able to put all of that aside and stayed the course of helping out each other. I don't think you or I could have been any happier, two cousins together having the time of our lives going out to exciting highlights in the city, meeting guys who claimed to be professional guys to learn they were players, but with our smarts, you and I did not allow them to take us down. Now, I have to say I think those times were the highlight of it all." As they continued talking the seat belt light came on for all to fasten up as they would be landing in about ten minutes.

Sandra said to Delores, "Our three hour flight for some reason did not seem long and now here we are ready to land. Just think about it Delores, my little brother has graduated from college and now he is at the point of journeying on into his career. I cannot believe how quick time has flown by because it seem as if it was yesterday that he was still in high school and now, he has made a great accomplishment. Since we are off until Wednesday, why not spend time shopping to see what we will buy for his graduation? Delores, I don't have a clue to what to get him."

"You think you don't, what about your cousin Delores?" Surely I don't know but I think if we put our heads together we will come up with something as we shop."

Soon their plane touched down and they were on the grounds waiting to be given the signal to pull up to the unloading gate before they could unfasten their seat belts to start getting up to get off. As the two of them walked by the stewardess, they were greeted with, "Thank you for flying with TWA and have a good day."

Once Delores and Sandra got inside the terminal to retrieve their luggage, Delores said out loud, "We are back home to New York City. We flew to Louisiana and now we have returned to a bigger city with bright lights and so much excitement." When they picked up their luggage, they walked outside to halt a cab that would take them home for they needed to spend the rest of the day doing nothing because they did not get the rest they needed because of the excitement that was surrounded by Greg's graduation and with something like this, you will not be in the loop of getting rest because that was not to take place but to come later on once all the excitement has subsided.

After the cab has stopped for them and the cabbie placed their luggage in the trunk of the cab, they head on into the city of Manhattan where Delores had purchased her condo some time ago in a safe environment where she would not have to worry about things getting out of hand at night while she rested and she wanted to let her cousin Sandra see that she would be safe once she had moved in with her for a few years. She had her game plan to entice Sandra to remain there with her and not return back to Mississippi and instead have a rewarding life there. It was Delores' game plan, but it was not the least part of Sandra's game plan. As they drove through the city, Delores pointed the highlight spots out to Sandra in hopes of changing her mind.

Delores said to Sandra, "Isn't this city full of all the things that you read about?"

"Delores, I appreciate what you are trying to do and I really respect you for it, but to be honest with you, this is just not for me because my heart is not here and if I continue to remain in hopes of feeling different, I am afraid I would get depressed from being locked in a place that I am not in love with. All of the important parts of this city that you are showing me are nice but I have to go and please, let's you and I think on how good it was to see your parents as well as my parents. Delores, you and I flew to Louisiana for a worthy cause and to put a spin on it that was my highlight to see my baby little brother march across the stage to receive his degree just as you and I did when we both graduated. I don't think anything in this city could even come close to what you and I both experienced in Louisiana. I want to let my last two weeks here in New York City be a memorable time where I can leave with my head held high to know that I have made a difference in the lives of a lot of people here from a little black girl from dear ole Mississippi."

"There is one thing that you cannot escape and that is the south from which you came from with a good background in education that prepared you to obtain the position you now hold. I have to say, I am southern breed and there I will continue to be that type of person because my loyalty is there."

"I guess with these last two weeks, I better get used to being alone again after you leave," Delores responded.

"Delores, you were never alone before I came, it is just that you lived alone, but you always had company you know because you were raised to call out the one name that you know would hold you in the palm of his holy arms."

"Don't go any further because I get the point my wonderful cousin Sandra because you always seem to put your final touch on things. I know without a shadow of doubt, you will be happy because I know you will. Please don't get mad or take it the wrong way with what I am about to say because more and more as I look at things about you, even if Wayne asks you to marry him, you will be happy because he is and will be a good provider regardless of how I feel toward him."

Once Delores has finally given in to her cousin Sandra about whether or not Wayne will asks her to marry him, she was convinced that this just might be the right thing for Sandra to make her life complete. After all of this back and forth talking, they decided to go shopping for Greg's graduation if as the two of them decided on something that he would always remember them by, two New York fitness outfits of different colors so when he decides to spend time in the gymnasium, all the fellows there will think that he is from New York. After shopping the two of them returned home to prepare for the last episode of Sandra's last days there as she will be pulling out come next Saturday morning headed home to meet up with her future husband. As Delores and Sandra had returned home the two of them sat down to rest from having a long period of the day from shopping for Greg. As they looked over what they had purchased for him, Delores asked Sandra, "Do you think he will like this color?"

"Knowing my brother as I do, he will like any color that you give him because he will just be so overwhelmed with what you and I decided to buy him. This will surely be a show stopper for him to show himself off to everyone," Sandra said laughing.

"Sandra," Delores responded to her to say. "Girlfriend, come next Saturday night, my home will be as empty as a bird's nest because you would have arrived home by the time I will start missing you."

"I know Delores," Sandra responded back to her. "I too will miss you as well. Have you called Wayne yet to let him know of your departure time and your time expected arrival there?"

"I am going to call him here shortly so he will have all the facts he needs to know about."

"So you still don't intend to let your parents know of your departure? I think they will be happy once they see me drive up into the driveway with Wayne so that Greg, my parents, as well as his parents can have a reunion."

"Sandra when does Wayne plan on telling Greg about you and him?"

"I am quite sure he will break it to Greg this weekend as the two of them get together for a joyful graduation gift time. I sure hope that Greg will accept the news and handle it well without going off as a Fourth of July rocket," Delores said to her.

Sandra responded, "It won't be like Greg doesn't know anything about him because they have known each other basically all their lives. You know Delores, you keep talking about Wayne but I have yet to say that if I am asked by him that I will accept his proposal, not knowing if will be the right thing for me to do because I have to really give myself some time to think about the possibility of getting into something that I just might sorry about later on down the road."

"Come on Sandra," Delores answered her. "You won't be sorry because you will have a good life in spite of how most people will accept the two of you, but if Wayne want care then why should you be so concerned? I say to you again, as you have reminded me many of times about the changes in the south, I think those old, narrowminded people will have no other reasons to turn up their noses, but to bring them down out of the air to let live and let go, as they see their sons and daughters jumping the flood gates to swim across the other sides that had been closed off by that old southern traditions."

"You know Sandra I have heard this old saying many of times about the south will rise again because they lost the war, but this time is surely rising from the cross over into different directions of people. Maybe while things were being shut down to most of the people, someone should have looked into the future to see the rising of the sun and the going down of the sun. Sandra took toward Delores and asked her exactly what was she going on about.

"Sandra if you didn't notice things while we were in Louisiana, attending your brother Greg's graduation and noticed the night your parents gave him a nice graduation dinner to see all of those white girls all over him on the dance floor."

"I noticed them having a fun time but Delores I wasn't thinking on all the things you noticed because I saw them having a good time and showing their appreciation for my parents booking the establishment there."

"Whether you know it or not, since things have changed, those girls are getting wild because you know that they have always wanted to get next to that smoked meat."

"Delores, I have to say this much, I have one crazy cousin."

"Look at yourself my dear cousin Sandra that skinny white boy has been waiting to get his hooks in you because let us face it and we know it is true, those southern white guys have always wondered about those brown skinned beautiful girls too. You know it has been said by weather metrologists that there will be a change in the weather and now it has surely been a change in the south," Delores kept on say.

Finally, Sandra said to her, "I think I have had enough of your say and I am going to call Wayne to give him an update."

"You go right ahead girl," Delores said to her, "because that storm will soon land." Sandra excused herself from the presence of Delores because she knew how noisy she could be and she went into her bedroom to make her call.

Once she had called Wayne and he answered, he said, "Sandra it is so good to hear your voice as I was wondering if and when you would call me to give me your schedule so I will not be late."

"Wayne, I will be leaving here from New York next Saturday morning on the nine o'clock train and I hope to be arriving there around three thirty in the afternoon.

"I got it all written down and you can be sure that I will be there waiting long before your train pulls in."

"Sandra I have so much to tell you when you get here as we are on the way to your parents' home."

"Would you care to share some of the good news with me now?" she asked him.

"No, because it will spoil the whole setting of things."

"I guess then I have no other alternative but to just wait."

"Wayne what are you up to?" asked Sandra.

"I am not up to anything that will make you think less of me," he replied.

"You know Delores and I went shopping for Greg to get his graduation gift and I am sure he will like what we bought him."

"May I ask what you guys bought him?" asked Wayne.

"We saw these beautiful exercise leisure outfits and purchased two of different color that have the logo on the back that says: You are now a New Yorker. We thought he would get a thrill out of them. Did you get him something Wayne?" asked Sandra.

"I haven't bought anything yet for him but I think I will call him tonight to tell him."

"Whatever you let him know what you plan to give him, I think that he will welcome it." Wayne replied to Sandra how so much he hoped so.

As the two of them had finished with their talk, Sandra said to Wayne before she hung up to ask how were things going there with his job.

"It is fine and I have put in a transfer closer to home so I will be close by my parents as well as you and all the others."

"Do you think you will get it?" she asked him.

"I am hoping to as my boss told me that my work record tells the story."

"That is good news to hear Wayne."

"Now that I have your schedule, I will let you go so you can start getting yourself together to leave. I will see you next Saturday then. "Wayne said good night to Sandra with a smile on his face knowing that all of his plans were beginning to work in his direction. Hopeful when he tells Greg all about it tomorrow when he get there to visit his parents, the two of them could just go someplace to have a one on one conversation. Wayne knows that it will be a hard nervous thing for him to bring up to the one brother he had always loved because he did not have a brother of his own so he was adopted as a brother by Sandra and Greg that makes it so hard to tell him with hopes of getting a good feel from this little brother of his.

Wayne thought after he had finished speaking with Sandra to not wait until the next day, but he should call Greg this night to talk with him, so he will be prepared to hear what he has to tell him when in his presence. Wayne dialed Greg's home number and wouldn't you know it, Greg picked up the phone and answered." Hello brother man," Greg said to Wayne. "What do I have the pleasure of your call this night?"

"Listen little brother," Wayne said to him. "Tomorrow when I get there as I plan to visit my parents over the weekend, I would like for you and I to go someplace where there is only you and I so we can talk because I have something to tell you and when I tell you all about what I have kept from you, I hope you will accept me as always and you will not make any changes in the way you have felt about me all these years."

"My big white brother, what is it you would like to talk to me about?" Greg asked him.

"Let's just say for now, it will be your graduation gift."

"Oh boy, you are going to tell me you decided to buy me a car."

"No, nothing like that but I think what I have to tell you it will be better than any car or something else. It will be a lifetime guarantee."

"Well my brother, I guess I have to wait until tomorrow comes because right now, I don't see you telling me anything to prepare me for my big surprise." After the two of them had finished with their conversation, Greg walked into the living room where his parents were sitting talking to say to them, "Guys, I just got the craziest call from Wayne telling me he wanted to talk with me tomorrow about something he had been holding inside of him for so many years."

His father asked him, "Did he tell you anything about was on his mind?"

"That is the part that I just don't understand because it is not like him to hold things back from me of all people because he and I have always told each other our secrets. I wonder what this big secret is that it has to wait until tomorrow?" Greg asked his parents.

As he turned around to walk out of the living room, his mother and father said to each other, "I think once he has been told, this just might be a shock."

"Yes," his wife Catherine said. "But I don't think it will change their relationship the least bit besides, it just might make the two of them become more brotherly love."

Elijah said to Catherine that they must continue to pretend that neither of them had no knowledge of all that was told to them by Wayne. "I am sure the same thing with his parents stand as well because you know that the four of us being parents have been so secretive for this whole ordeal. Neither has Florence has spoken to you about it nor has Samuel spoken to me about it. We four parents have locked this secret up in the fault to only be taken out by Wayne. Maybe tomorrow once Wayne and Greg speak, then Wayne will know about Greg's intentions on marrying Sadie, which is coming too quickly. Well Catherine, it looks as if the two of us no, the four of us will be having all these wedding bells ringing all around this place."

"Elijah?" Catherine asked him. "Do you think once Wayne tells Sandra she will accept his proposal and at least give it a lot of thought before she gives him an answer?"

"I think everything will work out for the two of them as well as for Greg and Sadie. Well Catherine, I feel a chill in the air and it will get colder than ever before. Once this is out you and Florence had better get on the stick and start planning for all this excitement that will go on in this community."

The silence of Wayne has finally pushed its way right up to the top of his list as he and his best friend and adopted brother made an exact time to meet for their talk as Wayne will open up to let all those hidden flies fly out in the direction of Greg to get his take on him proposing to Sandra, the girl whom he had called all of his life his little sister, hoping that Greg would accept it and wish him the best. As he thought about it as he drove toward his parents' home saying it can be the worst thing ever for him to do. There was one thing that Wayne was banking on and that was the fact if Sandra accepts then Greg just might go along and forget about being mad with him if that would be the case. Once when Wayne reached his parents' home and drove up into the yard, he looked toward Greg's parents' home to see him standing out in the yard waving to him and yelling, "Hey brother, I don't want to wait to hear what you have to tell me that has been heavily weighing on your mind as this is a good time for you to come on over so you and I can sit out on the front porch as we use to do so you can start telling me."

Wayne said to him, "That sounds good but first, I have to let my parents know that I am home and then pending what all my mother and father have planned for me, I just might not be able to come over tonight so you and I will have to wait until you and I have had our breakfast before we can get together. Besides, I will be here all weekend so if our plans doesn't work out for tomorrow, there will be Sunday where you and I can get together before I leave to return back to my place to tell you."

"Oh no my brother," said Greg. "You and I are going to have this conversation tomorrow one way or another because I want to know what has been holding you back from dating girls."

Wayne said to him as they talked afar that it wasn't anything that bad, but he sees it as a beautiful thing. "Since you put it that way then I guess it will be acceptable because you are my brother and I know you wouldn't tell me anything that will hurt my heart and soul," Greg responded to him.

"I think you will be very pleased Greg. Besides me telling you about my situation, why haven't you told me about your plans to marry?"

"I will bring that part of my life up to you tomorrow after you tell me about this big surprise of yours."

"By the way, I want you know how sorry I am about not being able to attend your graduation due to my job."

"I understand my brother because you have a very important position because these farmers depend upon your expertise. I had a good time as my parents planned a good after party for me, as some dance girls entertained the highlight of the night by keeping me on the floor dancing until I almost fainted. I had to show off because Sandra and my cousin Delores were present but neither one of them would get up to dance with me because they knew that I would show them up so they remained seated."

"You are something else Greg," Wayne said.

"Did you know that my sister would be there?" Greg asked him.

"Yes I did because you know she and I always call to see how each one is doing. Listen brother," Wayne said to him. "I think I better go inside to see my parents. You and I will meet tomorrow morning after breakfast."

"Wayne," Greg said to him. "Why don't I come over to your house for breakfast that way, we will not have to meet up? You know your mother will welcome me to eat some of her good old hot cheese biscuits."

"If you want to I will let mother know."

As Greg turned to walk into his parents' home, Wayne turned to do the same as he thought in his mind, "Gee I hope this will go well."

Once Greg had gotten inside, he walked into the kitchen where his mother and daddy were sitting at the table having a cup of hot tea as they ate a slice of her potato pie to ask him, "Did you and Wayne have a good talk?"

"How do you two know that we were out there talking?" he asked them.

"We noticed you two from the kitchen window."

"Guys," Greg said to them, "There is something going on and I have yet to put it all together but I know there is more than what Wayne wants to tell me. Do you guys know anything that can ease my mind?"

Greg's mother said to him, "Son, why are you always trying to put more to something where you have no knowledge of?"

"I don't know mother but I guess I will find out tomorrow. By the way, I plan on having breakfast with the Hunts in the morning that way Wayne and I can get an early start on his secrets. I think I will go to my room and call Sadie to see what she is up to," Greg said to his parents.

"By the way son," his father asked him about all of Sadie's plans until she is ready to start in her position as the head administrator within the Board of Education.

"Well Daddy, she is fortunate because come next week she will begin fulfilling some of her tasks long before school is on the way."

"In other words, she will be gainfully employed while you have to wait until you begin your job come September? That is good son, you two preparing to build up yourselves by saving your money until you two are ready to walk down that aisle. You know your mother and I do not want you two to worry about finding a house to move into because we will be looking out for the two of you in hopes of finding you a place where you can afford."

"Daddy and Mother that will be a while off because Sadie and I want to get our feet wet in the work force. A whole year will be the time she and I will set our date. Have you two heard from Sandra since she and Delores returned back to New York?"

"She called to let us know that the two of them arrived back safe and sound and next week the law firm that Sandra works for will be giving her a farewell party."

"If they are giving her a party next week then when is her due date to arrive home? Greg asked.

His parents knew they could not tell him because then he would surely know they knew about what Wayne is holding secret so to be true to their words they said, "We don't know because she didn't say. I am sure she will let us know." Once Greg had left, his parents looked in each one's eyes to say, I hope you know that we have kept from our son the biggest secret ever.

"Catherine, we have to continue to keep this in the dark from him."

"You know Elijah," said Catherine. "I will be so glad when this whole thing has finally ended so Florence and I can reunite as one instead of pretending neither of us know the other's secret."

Elijah said to Catherine, "I do know this much, I hope Sandra will do the right thing and not disappoint that young man because if she refuses him, who knows exactly what he will do?"

"We just will hope for the best and everything will finally work out for everyone's sanity," Catherine responded to Elijah.

The next morning had appeared and Greg was up already preparing to walk over to the Hunt home to have a good breakfast with them because he and Wayne had a meeting together to share what has been eating on Wayne's mind all of these years in secret. As the two of them raced to see who would eat the most of Florence's good old cooking, Mr. Hunt said to Greg how glad he was to see him with his feet under the table of his home sharing in his wife's cooking enjoying it with his son. "If you two guys still feel that you need more to eat," Wayne's mother said. "I will be more than happy to get up and prepare more."

"Oh no mother," Wayne said to her. "I am sure Greg and I have already eaten more than our share."

Greg said to him, "You speak for yourself because I would like very much to have two more of your hot cheese biscuits."

"No problem there Greg," she said, "because here they are," and she turned around to take them off the stove to give to him.

Wayne said to him, "Listen my brother after you have finished eating those two biscuits come on and go with me because you and I have some talk to deal with."

Greg sad to Mr. and Mrs. Hunt, in lieu of what Wayne was talking about to ask if they knew. Since all the things Wayne had mentioned to his parents in secret, they had to pretend they didn't have a doubt to let Wayne break it to Greg himself. Well after breakfast was over with and Greg thanked Mr. and Mrs. Hunt for allowing him to have breakfast with them on Wayne's invitation, it was a privilege.

"Why Greg," Mrs. Hunt said to him. "You know that you are a part of this family and at any time you feel like coming over to eat with Samuel and me when Wayne has returned back to his place, by all means you have that right too because you know your mother and father don't mind."

Wayne pushed himself back from the breakfast table and said to Greg, "Alright now, you have eaten enough so we need to get going."

Wayne's mother asked him, "Where are you two going for this important talk Wayne?"

"I thought Greg and I would just take a walk to our favorite place where we shared a lot of time playing as children under that old oak tree."

As the two of them walked out of the house, Wayne's father said to his wife, "I really hope when Wayne lets on to Greg about his secret in wanting to marry his sister, it will not make Greg to blow up at him to hate him."

"I don't think that will happen honey," she replied to Samuel. "Besides, something like that could never happen after all those years spent together as brothers and sister. I think Greg at first will be shocked, but once he has accepted it, he will be alright."

Samuel said to his wife, "I trust and hope you are right. Let you and I hope for the best. I am sure Catherine and Elijah feels the same as you and I."

Soon Wayne and Greg had gotten to that favorite oak tree as they had so many memories of to take a seat right down on the grounds as they did as young boys. Greg opened up to Wayne to say, "Now we are here and I want you to tell me all of your secrets and please don't hold back." Wayne asked him would he get mad with him once he find out all about what has been in his mind. "It all depends on what it is," Greg responded.

"Then I better not tell you Greg."

"Oh now brother, you are not going to do this to me so get busy and let me have it, I promise you that I will try to understand to go along with you."

"Okay my little brother here it is so brace yourself."

"Do you remember how you used to dog me out about not dating any girls in college or where I live now as there are so many around me?"

"Yes, but I just couldn't understand what was your reason for not wanting to date any of those white girls."

"It was due to the fact that I am in love with your sister Sandra and I have been all of my life from the time we three met and grew up together. She has always been on my mind and in my heart to the point I just cannot function each day without thinking about her. I ask that you don't be mad with me because I felt this was the right thing to do was to tell you what was going on with me. Now since I have let out my secret to you, now is the time foy you to hit me or tell me to get lost as you don't want to have anything else to do with me. Greg I am waiting for your response," he said as Greg sat quietly as if he was in a state of shocked.

As Wayne sat quietly waiting to see how Greg would respond, he got up to start to walk away and suddenly Greg said to him, "Come back and sit down."

"Listen Wayne, I am totally shocked from what you have just told me and I just had to take it all in because I had never expected anything like this to be told to me by you as being in love with my sister, your adopted sister to wanting to marry her. Have you said anything to Sandra about this?" Greg asked Wayne.

"No I have not and I am asking you to respect my feelings and let me tell her my way."

"What about your mother and father, do they know or have you said anything to them about this shock?"

"I said something to them about two weeks ago."

"How did they accept the news? Like you, they too were shocked, but as I talked about it more to them, they were alright with it. Besides, they said that they would rather see me married to Sandra than one of those white girls knowing that I would not be happy, but marriage was the thing to do because of society rules. They wanted me to not follow society's rules, but to follow my own rules that would allow me to have a happy life."

"So now, if I accept it that will mean you will become my brother in law as you and I will no longer be brothers."

"Greg you and I will always be brothers because that is something that will never be changed, only instead of calling each other brothers, we will refer to each other as brother in laws."

"Wayne, I am shocked and right now I don't really know what to say, but I can tell you this much, if my sister Sandra accepts you to become her husband I won't have any other choice but to accept you so for now, I will be happy for her and when she says yes to you, then I will be much happier. By the way, have you mentioned any of this to my parents?"

"I don't want to tell you but I have and they were in the same agreement with each other as were my parents."

"So everyone knew but little old me I see," he responded to Wayne.

"I thought it would be in the best interest of your parents if they remained silent on this even if you come to them asking questions. Greg I had to take this route because if I had opened up to you in the beginning then you know you would have told Sandra and everything would have been a mess."

"I respect you for keeping this secret from me, but in the back in my mind all these years I knew something just was not right with you but I didn't know it was my sister."

"Greg I would like to ask you a very important question, and I hope you will give me a fair answer."

"What is your question Wayne? I promised you that I will give you a true answer."

"Would you rather I did not marry your sister Sandra if she accepts my proposal?"

"I see what you are trying to do is to put me on a spot just because you are a white boy."

"No, not really," Wayne said to him." I am just asking you the question as I need to hear an answer."

"Listen my brother or soon to be brother in law, I would much rather to have you as her husband regardless if you are a white boy just as long as you treat her with the respect she deserves and love her. At least I know you and what kind of person you are. If she marries someone else to whom I have no knowledge of then I would have a lot of reasons to not trust him. To your answer, I would be more than happy to have you marry my sister. You could have shared this with me a long time ago but I respect you and I am not mad with you. Besides, I will be getting married to a mixed girl in about another year so race to me is not the answer to happiness. When are you planning on breaking the news to Sandra?" Greg asked.

"Listen, please keep all of this a secret even with your parents and don't let on to them that you know because I want this to be a surprise to Sandra."

"When do you plan to tell her my future brother in law?"

"I will meet her next Saturday as she arrives home from the train from New York, your parents don't know when she is coming here because she and I want it to be a surprise to them that is why she asked me to meet her as I told her I needed to tell her something. Not even you can go with me to get her because then she will know."

"Alright my brother in law, I am quiet on the whole matter."

"I feel less stressed now Greg because I finally got it all out of my system so I can talk about it."

"When my parents ask me why did you and I walk down by the oak tree to spend time, what should I tell them Wayne?"

"Tell them nothing about what you and I talked about but to say we just wanted to renew old times down under the oak tree." As the two of them walked back to the house Wayne decided to walk over to Greg's home and sit out on the front porch to swing as they did when they were young kids.

As Greg's mother came to the front door to see what was going on, she asked the two of them, "What are you guys doing keeping all of this fuss out here that might cause the neighbors to take a look?"

"Mother, we are just having a good time talking about all the crazy things we did when we were children."

"Wayne?" she asked. "What is your mother doing after my son went over there to have breakfast with you guys?"

I think she and my daddy will soon be going to the supermarket to buy foods so she can prepare one of her big dinners for tomorrow so I will have enough to take back with me."

Greg said to his mother, "Why don't you make a banana pudding so Wayne and I can eat the whole thing before he leaves tomorrow?"

His mother responded by saying, "I do declare that is all you two guys think about all the time is eating. I feel so sorry for your wives when you two get married if you ever will because your wives will do nothing but cook all the time," she said as she laughed. "Not only like your mother Wayne, I think I too help her to do the worst thing, creating eating machines as you and Greg are definitely the pattern."

Once when Greg's mother left the two of them alone, Wayne said, "Do you think she know that you and I discussed what you told them?"

"No I don't think so because if she did she would not have said about if one day you and I got married all our wives would be doing would be cooking."

"Still Greg you have got to be careful in what you say to her because she is a smart woman you know.

As the two of them continued to have fun, Wayne's father walked across the road to Greg's father's house to see Elijah. He walked out on the porch to join him as they too sat in the company of their sons. Greg said to Wayne, "I guess this is the Saturday where fathers and sons come together to hang out."

Greg's father said to him, "Young man just because you have grown up into manhood and you have finished college by my money, don't think I can't handle you," Wayne's father had to support Elijah, by saying the same thing to him.

"Oh know, Wayne and I are not saying anything about whether or not you two are not able to challenge us, we were just making an assumption. Don't get mad Daddy," Greg said.

"You too Daddy," Wayne said.

The time finally came as Wayne received that called he had been waiting for from Sandra to let him know that she would be departing from New York Saturday morning heading home for good. After all of the glitter and lights that had been shined upon the life of Sandra by her employers and friends, she would be going back home to her family not to return back to New York for any cause. Delores had to give her cousin a special gift, a speech that would always be with her until the end, giving thanks for all the wonderful joys she brought to her while spending time with her for a period of time. Sandra was given the key to the city by the mayor and other fine gifts by her employers as she was presented with a cashier's check in the amount of the sum of one hundred thousand dollars appreciating her for opening up a new business world in the law firm she reestablished. It was a last good night with Delores and Sandra because in the morning, she would be leaving behind a wonderful and caring cousin Delores to be with her family back there in Mississippi that she had missed so much, and there was a whole new future waiting for her once she arrived by someone who will sweep her off her feet as he hoped she would accept his proposal.

That night, Wayne had a hard time sleeping because he was so afraid that he would not be ready to meet his future wife on time. As he tossed and turned, Sandra's family had that same feeling as well as his own parents not knowing if he would be rejected by the one girl he had always loved. Greg himself would wake up time to time wondering if his sister would want to marry the guy they had always guarded as their brother now forgetting all of that to become a loving wife to him not because he was white, but because he had been viewed all these years as a brother. Greg kept thinking that for Wayne's sake, she would give in and give him what he wanted to hear. "Besides, I think he and I will become good brother-in-laws because come another year, he will see my wife as a good sister-in-law as well. I think this will be a happy time here in this community once the two of them are married as nothing but buzzing will be all around. Well, I think I will try and get some sleep because I know Wayne just might be having a hard time knowing that come tomorrow afternoon, he will be driving over to the train station to pick up my sister."

Back in New York, Sandra and Delores were busy packing up everything to make sure she wouldn't leave anything behind. The two of them stayed up most of the night spending time laughing and talking as Delores was busy wishing Sandra the best of life as she might be the wife of Wayne as she had been told many of times by Delores, but she did not believe it so come tomorrow once she sees him, she will know once and for all. There were a lot of things that Sandra had accumulated from the years she had spent there in New York, until she had to have some mailed home through the mail because it was impossible for her to carry all by train. As she and Delores talked, it was such a delight as Delores responded to her to say, "They really did you good my cousin by giving you all that money. If anyone really deserves it especially for all the things you had done for them, it was you because if you had not walked into that office that day when I set up your interview with them, they would not have been who they are today. Now, once you get back home before you start with your new job, you will have quite a bit of money to get you and Wayne off to a good start."

"Delores, please stop saying that because you don't know it for sure that Wayne wants to marry me."

"My dear cousin Sandra you just might not know it but I do and this you can count on. I see you have already called him to let him know the arrival time tomorrow."

"Yes I did because I promised him that I would since he didn't want me to tell anyone. Now, can I ask you one thing Sandra?"

"What is it this time Delores?" she responded.

"Doesn't it strike you as strange that he asked you not to let anyone know that you would be arriving there tomorrow?"

"No, not really because he said that he had to tell me something and he just wanted the two of us together when he open up to me."

"Bingo Sandra!" Delores said. "That will be the question," she said laughing.

"I think it is something else pertaining to his request to be reassigned closer to his home. I bet it is that Delores," she responded back.

"Girl, Wayne is requesting for a reassignment to be closer home to be close to you once you are settled and start teaching school so when the two of you are married, he will not have to worry about you traveling far away from him."

"Delores, can you and I just put this whole thing on hold for now? I am making sure I don't leave anything behind and especially the gifts you and I purchased for Greg's graduation present."

"Sandra do you know what gift Wayne gave him?"

"No I do not and nor do I want to know because I know I will find out soon enough from Greg. Well, if I am going to be up and ready to move on out tomorrow morning to make sure I catch my train then I think I better get some of this New York sleep for the last time," she said laughing. While thinking about all the things he would be telling Sandra once he laid eyes on her tomorrow, Wayne was becoming a little nervous about being rejected by her as he might know what to do or how to handle himself. As Wayne walked around mostly the whole night, he kept a positive mind because in his heart he felt that she would not reject him but would agree to all of his kept secrets about her.

Finally, he made up in his mind that if he didn't try and get some sleep it would all be wasted because he would not have the energy to tell her due to the lack of sleep so he forced himself to sleep as he set his alarm clock to go off a certain time to wake him up. Soon, Saturday morning had appeared and his clock came off right on time and he knew it was time for him to roll out of bed and on into the shower to be fresh and clean as he would soon head on out to meet the train that would be bringing home his future wife to make his life joyful. Although he had a few hours before he would drive on to the station, he decided that he would sit down to have a good breakfast to calm his nerves that way, he would not be so afraid. He thought that he would give his not yet brother-in-law a call to see if he had kept his promised not to say anything to them about what is coming to surprise them this afternoon. Once he called to the Hunt's home Greg picked up the receiver to say hello to find that it was Wayne. "What are you up too this morning my brother?" he asked.

"I am really not up to anything, but getting ready to walk into the kitchen and eat up everything. What about you Wayne?"

"I am just passing time to get ready to go to the train station when it nears time to pick up Sandra."

"So are you still planning on telling her once she is in your car?"

"I plan on letting her know before I burst."

"I wish you the best, I better go because mother is calling me to come to breakfast. We will speak later on and when you bring Sandra home I know it will be a happy time." Once Greg walked into the kitchen his mother asked him who he was talking to so early on the phone in the morning before breakfast. "It was only Wayne."

"What did he want by calling you?" his father asked.

"Nothing except to know what plans I have for today."

"When do you plan to go see Sadie, who you said she was going to be your wife in a year?" he asked.

"Daddy, I have that all of that under control because she and I have already made plans while we were in college as to what we wanted to do."

"So son, his mother asked him, are you telling me that neither of you want to involve us into your wedding?"

"No, nothing like that I am just saying Sadie had said what she would like and how she would want things to be carried out. You do know Mother that you and her mother will be working close together in this matter I hope you know. "There was little that Greg knew about what his parents had already done to congratulate them on their marriage by purchasing them a lovely home not too far away from them with the money they had saved long ago for him, as well as for his sister Sandra also to get them started in life.

The only difference with Sandra and Wayne as they thought Greg didn't know the two parents had gotten together and they already purchased for

Wayne and Sandra the home of their dream without either of them knowing anything about it, as the two parents put their monies together to give their son and daughter the gift of their lives to present them their keys to their home once they are married. As they will all come together once Sandra arrives home with Wayne bringing her to finally let go of the secrets they shared without telling each other due to Wayne's restrictions until now. This was a sure way for Wayne to ensure that all of his hidden secrets were safe.

Now that day has finally arrived and the cats would be let out of their bags to breathe this afternoon once his car pulled up into the driveway where everyone would be in awe. As the Logans ate their breakfast, over at the Hunts home the same thing was taking shape as they too would be shocked once they saw Wayne's car pulling up into the Logan driveway to cause his mother and father to walk over to greet Sandra as they will be hugging her and shout gladness to see her return finally back home as they will congratulate her on her teaching position, also acting surprised to welcome her into their family as a daughter-in-law not yet to be exposed. Of course on both sides, they all had to pretend this news would be a surprise as they did not know, but they knew all along to let Sandra believe they did not know anything about what Wayne was doing. It was about time for Wayne to head out to the train station to meet Sandra as when he got there, he parked his car and stood silently out front of the station where the train would come to a stop to see her and take her into his arms because now that so many things there had changed, he didn't care who noticed him hugging her as a white guy because he wanted them to know who felt like it was not the right thing to do, he was hugging and embracing his future wife and he could have given a flip toward their attitudes of refusing to make a change.

As he stood there and finally saw the lights on the train shining bright, he knew it was her train and he was getting all nervous to see her because it had been four years at the most since he set eyes on her, as he wondered would he recognize her or would she recognize him. Once the train came up and stopped, the passengers started to unload as he watched for Sandra to walk off and suddenly, she walked off and right into his awaited arms as people watched to say in their minds all those who still had that we will never accept these changes of the south, has he lost his mind to be hugging that black girl right here in front of us? After the two of them had finished hugging and after he finished with his kisses on her cheeks, the two of them walked inside to get her luggage to place them in his car as Wayne backed out and started down the road.

"Sandra," Wayne said to her. "I thought I would never ever see you again since you had moved away to New York, the city with big lights and lots of entertainment. I thought your cousin Delores would persuade you to remain there."

"Wayne those were her plans not mine. My heart was always here in this land because this is where I want to teach and use my talent to help children so I could never allow myself to remain there in that city although it was rewarding and I made a lot of accomplishments within the law firm that I was placed over by my two lawyer brothers- my bosses- as I helped to build up their clientele to become one of the best in the city."

"Sandra listen to what I have to say to you and I want you to think about it."

"What is it Wayne?" she asked.

"Right now your parents doesn't know you are here as well as my parents because I wanted all of this to be their surprise and I want to marry you because I have always been in love with you even from day one when the three of us played together as young children. I had always wanted to be with you and now since you and I have grown up and finished college to have our own careers, I want you to be my wife. If you don't feel as if you want to marry me or you don't think that I am good enough for you then I guess I will understand to the point that I will just have to move forward. I want you to know since you have been gone, I have not dated anyone, especially these white girls, because they just did not do anything for me. You know me and I know you so there is no room in our hearts for hate because neither of our parents are that way with you being black and me being white. Love as I see it is love and when two people fall in love there is a special bond that cannot be broken by anyone else."

"You know Wayne," Sandra responded to him to say, "My cousin Delores had been right all along when she kept telling me that you had fallen in love with me but I couldn't see it as I looked at it as her just being nosy to see what I would say."

"May I ask you something if you don't mind Sandra?"

"No, I don't mind."

"While you were there in New York, did you ever date any guys that you had an interest in?"

"Wayne, I met a lot of so called business minded type guys who only wanted to use smart girls to meet their needs. Of course, I was not one of those girl to allowed myself to get caught up in that storm of life so I passed them by."

"That is good to hear because now I know that if you marry me you won't ever have to worry about a thing because I have a good job which I am now being transferred closer to home and once you and I get marry and you begin teaching, you won't have too far to travel as we will always be together at night to make our lives blossom."

"Wayne if I said to you that I didn't think about you often while I was away, I would be lying because the more my cousin Delores would drill me about you, I felt a strong feeling for you but I played it off to her because I didn't want her to think she was right and all the time she was."

"What then are you telling me Sandra?" he asked as he pulled to the side of the road and stopped his car.

"I don't have to think about it at all because I will marry you because if I would ever marry anyone, it will be you."

"So it is complete now that you have given me your answer?" he asked her.

"Yes, I will marry you and right at that moment without hesitation."

He pulled her into his arms and gave her a long kiss as she said to him, "You better stop because people are passing by and what do you think they will be saying?"

"Who cares, I am kissing the future Mrs. Hunt and once we get to your house you and I will fill both homes with nothing but joy."

After that happy span of time, they drove off with smiles on their faces to let the two families know that there will be a wedding as soon as possible. "Sandra baby, let's get married next month before school starts that way we will have time to look for a place to live." Little did he know that place had already been established and all the two of them had to do was to move in after they had their honeymoon.

"All these years and all the times I have been so uptight thinking that I would be rejected because we all grew up as brothers and a sister to have to come to this point in our lives to learn not only was I in love with you, but you fought your feelings for me and thanks to your cousin Delores who you know didn't care that much for me to bring it out to your own attention. I don't know why she refused to like me, but with all the things that were going on when she was here, I sort of understand and hope now she likes me."

As Wayne and Sandra continued to talk and drive home to surprise everyone, the joy and happiness in Wayne's final moments were here and he was as happy as anyone could be from the good news as he was not expecting turned out to be what he had hoped for. Once in sight of Sandra's parents' home, she was so joyful because she will finally be in the place where she had to leave due to the less opportunities than there that had made her leave for a better way of life. After all those years being away, her mark in her life has been made and now, things had changed over the years she had been away to allow her to return to pick up from where she had started from. Soon Wayne had pulled up into the driveway blowing his horn as Greg came outside to see what was going on and yelling to his parents, "Come out here guys to see who is standing in the yard." As they came out, her mother as well as her father just could not believe their eyes that their daughter was home smiling as they all grabbed each other hugging and crying with happiness.

Her mother said to her husband, "Look honey, our little girl is home now as she surprised us." As all of them just continued with happiness Wayne took a look at Greg and winked his eye because Greg knew all about it, but dared not to tell as he had promised his soon to be brother in law.

After they had finished with their crying and hugging, Sandra said to her parents and her brother that she had to tell them something very important. Of course what she would tell them would not be any surprise to Greg because he knew what would be coming out of her mouth but then first, Wayne opened up to say to Sandra, "Please, I want to tell them." Wayne started by saying, "Mr. and Mrs. Logan, I have asked your daughter Sandra to become my wife and she agreed."

Greg, playing as if he did not know anything of it, asked Wayne and said, "Are you saying what I think you just said in asking my sister to marry you?"

"Yes my brother and soon to be my brother-in-law. Wow! I am overwhelmed! Mother and Daddy," he said to them. "What do you suggest in this matter?"

"If they are in love and if they want to get married, we are happy."

"Well, it looks as if happiness has finally come home to take its place. There will be a wedding in this community soon. Let me go inside and call Florence and Samuel to tell them of the good news so she and I can get busy in doing what must be done to prepare for that glorious day. Come on Wayne let me help you to take Sandra's baggage out of your car so the three of us can get the ball rolling."

As the three of them were still in the front yard, Sandra's mother had called Wayne's mother and father and soon they were running over to the house in excitement as if they did not know all along to the news. Wayne was so excited that even himself didn't know how to go about dealing with it so he just played along with the others. As Wayne's parents walked into the yard, Elijah and Samuel took a short walk away from them to make a time when the two of them would go house hunting for the two soon to be married couple as a wedding gift to them. Elijah said to Samuel, "You know, we will be doing the same thing next year for my son Greg when he and Sadie tie the knot."

Samuel said to him, "Hey, then you and I will just have to do the same thing over again."

As the two of them walked back over in the presence of the three while Florence had gone inside with Catherine, Greg, and Wayne, Sandra asked them, "Why did you two guys walk away to yourselves to talk?"

"Hey guys, don't worry about what Samuel and I were talking about because it was a very important conversation we had to take care of. We know that your mothers are inside making all kind of plans, but Wayne and Sandra have you two decided on a date and time you two want to do this thing?" asked Elijah and Samuel.

Wayne said to his father, "I have been relocated back here in this area to work as I will be moving back in with you and mother until Sandra and I get married to save our money for a home."

"What about you my daughter?" Elijah said to her.

"I am in the same situation as Wayne to work to save some money for a new home." The two fathers said to them how grateful they were to them wanting to do that, but as fathers, they wanted to help out too. Sandra had just been given a cashier's check for one hundred thousand dollars from her employers.

She would let Wayne know once she get settled. "Daddy, Wayne and I have decided to get married in a couple of months before school starts so we can start finding our way in this thing called marriage."

"I think I better go inside where his mother and your mother are to talk with them while you guys remain outside here and talk, Sandra." Once she left Wayne's father said to him that he was so happy for him and he along with Elijah know that he will make Sandra a happy person.

Greg said to Wayne, "I know you will because my eyes will be watching."

"I consider this as being a good homecoming day for your daughter and for my son, Samuel said.

Wayne said to Greg, "Why not come go with me to my place to help me to start packing up my things because you know next week I will start working from this location?" As the two of them drove away, it gave Elijah and Samuel time to rearrange their schedules for the next week to start looking for that perfect home for the newlyweds.

"Let you and I leave all of the wedding details to the ladies because they will do a fine job because that is just who they are. I know this wedding will be grand. So Elijah, it is set for you and I to go out Monday morning to get this house, right?"

"We have the money and who will turn the two of us down Samuel?"

"We are about to make history in this community pretty soon my friend," Samuel said to Elijah. "And pretty soon there will be some little ones running around carrying both genes."

As the three females carried on inside, Florence asked Sandra and her mother Catherine about having the wedding on a Saturday afternoon so it would not interfere in the scheduled Sunday service. "What about it Sandra?" her mother asked.

"I think that is a good idea; that way everyone will have plenty of time to regain their momentum from attending my wedding.

Florence said to her, "I will be responsible for all invitations and ordering the wedding cake, getting the hall set up for the reception including music and accepting all wedding gifts."

Catherine said to her, "I don't want you to do everything because I need to be fully involved."

"You will be Catherine," Florence said to her, "with the decision of her wedding grown, her maid of honor's dress, and other girls' dress colors.

Florence said to Catherine, "What a good time it will be in this community when this wedding takes place next month."

"Sandra," she asked. "Have you and Wayne decided on a place you want to spend your honeymoon?"

"No Mrs. Hunt because he and I have made a decision to put it off until a few months down the line because I will be teaching school and that would interrupt my schedule. We decided to wait until the school session is over with and then we will take off."

While Wayne and Greg were packing up moving all of his things back home, the two fathers had gone on a house hunt to locate one they had seen in the nearby community that they thought would be a nice home for the two of them so they headed off to the bank which held the deed to it to make an offer and to pay for it cash on the head, because there were funds set aside especially for that purpose. Once the bank made the arrangements for them to take a look inside to get their approval on things by a bank examiner, they returned back to the bank and pulled the money out of each one's accounts to pay for it as paperwork was given along with the deed to it in the name of Wayne and Sandra Hunt's name as wife and husband. After all of the finishing touches had been taken care of, the bank president shook their hands and gave them the keys to the house. After Elijah and Samuel had gotten outside, Elijah said to Samuel, "I think you should hold the keys and in the midst of the reception at the hall when gifts are presented, I think you and I shall walk up to them to present them their new home."

"Now that is a good idea," Samuel said to him. "I know they will not know what to say."

"Samuel, you know while the ladies are doing their things next week and Greg will be busy looking around because Wayne will be at work so why not take him with us to purchase furniture for their new home because I as well as you know exactly what the two of them like. When the two of them walk in that night to celebrate their wedding night to see all the nice things that had been placed inside for them, they will just be so overjoyed until they will not know what to say or do. You know you and I did not make a dent in the money we have saved for them Samuel," Elijah said.

As Wayne and Greg packed up his things, the two of them just had a good time with their talks as Wayne said to Greg, "I hope you know you will be my best man because who else would I get that I would be happy standing up for me?"

"I don't know of any my brother," Greg said to him. "Because you and I have known each other all of our lives. It will be my pleasant in my heart to stand for a great guy who is white. You know Wayne, I knew something just wasn't right with you as I thought about how you acted around my sister so many times but then I thought that you were busy trying to protect her and all the time you had been loving her so now that apple that you held tight and high on that tree finally fell to the ground to let everyone know that there will be a wedding taking place in the next month. You know that come next year you and my sister will be attending Sadie and my wedding too."

"I can see it now written all across the skies, happiness has finally come to the Hunt and Logan family members, a mixture of love," Wayne said as he continued to finish packing because he wanted to get back to his beloved future wife to sit down together to make sure they would have everything available to pull this off.

As the ladies continued with their assignments, Sandra opened up to her mother and her soon to be mother-in-law to tell them that money would not be a problem for her and Wayne because she was presented a cashier check's for one hundred thousand dollars by her employers for the work she had done to reshape their law firm. Of course the two mothers could hardly believe what they had heard, but they were happy because they knew that things would be easier for them to get started. Wayne's mother said to her, "I know Wayne himself has saved quite a bit as well because now I understand why he was saving so much each week, it was because of this event."

"Well Catherine, Florence said to her. "At least our children will not go into a marriage broke as you and I did when we got married in the time that we did because there was not a lot of money within the families." Of course the two mothers dare not let on that once they are married they will be presented keys to their new home paid for in full from the money saved for them.

Things were being enacted to this glorious day as Sandra decided to make a call to her cousin Delores to let her know of her decision to marry Wayne as she had always said to her that she knew she would because she had that gut feeling as it has come true in all she and Sandra talked about while she was there in New York. Sandra knows in her heart that Delores would be happy for her except she never thought that she would ever marry a white guy, especially the one that she did not give a second hoot about as she blamed everything what was going on there in Mississippi at the time when she graduated that caused her to move away.

"I guess if we would just let time take its course then in the long run things will get better and so far by seeing what has taken place with my cousin Sandra, I can truly say I have a change of heart. At least now I will know the way things were long ago will never be that way again because there will be a mixture of genes flying around in everyone's family." As the two talked about this big wedding to soon take place, Delores wanted to know the date and time because this is one wedding she will not miss.

"Wayne and I have decided to get married next month as he has been relocated back home in this location to work and I waiting for school to open that will be close by."

Wayne's mother Florence and Sandra's mother Catherine were busy putting things all in motion as names were being placed down to receive invitations, and arrangements of all flowers were being ordered as well as the reception hall to be decorated by hands of the ladies in the community that were so excited to hear the good news. The news was not about a white boy and black girl, but a wedding of two young and in love individuals uniting in marriage for life. Wayne and Sandra knew that this event would surely be the talk of the town as the newspapers will be carrying it for every citizen to see. In the meantime, Wayne and Greg, his soon to be brother-in-law, were busy packing up his things to be moved back to his parents' home to clear out of his apartment because he would no longer be living there as his work will be continued and carried out in the location of his community.

Well! It looked as if everything has been put in place and all that need to be done as the wedding day was nearing to make sure everyone was on board. All the groomsmen has been chosen as well as the best man which would be Greg and all the bridesmaids been chosen to include the maid of honor. The heat was on as Wayne could not hold his composure whenever he was in the presence of Sandra knowing that just in a few days, they would be Mr. and Mrs. Hunt. Everyone within the community was in full expectation to attend. This will be a well talked about wedding long after it has ended. Sandra and her brother Greg had a good conversation as she talked with him about what will take place with he and Sadie come next year when they too will share their vows to each other to begin their long life together that would make their parents as well as Sadie's parents happy to hope for the future of some grandchildren to carry on the Logan name for generations to come.

Greg said to Sandra about his reservations about Wayne wanting to marry her and then he thought about it long and hard after the two of them talked about it to give his blessings because if there was anyone he would want his sister be married to, it was him because they all grew up together and felt he would make her a good husband.

"Sandra, I gave Wayne my blessings and I am hoping the best for the two of you. Look at things this way my big sister, not only will I be losing a sister but I will be gaining a true and worthwhile brother-in-law that I already know and it is not because of his color, it is because of his good character. I can't think otherwise why these two families should be sad because there is no reason why that through these years, there has been nothing but joy and good standards among everyone. I am so proud of you because the time you spent there in New York with our cousin Delores, you did not allow her to change how you felt about Wayne although you did keep yourself hidden in secret from her, but you continued to hold on to what you had trusted and believed in all these years, the love you shared with Wayne. Now, as you and I sit here talking about it, the time has finally arrived to no longer for you to hide your secrets because now, everyone knows and come next week, it will be shown as you walk down that aisle to take his hand to become his bride. How do you feel Sandra?" Greg asked her.

"I suppose I feel like you will be feeling overjoyed once you say I do. Just take a look at this whole thing, my sister has come home to take up her job to tech high school and her soon to be husband has been moved closer to do his work right here in this location to be close to his wife. I think Wayne planned out his strategies just well because he is finally going to get what he has always wanted, my big sister. Sandra there is something I need to tell you, but you cannot let on to Wayne of it as I am not supposed to let you know because it supposed to be a secret, but as kids you and I have never kept anything from each other."

"What is it you want to tell me Greg?" Sandra asked.

"Daddy and Mr. Samuel went to the bank yesterday and paid for that nice beautiful white house that had been taken back by the bank to make it a wedding gift to you and Wayne."

"Oh no Greg they didn't do that did they?" Sandra asked.

"Yes they did and it is for you to be silent on this thing to act like it is a shock when they present you and Wayne the keys at your reception."

"I just don't know what to say because I am just shocked. Where did they get the money to do it?" she asked.

" There has been money set aside that neither you, Wayne nor I knew about and it was so much until the two of them split the total amount half. Sandra I was with them when they purchased the furnishings for your new home and believe me when I say this sister, you are going to love what the two of them have done. I know once mother and Mrs. Florence see it, they will just be so overwhelmed with their husbands. I am wondering what I should get you two for a wedding gift as well," Greg said to her.

"My brother, just being the best man to Wayne will be the best gift you could ever give. I want yours and Sadie's wedding to be as great as Wayne's and my wedding will turn out to be. There is no doubt in my mind you will want Wayne to be your best man."

"If I wanted anyone to be my best man, you know it will be my brother-in-law because I know everything will be alright."

"You know Greg since you and I are having this little talk, has it ever dawned on you that with what Daddy is doing for me, he will do the same for you once you are ready to take Sadie for your wife? Knowing just how he and Mr. Samuel work, the two of them would try and find a home near Wayne and me so we all can be located closed by."

"You know our Daddy don't you Sandra?" he asked. "After spending a lifetime with him, how can I not know because you and I have been the apple of his and mother's eyes, just as Wayne has been to his parents."

"Does this mean that I can come over anytime I want too to have dinner with you and Wayne?" Greg asked her.

"Well, not too often but yes, you can stop over anytime you want . You know if Wayne didn't see you often, he would be worrying about what has happened. Now, you and I really don't want that to happen now Greg. I think you and I have had our long talk and I think I better get back inside before mother and Mrs. Florence think I have ran away to keep from helping out."

"I have to report to the school board tomorrow money to be given my assignments as a high school English teacher. Boy, I have waited for this opportunity for a very long time and now it has finally arrived where I will be standing right up there in front of the classroom giving out my instructions as to the assignments I will be handing out to be written in the right way."

"Look at my big sister, the all-time English teacher as I know she will be the talk of the education board wishing that they had her on board many years ago that way, things would have been better for the children that did graduate. I guess I can say to you my sister that there is a new sheriff in town and on board to make sure the students who will be graduating will have the right tools to go out there in the job market to be ready to take on their responsibilities because they know that what they had been taught will surely get them far."

"Take a look at yourself Greg," she replied to him, "because you too will make good strides with your students; in teaching all technical math learning you will teach them to be prepared for the changing world."

The more that everyone talked about this wedding to be then the time has finally showed up with everyone busy being put in place to know what they were supposed to be doing when all the excitement takes place. Sandra was not seen for a few days by her soon to be husband because she was out of sight as all brides are supposed to be just before their wedding takes place. Her gorgeous, whit,e flowing gown had arrived by the person who designed it as well as the dresses of her maid of honor as well as her bridesmaids. While her four maids of honor and bridesmaids were all locked inside of Sandra's family home waiting for everything to kick off, Wayne along with his best man Greg, his soon to be brother-in-law, and all others of assistance, were also over to Wayne's parents' home as well as Mr. Elijah, a house full of men getting prepared to go over to the church to get themselves in place before the bride and her group will show up. It looked as if the church was filled to the top as everyone who know of this wedding taking place was there to include whites as well because this was surely a thing that has surprised everyone. Some came to watch to see how things would turn out and then some came to wish them well. Anyway, they were there as well as the news teams and newspaper cast to write about this wedding of the century taking place right now in the state of Mississippi.

As the minister came forth to greet all who were present, he said to them, "I know most will think that this wedding is just not right because who these two in love individuals are, but if we follow the rules of the good book, we will know that this affairs is not for anyone to say, what is right and what is not right. Let all of us look at this exciting moment in our time to soon take place, as the joy of love that has developed over many years, not because of a beautiful black girl, but because the young man that chose her to be his wife is white, leaving him to not judge her because of her complexion, but he fell deeply in love with her for who she is, a smart, intelligent person who he know will brighten up his life and be a good wife and mother to his children when the time is right."

After the minister had finished speaking to the audience, he was given a nod that the bride and her guests had arrived and now were inside waiting for their cue to enter. If anyone was nervous it was Wayne as he stood still as Greg his best man kept him focused to whisper to him, "Hold on my brother-in-law because this is surely your day as you have always wanted it to be." All the escorts were present dressed in black tuxedos, as were Wayne and Greg, the only difference was Wayne and Greg's tuxedos had long tails to offset the queen's white, long, flowing gown. As the ushers started to escort the bride's mother in to take her seat to follow by the groom's mother and his father, because the bride's father would be escorting her down the aisle to give her hand to her soon to be husband. Delores had to be there as she came directly to the church as she arrived so Sandra would see that she kept her promise to her. Soon the minister turned around to give the organist the go ahead with the music as one by one the bridesmaids walked in holding a hand full of white roses as chosen by the bride. After the maid of honors took their place then came the bridesmaids that would stand close by the bride to be followed by a little chosen black boy and a little chosen white girl to walk in front of the bride dropping rose petals in front of her as she and her father marched in with him being in a black tuxedo also as they walked up to the front of the minister where Wayne, his best man, and others stood.

The minister asked, "Who give this young girl's hand away?"

Her father said without any hesitation, "I do," as Wayne took Sandra's hand to become joined as one as the minister cited the ceremonial wedding vows. Pictures were being taken as they finally were united in marriage by a kiss as the church crowd clapped their hands to well wishes. Just as Wayne and his wife Sandra turned around for everyone to see them, their parents jumped to their feet to give their best wishes by kisses and hugs as they were about to march out of the church on into the waiting limousines that would take them to the reception hall where thing would be celebrated, Sandra's mother as well as Wayne's mother Florence said to each other how so grateful they were to see this wonderful time with their children as it finally happened to be no more secrets to be kept.

As the bride and groom, now Mr. and Mrs. Hunt, grooved off to the reception center, all other attendants followed directly behind them as the newspaper crew followed along as well. Of course the parents of the bride and groom were also driven there in their limousine as Delores and her parents accompanied them because they too were a part of the family and they wanted to be included. Some of Wayne's cousins on his mother's side were in attendance once they came to grip with it as well as one or two of his father's relatives, the one who had gotten adjusted to the changes." The day was a nice day because the sun was shining bright and the humidity was not bad so there was not much of a need to try to stay cool because it was such a good day for a good wedding as it turned out to be just that, a good day. Once they arrived to the center to see a lot of people had already arrived there, Wayne and Sandra were riding in the maid of honor's company because it was her responsibility to see that the bride was alright for the entire time. As their car pulled up, the driver got out to open the door as the maid of honor stepped out first, and then the bride and the groom followed to be escorted inside as the best man and all the maids of honor escorts stood together to follow inside behind the groom and bride into the hall where people were there to greet them, as the two of them walked over to the long table where they would be seated with both of their parents, best man, bridesmaids, maid of honor, and flower guys to wish them well. The table was decorated so nicely as Wayne's mother saw to that with all of the foods arrangements. The wedding cake was the choosing of the bride's mother because she knew exactly what flavor they would like as she chose a four stage cake with a status of a white groom and a black bride on top. The music was chosen by what flavor of songs the younger folks would like to dance to. The minister was still present as he stood before the microphone to address the crowd and give best wishes to the bride and to the groom to wish them the best life together. After that, he gave the floor to them to come out to share moments together to be watched by everyone as they hugged and had kisses for each other. Delores was so amazed by the whole thing she said to Greg as she sat close to him, "You know cousin, I was wrong about that skinny white boy."

Greg responded back to his cousin Delores by saying, "You were so wrong and I really think you should walk right there up to him to tell him all about how you once felt toward him and ask for his forgiveness."

"Do you think he will accept my apologies my cousin?"

"Of course he will because he is now my brother in law and I know how he is as we grew up together. When I get the chance to, after all of this excitement has ended, I will make it my point too. Besides, I know Sandra will appreciate it a lot now that he is her husband and a part of the family."

"I guess everything turned out to be a worthwhile fight with me as I can accept that I lost that battle. Just look at the two of them," she continued saying to Greg how good they look and how she knows now what a good husband he will be to her.

Greg said to her, "Now cousin, you know come next year I will be in her shoes with my wife to be too and you must attend my wedding."

"Greg I have to say to you as I take a good look at your future wife as she sits nearby watching Greg from afar as he communicated with everyone just how happy she too will be and to be the sister in law of his sister." As thought ran through Sadie's mind, she said without any doubts she know that once she and Greg are married, they will be one big happy couple.

As things were getting wild and everyone was out on the dance floor dancing along with the newlyweds, foods were being served and soon at the end, it was time for the bride and groom to cut their cake to serve each one a piece as it is a tradition from long ago been established. All the gifts that people brought to honor them were placed on a large table as their parents were in charge of that part of the reception. Soon Mr. Hunt, Wayne's father, and Sandra's father Mr. Logan got together to decide when it was a good time to present the two newlyweds the keys to their home where they will be spending their wedding night. Once the two of them leave the reception hall they will be driven to their new location by the limousine driver and dropped off as

Greg now as Wayne's brother-in-law will drive his car over to their home as he will be picked up by their parents because the two mothers wanted to check out their new home.

Just as the cake was cut and served, Wayne's father as well as Sandra's father walked up to the microphone to make their announcements as they thanked everyone for their support to this wonderful wedding to the couple that just got married. As they kept speaking, finally it was time for the gifts to be presented so the two mothers came up to the microphone to give their thanks to all that helped put this fabulous wedding together and all the gifts that has been received. They also said to the audience, "All the gifts will be taken over to them at a later date but first, we will give them time to acquaint themselves with each other."

Mr. Hunt and Mr. Logan walked up to Wayne and his new bride to say to them, "Wayne your father and Sandra your father are here to present to you the keys to your new home as it is fully paid for and the deed is in the two of your names. This is our gift to you two. "Sandra and Wayne were so shocked but as Sandra already knew from her brother Greg she had to pretend she didn't have a clue.

The two of them just hugged bother fathers and thanked them for all the things they had done and to said, "We are truly surprised about this house because we thought we would be living in an apartment until we found one on our own."

Wayne holding Sandra's hand said, "I just don't have words to say to you guys except that we love you with all of our hearts." Sandra was so overjoyed until tears came falling out of her eyes.

As the party was ending the bride and groom stood in front of everyone to say how so grateful they were to all who had attended and to all who thought they were so deserving of all this attention today." Everything has been beautiful and we as a new married couple are just so happy."

Wayne said to everyone, "Please don't forget come next year at this time, there will be another wedding right here to honor my best man and now brother-in-law Greg as he and his soon to be bride will be in Sandra's and my shoes to become Mr. and Mrs. Logans." Greg was so excited until he called Sadie to come up to stand next to him so everyone could see her, as he was laughing from ear to ear.

Sandra had to say a few words. "I want to thank everyone who participated in my wedding especially my maid of honor, my bridesmaids, and the ushers because Wayne and I could not have pulled it off without your assistance. We are so much appreciative. Especially I would like to give special thanks to my first cousin Delores who came in from New York to attend our wedding." Once Sandra said that Delores was all in her happy smiles as she motioned to her with a thank you hand.

As she and Wayne danced their last dance together with all attendees and her honored guests along with both parents dancing, they made their way to the entrance to say goodbye as they would be taking their wedding ride to their new home and then as Wayne's parents walked out the door to greet them goodbye and wished them well, Wayne turned around to them as he whispered to them in a soft tone of voice to say to them where everyone would not hear and said, "I told you and Daddy as you always hounded me about marriage as I told you then as you did not understand why I did not date was because I knew that the love that I had for my now wife was worth the wait."

www.ingramcontent.com/pod-product-compliance
Lightning Source LLC
Chambersburg PA
CBHW070126180125
20532CB00035B/641